MS World History II
Student Guide

Second Edition

Illustrations Credits
All illustrations © K12 Inc. unless otherwise noted

About K12 Inc.
K12 Inc., a technology-based education company, is the nation's leading provider of proprietary curriculum and online education programs to students in grades K–12. K[12] provides its curriculum and academic services to online schools, traditional classrooms, blended school programs, and directly to families. K12 Inc. also operates the K[12] International Academy, an accredited, diploma-granting online private school serving students worldwide. K[12]'s mission is to provide any child the curriculum and tools to maximize success in life, regardless of geographic, financial, or demographic circumstances. K12 Inc. is accredited by CITA. More information can be found at www.K12.com.

Copyright © 2016 K12 Inc. All rights reserved. K[12], the K[12] logo, and Unleash the xPotential are trademarks or registered trademarks of K12 Inc. or its affiliates in the U.S. and other countries. Other names may be trademarks of third parties.

No part of this document may be reproduced or used in any form or by any means, graphic, electronic, or mechanical, including photocopying, recording, taping, and information retrieval systems, without the prior written permission of K12 Inc.

ISBN: 978-1-60153-497-2
Printed by LSC Communications, Harrisonburg, VA, USA, April 2018

Table of Contents

Student Guide

Unit 1: Beginning
Lesson 1: Getting Started

History is the study of the human past—the story of change over time. It's a story based on evidence. Our physical world is the setting that helps shape the story, and real people are its heroes. Historians ask questions about all of these elements. Why did Europeans of the Middle Ages build cathedrals? How did the shoguns of Japan maintain their power? What inspired explorers to set sail across the seas? Join our odyssey through history. The questions are endless, and the answers amazing.

You will be helped along in your journey through history by the book—*The Human Odyssey: Our Modern World, 1400-1914*. In it you will find out why the Middle Ages came to an end. You'll see the beginnings of modern democracy. You'll meet extraordinary leaders, inventors, scientists, and the ordinary people around them. This book will be your passport to faraway places and long-ago times and to places and times quite near.

Lesson Objectives

- Review basic geography skills.
- Define *history* and identify reasons for studying history.
- Review the late Middle Ages in Europe and Asia.

PREPARE

Approximate lesson time is 60 minutes.

Materials

For the Student

- Your Passport - Answer Key
- Your Passport to The Human Odyssey
- The Human Odyssey, Volume 2 edited by Klee, Cribb, and Holdren
- Reading Guide
- Reviewing Map Skills

Keywords and Pronunciation

Abbasids (uh-BA-sids)
Avignon (ah-vee-NYAHN)
Byzantine (BIH-zn-teen)
caliph (KAY-luhf)
Christendom (KRIH-suhn-duhm)
Genghis Khan (JEHNG-gihs KAHN)
Kublai Khan (KOO-bluh KAHN)
Pisa (PEE-zuh)
Renaissance (REH-nuh-sahns)
schism (SKIH-zuhm) : a division or separation
Tatars (TAH-tuhrz)
Yuan (you-EN)

© 2016 K12 Inc. All rights reserved.
Copying or distributing without K12's written consent is prohibited.

LEARN

Activity 1: History and You *(Online)*

Activity 2: The Introduction *(Offline)*

Instructions

Read On

Read the Introduction, pages 15 to 23 and complete the Reading Guide. When you have finished, use the Lesson Answer Key to check your work, and then place the Reading Guide in your History Journal.

Day 2

Check Your Reading

Review what you learned in the reading assignment by going online and completing the Quick Check: Middle Ages activity.

Focus on Geography

Complete the Reviewing Map Skills sheet. Check your answer with those in the Lesson Answer Key.

ASSESS

Lesson Assessment: Getting Started, Part 1 (*Online*)

Complete the computer-scored portion of the Lesson Assessment. When you have finished, complete the teacher-scored portion of the assessment and submit it to your teacher.

Lesson Assessment: Getting Started, Part 2 *(Offline)*

Complete the teacher-scored portion of the Lesson Assessment and submit it to your teacher.

© 2016 K12 Inc. All rights reserved.
Copying or distributing without K12's written consent is prohibited.

Name Date 

The Human Odyssey, Volume 2: Our Modern World, 1400 to 1914

Before you begin your odyssey through history, start with a little odyssey through your book. Use *The Human Odyssey, Volume 2: Our Modern World, 1400 to 1914* to help you answer the following questions.

The book has four parts and each part is divided into chapters. Use the Table of Contents to help you find the answers to the following questions:

1. On what page does Part 4 begin?
2. In the Introduction to Part 2 there is a photograph of a small ship used by fifteenth-century Portuguese explorers. What is the name of this type of ship?
3. On what page does the Prologue begin? What are the major topics in the Prologue?

You may find that some of the words in the book are hard to pronounce. For help, look for the pronunciation in parentheses right after the word. You can use these, along with the Pronunciation Guide on page 712, to help you sound out the words.

4. Look at the following word in the second column of page 484 – *bourgeoisie*. Use the pronunciation in the parentheses after the word to sound out *bourgeoisie*. Check the Pronunciation Guide on page 712 to help you recognize the sounds associated with specific letters and letter combinations used in word pronunciations.

The book is full of photographs, illustrations, maps, and other pictures. All pictures have captions, although the caption may not always be right below the image.

5. What does the map on page 152 show?
6. Who is the figure in the image to the left of the first column on page 318, and what is he doing?

There is a time line at the end of each part. Use the time line for Part 2 to answer the following questions:

7. Which of the following three events happened first?

- England's navy defeats the Spanish Armada.
- Slave trade begins between Africa and the New World.
- Columbus sails from Spain to the Americas.

© 2016 K12 Inc. All rights reserved.
Copying or distributing without K12's written consent is prohibited.

Name Date 

8. In what year did Nicholas Copernicus publish *On the Revolution of Heavenly Bodies*?

Use the Atlas that starts on page 690 to answer the following questions.

9. In what direction (north, west, northeast, etc.) would you be heading if you traveled from Kandahar, Afghanistan to Ahmadabad, India?

10. What map projection is an elliptical equal-area projection that distorts shapes near the edges?

11. What two climate zones comprise most of Australia?

What was the Reformation? When did Leonardo da Vinci live? What is the definition of *tyranny*? Your book has two sections that can help you find the answers to questions like these—a glossary and an index. Use these two valuable resources to help you find the answers to the following questions.

12. Write the definition and pronunciation for *boyars.*

13. On what two pages can you read about Kublai Khan?

Nothing helps us understand the past quite like a good story. In your book you'll find lots of stories, including some in document excerpts in special sections called "A Page from the Past." Look on page 496.

14. What is this story about?

You have completed your short odyssey through the book! There is a lot of history in this book, and ahead of you lies an entire year of world history. Why should people study history? And what exactly *is* history?

Go back online and complete the History: What is It and Why Study It? activity to help you find the answers to those two questions.

© 2016 K12 Inc. All rights reserved.
Copying or distributing without K12's written consent is prohibited.

Name Date 

Reading Guide

Day 1

Read On

1. Explain how Christianity spread throughout Europe.

2. What caused Christendom to be a troubled realm at the end of the Middle Ages?

3. What elements helped the Byzantine Empire rise to power during the early Middle Ages?

4. How did the Muslim world help keep learning alive?

5. What factors caused the fall of the Mongols' empire?

© 2016 K12 Inc. All rights reserved.
Copying or distributing without K12's written consent is prohibited.

Name Date 

Reviewing Map Skills

Maps help us understand the Earth by giving us a picture of the size and shape of land and water. Globes can show the Earth fairly accurately. But it is impossible to transfer the round Earth onto flat paper precisely. Since every flat map has to be distorted in some way, mapmakers always have to compromise. They have to decide the best way to show the Earth. Some map projections are better for some purposes, others are better for other purposes.

Map Projections
When cartographers make a map, they project the geographic grid of the round Earth onto a flat sheet of paper. Small areas or even single continents can be mapped fairly accurately. But mapping the whole Earth at once presents problems of distortion. To deal with distortion, cartographers have devised special ways of representing the round Earth on a flat surface. They are called *map projections*. There are many different projections. Let's consider the strengths and weaknesses of some of the most popular ones.

Study the different map projections in the textbook on pages 706-707 and answer the following questions:

1. Look at the map of North America on page 696, and find the island of Greenland to the northeast of the continent. This is a fairly accurate representation. Now look at the maps on pages 706-707. In which projection is Greenland most distorted? In what way?

2. Which map projection would give navigators trouble if they tried to trace a water route between two places?

3. On which two map projections do the landmasses look most similar?

Longitude and Latitude
If you look toward the equator from the North Pole, you will see that the circles running around the globe get larger as they get closer to the equator. We call these circles *parallels of latitude.* All points along a parallel are the same distance from the equator. The parallels tell how far north or south any given point is from the equator. Each parallel is identified by the number of degrees (°) north or south it is from the equator (0°). The poles are 90° from the equator.

On a globe there is a set of lines that crosses the parallels. Rather than running east and west, as lines of latitude do, these lines run north and south. They divide the globe into sections like an orange. The lines are called *meridians*. The meridians are also called the lines of *longitude* and they are used to determine distances east or west of the "zero" or prime meridian.

4. Look at the map of Africa on page 699. What are the latitude and longitude coordinates for Cairo, Egypt?

5. Find Liberia on the map of Africa. Is it located east or west of the prime meridian (0°)?

6. Find Zimbabwe on the map of Africa. Is it located north or south of the equator?

© 2016 K12 Inc. All rights reserved.
Copying or distributing without K12's written consent is prohibited.

Name Date 

Absolute and Relative Location

The world is a big place. How do we know exactly where we are on the planet? How do we describe to someone else how to find a particular spot? How do we explain the relationship between one place and another?

Geographers refer to the concept of location in two ways—*absolute* location and *relative* location.

Absolute location is the precise location of a particular place. Latitude and longitude allow us to pinpoint absolute location. No two places on Earth have exactly the same latitude and longitude. A ship at sea that radios its position as 20° N, 60° E, for example, will not be confused with a ship somewhere else. There is only one city—New Orleans—located at 30° N, 90° W.

Latitude and longitude are not the only way to express absolute location. Think about other ways you pinpoint your location. You probably use your address fairly frequently. Someone else's house could be on a street with the same name and perhaps even have the same number as yours does. But no two houses have the same number, street name, city, and zip code. Your complete address is another way to express *absolute* location.

Sometimes, however, it is more useful to give the relative location of a place. Suppose you want to tell a friend how to get to your house. You could just tell your friend your exact address, or absolute location. But you might decide that giving him the *relative location* would be more helpful. You describe the location of your house in relation to other places. You might say that you live on the street just past the park, or tell him to turn left at the golden arches and look for the big oak tree. Your house is just after the tree on the left. You are describing a relative location.

Relative location can also refer to larger geographic areas. For example, Vienna, Virginia, is roughly 10 miles west of Washington, D.C. New Orleans is about 700 miles downriver from St. Louis. We frequently use relative location to describe the position of countries. The United States is south of Canada. Egypt is west of the Red Sea and east of Libya. Relative location is not as precise as absolute location, but it is sometimes more useful.

7. Use a world atlas to identify each place. Where appropriate, give the city and the country.

You are part of a worldwide spy operation. You've just been given your new assignment. You and your partner are to track and capture Mr. X who is on the run. You pack your bags—taking clothes for both warm and cool weather since you aren't sure where you will end up—and fly to ______________________________, located at 36° N and 140° E. There you meet up with your partner. You decide to split up because you've heard two rumors about where Mr. X is holed up. Your partner catches a boat to ____________________________, at 25° N and 122° E. Meanwhile, you catch an airplane and head to the continent of ______________________________, where China is located. Mr. X was there—cold and using bottled oxygen—hiding out in the ________________________, which border China to the west. Unfortunately, you just missed him. You and your partner decide to regroup, so you rendezvous in ______________________, located between 15° and 30° N and between 150° and 170° W. You spend several days surfing

© 2016 K12 Inc. All rights reserved.
Copying or distributing without K12's written consent is prohibited.

Name _______________________________ Date _______________________________ 

and talking to the locals. Word on the street is that Mr. X is cruising in the middle of the ____________________ ____________________, located at 20° S and 70° E. You haven't heard exactly where he is going, so you head to ____________________, located at 1° S and 37° E, where one of your satellite offices is located. Meanwhile, your partner takes off for Cape Town, South Africa, located at____________________ (latitude/longitude) to visit with an old friend while awaiting Mr. X's next move. Within days you learn that your information was wrong. Mr. X was last located on a boat at 40° S and 20° W in the ____________________ ____________________, and the boat is traveling west toward the____________________ ____________________continent. You and your partner charter an airplane and are waiting for him at____________________, located at 23° S and 43° W. Your mission is almost complete. You transport him back to the United States, located on the____________________ ____________________ continent, and turn him over to the head of the spy ring, whose home base is in ____________________, located at 39° N and 90° W. You say goodbye to your partner and head home to wait for your next assignment.

The following places are identified by their relative locations. Use the clues (and a world map if necessary) to name each country.

8. This country/continent is located in the Pacific Ocean. New Zealand lies southeast of it.

9. This Asian country is between Russia and China.

10. This country, located on the continent of Africa, is bordered by the Democratic Republic of the Congo on the north, Tanzania on the northeast, Angola on the west, and Namibia and Botswana on the south.

11. This country is located on the continent of Europe. Germany is to the north, Italy to the south, France to the west and Austria to the east of the country.

12. This country is north of the United States on the North American continent.

13. This country borders the Atlantic Ocean on the South American continent. Guyana, Suriname, and French Guiana are to the north.

Climate Zones

Climate maps are used to show dominant weather patterns in certain areas. Use the Climate Zones map on page 708 to answer these questions.

14. What are the major climate zones at 60° N latitude?

15. Describe the climate at the equator.

© 2016 K12 Inc. All rights reserved.
Copying or distributing without K12's written consent is prohibited.

Name Date 

16. The ocean currents below 60° S latitude would be cool. True or false?

17. Describe the climate in the northern half of Africa.

The scale on a map is used to represent distances between points on a map. Use the scale on the North America map, page 696, to approximate the following distances:

18. Between New York City and Washington, D.C.

19. Between Edmonton and Winnipeg

20. Between San Francisco, California, and Tijuana, Mexico

Continents and Oceans
A continent is one of the seven principal landmasses on Earth. The seven continents are Asia, Africa, Australia, Antarctica, North America, South America, and Europe.

The ocean is the body of salt water that covers 70 percent of the Earth's surface and is divided into four primary oceans. The four oceans are the Atlantic, Arctic, Pacific and Indian.

Study the location of the continents and oceans in your textbook on pages 690-691. Then go online and complete the Continents and Oceans activity.

© 2016 K12 Inc. All rights reserved.
Copying or distributing without K12's written consent is prohibited.

Getting Started

Day 1

Your Passport to *The Human Odyssey*

1. On what page does Part 4 begin?
   page 518

2. In the Introduction to Part 2 there is a photograph of a small ship used by fifteenth-century Portuguese explorers. What is the name of this type of ship?
   caravel

3. On what page does the Prologue begin? What are the major topics in the Prologue?
   It begins on page 8. First the Prologue briefly summarizes the content in the first volume of *The Human Odyssey*. Next the Prologue defines the term *modern* and explains why the second volume of *The Human Odyssey* is about the modern world. Lastly, the Prologue outlines the big ideas that the second volume of *The Human Odyssey* will cover.

5. What does the map on page 152 show?
   China and Japan, and the Ming Dynasty, 1368-1644

6. Who is the figure in the image to the left of the first column on page 318, and what is he doing?
   Isaac Newton; sitting, thinking

7. Which of the following three events happened first?
   Columbus sails from Spain to the Americas.

8. In what year did Nicholas Copernicus publish *On the Revolution of Heavenly Bodies*?
   1543

9. In what direction (north, west, northeast, etc.) would you be heading if you traveled from Kandahar, Afghanistan to Ahmadabad, India?
   southeast

10. What map projection is an elliptical equal-area projection that distorts shapes near the edges?
    Mollweide

11. What two climate zones comprise most of Australia?
    dry desert and semiarid steppe

12. Write the definition and pronunciation for *boyars.*
    Powerful landowning nobles of Russia (BOH-yahrz)

13. On what two pages can you read about Kublai Khan?
    151, 161

14. What is this story about?
    Olaudah Equiano, a former slave, describes incidents in the voyage across the Atlantic Ocean aboard a slave ship.

© 2016 K12 Inc. All rights reserved.
Copying or distributing without K12's written consent is prohibited.

Read On

Reading Guide

1. Explain how Christianity spread throughout Europe.
   Answers may vary but should include some of the following information. Amid the chaos of war waged by Germanic tribes, Christian missionaries spread the gospel of their religion. Monks started monasteries and schools throughout Europe. Bishops oversaw the building of cathedrals. Priests worked among common folk on manors and in cities.

2. What caused Christendom to be a troubled realm at the end of the Middle Ages?
   The Christian Church was engaged in infighting over the three leaders. Many people were dying of starvation due to the famine. In many towns, more than half the people had died from the "Black Death." War raged as England and France fought the Hundred Years' War.

3. What elements helped the Byzantine Empire rise to power during the early Middle Ages?
   The Byzantine Empire straddled Europe and Asia. Ambitious emperors expanded the empire. The Empire was a center of trade, and the trade goods went to and came from distant parts of the world. Scholarship thrived, and many learned men moved to Byzantium.

4. How did the Muslim world help keep learning alive?
   In the House of Wisdom, Baghdad's famous library, Muslim, Jewish, and Christian scholars translated texts from all over the world. Muslim scholars worked hard to advance every field of knowledge, including mathematics, astronomy, and medicine. Muslim translation and scholarship could be found in many Muslim cities.

5. What factors caused the fall of the Mongols' empire?
   The Mongols had a hard time ruling their vast domain. They weren't skilled at running the machinery of government. During the fourteenth century, the Mongols faced challenges in all parts of their empire. The Chinese expelled the Mongol Yuan dynasty. The Russians plotted to overthrow their Tatar masters. Ottoman Turks in Asia Minor grew restless under Mongol rule.

Day 2

Focus on Geography

Reviewing Map Skills

1. Look at the map of North America on page 696, and find the island of Greenland to the northeast of the continent. This is a fairly accurate representation. Now look at the maps on pages 706-707. In which projection is Greenland most distorted? In what way?
   The Miller projection is the most distorted because Greenland appears to be wider and shorter.

2. Which map projection would give navigators trouble if they tried to trace a water route between two places?
   Goode's Interrupted Homosoline

3. On which two map projections do the landmasses look most similar?
   Mollweide and Winkel Tripel

4. Look at the map of Africa on page 699, what are the latitude and longitude coordinates for Cairo, Egypt?
   30°N, 31°E

© 2016 K12 Inc. All rights reserved.
Copying or distributing without K12's written consent is prohibited.

5. Find Liberia on the map of Africa, is it located east or west of the prime meridian (o°)?
   West

6. Find Zimbabwe on the map of Africa, is it located north or south of the equator?
   South

7. Use a world atlas to identify each place. Where appropriate, give the city and the country.
   Tokyo, Japan
   Taipei, Taiwan
   Asia
   Himalaya
   Hawaii
   Indian Ocean
   Nairobi, Kenya
   34° S, 18° E
   Atlantic Ocean
   South American
   Rio de Janeiro, Brazil
   North American
   St. Louis, Missouri

8. This country/continent is located in the Pacific Ocean. New Zealand lies southeast of it.
   Australia

9. This Asian country is between Russia and China.
   Mongolia

10. This country, located on the continent of Africa, is bordered by the Democratic Republic of the Congo on the north, Tanzania on the northeast, Angola on the west, and Namibia and Botswana on the south.
    Zambia

11. This country is located on the continent of Europe. Germany is to the north, Italy to the south, France to the west and Austria to the east of the country.
    Switzerland

12. This country is north of the United States on the North American continent.
    Canada

13. This country borders the Atlantic Ocean on the South American continent. Guyana, Suriname, and French Guiana are to the north.
    Brazil

14. What are the major climate zones at 60° N latitude?
    Subarctic, tundra, and humid continental

15. Describe the major climate at the equator.
    Tropical and wet

16. The ocean currents below 60° S latitude would be cool. True or False?
    True

17. Describe the climate in the northern half of Africa?
    Very dry with desert-like conditions

© 2016 K12 Inc. All rights reserved.
Copying or distributing without K12's written consent is prohibited.

18. Between New York City and Washington, D.C.
    Approximately 234 miles or 375 kilometers

19. Between Edmonton and Winnipeg
    Approximately 750 miles or 1300 kilometers

20. Between San Francisco, California and Tijuana, Mexico
    Approximately 468 miles or 750 kilometers

© 2016 K12 Inc. All rights reserved.
Copying or distributing without K12's written consent is prohibited.

Student Guide

Unit 2: A Renaissance Begins in Europe
Lesson 1: Europe Reborn: Rediscovering Greece and Rome

During the fourteenth century, western Europeans developed a renewed interest in the ancient Greek and Roman civilizations. The "rebirth" of interest in classical learning sparked a period of tremendous creativity that lasted until the early seventeenth century. We know that period as the Renaissance. Italian geniuses like Dante, Giotto, and Petrarch forged the way with innovative ideas that gave Europeans a new understanding of human worth and potential.

Lesson Objectives

- Define the Renaissance as a period of artistic and literary achievement in Europe from the late fourteenth to the early seventeenth centuries, inspired by new interest in the classics.
- Identify Giotto as a fourteenth-century Italian painter who introduced lifelike figures to painting.
- Explain that the word *renaissance* means "rebirth."
- Identify Dante as the fourteenth-century Italian poet who wrote *The Divine Comedy*.
- Describe Dante's *Divine Comedy* as significant for introducing realistic characters to literature and being written in Italian, rather than Latin.
- Identify Petrarch as the fourteenth-century Italian scholar known as the father of humanism.
- Define *humanism* as a movement that stressed the wisdom of the classics and the dignity of humans and human potential.
- Review historical events.

PREPARE

Approximate lesson time is 60 minutes.

Materials

For the Student

- Document Analysis: Letter to Cicero
- Reading Guide

The Human Odyssey, Volume 2 edited by Klee, Cribb, and Holdren

History Journal

LEARN

Activity 1: Classical - Medieval - Renaissance *(Online)*

This lesson is designed to be completed in **3** class sessions.

Begin today's lesson by examining art and literature to find out how ancient Greek and Roman ideas inspired three great Italians to break away from the styles of the Middle Ages.

© 2016 K12 Inc. All rights reserved.
Copying or distributing without K12's written consent is prohibited.

Activity 2: Leading the Way *(Offline)*

This lesson is designed to be completed in 3 class sessions. We recommend following the schedule in the Student Guide. To keep track of your progress, you may want to check the box next to each activity title when you have completed the activity.

Instructions

Day 1

Read

Read Chapter 1, from the beginning to "Petrarch Seeks Classical Wisdom," pages 24 to 29, and complete the Day 1 section of the Reading Guide. When you have finished, use the Lesson Answer Key to check your work. Place the Reading Guide in your History Journal.

Giotto Breaks With the Past

Like most great medieval artists, Giotto frequently painted scenes from the Bible and other religious subjects. But Giotto approached his compositions differently and broke away from the old medieval styles.

Go online and study the images in the Giotto Breaks with the Past activity and answer the questions. When you have completed the activity and compared your answers with those in the Lesson Answer Key, you will have finished today's portion of the lesson.

Day 2

Read

Read Chapter 1, from "Petrarch Seeks Classical Wisdom" to the end, pages 30 to 33, and complete the Day 2 section of the Reading Guide. Check your work with the Lesson Answer Key and place the completed Reading Guide in your History Journal.

Historical Close-up: Document Analysis

Petrarch lived in a time when scholars were rediscovering classical texts that had been lost for hundreds of years. He was fascinated by the ancient texts. His work as a priest allowed him to travel throughout Italy. As he traveled, he searched for ancient Roman manuscripts. Petrarch was discouraged by the corruption he saw in society and the church. He became convinced that the classical thinkers of Greece and Rome possessed the wisdom to restore the light of virtue and learning to a corrupt Christendom.

Petrarch often wrote letters to Homer, Virgil, Livy, Cicero, and other Greek and Roman writers. One of Petrarch's letters is in your book, on pages 34 to 35. Use the letter to complete the Document Analysis: Letter to Cicero sheet. Use the Lesson Answer Key to check your work, and place the completed sheet in your History Journal.

Day 3

A Letter to the Past

Dante, Giotto, and Petrarch were three men from the late Middle Ages who were "ahead of their time." All three looked to the classical past for inspiration. All three realized that classical art and literature provided insight into human abilities and potential. The changes they embraced helped usher in the Renaissance.

Which of these three men interests you most as a representative of the idea that the times were changing? Write a letter to him.

In your letter:

© 2016 K12 Inc. All rights reserved.
Copying or distributing without K12's written consent is prohibited.

Introduce yourself and explain that you have been reading about the beginnings of the Renaissance.
Inform him that you believe he represents the changing times in Italy in the late fourteenth century very well, and explain why.
Describe the medieval attitudes and beliefs he challenged and some of the ways the ideas of the classical world influenced him. Be specific. Use examples.

ASSESS

Lesson Assessment: Europe Reborn: Rediscovering Greece and Rome (*Online*)

You will complete an online assessment covering the main objectives of this lesson. Your assessment will be scored by the computer.

LEARN

Activity 3. Optional: Europe Reborn: Rediscovering Greece and Rome *(Online)*

© 2016 K12 Inc. All rights reserved.
Copying or distributing without K12's written consent is prohibited.

Name Date 

Reading Guide

Day 1

1. What is the *Renaissance*?

Dante

2. What is *The Divine Comedy*? What is it about?

3. Dante grew up in the Italian city-state of ______________________.

4. What happened to Dante that led him to write epic poetry?

5. Dante was inspired by the writing of the classical Roman poets ________________, ________________, and ____________________.

6. ______________________ is Dante's guide in the first two parts of *The Divine Comedy*.

7. In what ways did Dante's epic poem reflect Christian beliefs during the Middle Ages?

8. How did the language of *The Divine Comedy* differ from other philosophical works of the Middle Ages? What effect did Dante's decision to write his poem in Italian have?

9. How were Dante's characters different from the characters found in most early medieval poems?

Giotto

10. Like most great medieval artists, Giotto usually chose ____________________ subject matter.

11. Briefly describe how most medieval art depicted people.

12. How were Giotto's paintings of people different?

© 2016 K12 Inc. All rights reserved.
Copying or distributing without K12's written consent is prohibited.

Name Date 

Day 2

Petrarch

13. Petrarch's father wanted him to become a lawyer, but Petrarch was more interested in ______
____

14. Scholars in Petrarch's time were discovering ______________________________
____

15. Where were the classical texts coming from?

16. What did working for the papal court allow Petrarch to do? What did he dislike about the papal court?

17. What did Petrarch believe could be gained from studying the ancient thinkers of Greece and Rome?

18. Describe the new educational program that Petrarch proposed.

19. How did Petrarch hold both a Christian view and a classical view of the world without conflict?

Thinking Cap Question

What did Dante, Giotto, and Petrarch have in common that set them apart from most scholars and artists of their time?

© 2016 K12 Inc. All rights reserved.
Copying or distributing without K12's written consent is prohibited.

Name ____ Date ____________________ 

Document Analysis: Letter to Cicero

Use the letter on pages 34 to 35 of your book to answer the following questions. Where appropriate, provide support for your answers.

1. The author of the letters is __________, who wrote them in _________.

2. The letters were written to __________________ who lived _______ years earlier.

3. Which sentence in the first paragraph of the document tells us that Petrarch did not give up easily?

Answer each question below and then copy a quotation from the document that supports your answer.

4. What does Petrarch think of Cicero?

   Answer: ____

   ____

   Supporting Quotation: ____

   ____

5. Did Cicero's manuscripts and letters still in exist in the mid-fourteenth century?

   Answer: ____

   ____

   Supporting Quotation: ____

   ____

6. Did many people in Petrarch's time read works by Cicero and his contemporaries?

   Answer: ____

   ____

   Supporting Quotation: ____

   ____

© 2016 K12 Inc. All rights reserved.
Copying or distributing without K12's written consent is prohibited.

Name ______________________________ Date ______________________________

7. What was Petrarch's outlook for the future and what did he attribute that outlook to?

   Answer: ______________________________

   ____

   Supporting Quotation: ______________________________

   ____

8. How do you think Petrarch would view the work of archaeologists today?

   Answer: ______________________________

   ____

   Supporting Quotation: ______________________________

   ____

© 2016 K12 Inc. All rights reserved.
Copying or distributing without K12's written consent is prohibited.

Student Guide
Lesson 2: Cities Spur Change

Look at the map of the Italian peninsula at the dawn of the Renaissance. What does it look like to you? It reminds many people of a jigsaw puzzle of a boot. Each piece represents a separate city-state. Some city-states were big and powerful and others were tiny but important. The people in all of the city-states considered themselves Italian and spoke one Italian dialect or another, but each city-state ruled itself. Powerful merchant families ruled many of the city-states. As these powerful families competed, fought, and intermarried, the political map of Italy shifted.

Lesson Objectives

- Explain that Italian city-states were often republics led by powerful merchant families.
- Describe the role of guilds in Italian city-states.
- Describe Renaissance cities as catalysts for change at the close of the Middle Ages.
- Identify on a map major city-states including Venice, Florence, Rome, and the German city of Augsburg.
- Describe major characteristics of some of the city-states and identify some of the important individuals associated with them.
- Define *manuscript* and explain why manuscripts were very expensive.
- Identify Johannes Gutenberg as the fifteenth-century inventor of the modern printing press.
- Explain the social significance of the printing press.

PREPARE

Approximate lesson time is 60 minutes.

Advance Preparation

- The next lesson includes David by Donatello and Birth of Venus by Sandro Botticelli. These famous works of art fall into the category known as a nude. While the general culture contains a great deal of material that demeans the human body, you may wish to help your student understand that at least since the time of ancient Greece and Rome, many outstanding artists have tried, in a variety of works, both secular and religious, to show the beauty, strength, and dignity of the unclothed human form.

Materials

For the Student

- Map of Renaissance City-States
- Reading Guide
- Venice: Queen of the Adriatic

The Human Odyssey, Volume 2 edited by Klee, Cribb, and Holdren

History Journal

© 2016 K12 Inc. All rights reserved.
Copying or distributing without K12's written consent is prohibited.

Keywords and Pronunciation

Assisi ((uh-SEE-see))
Augsburg (AWKS-bourk)
Bologna (boh-LOH-nyah)
city-state : an independently ruled city and the land around it
doge (dohj)
Ferrara (fehr-RAH-rah)
Fust (foost)
Genoa (JEH-noh-uh)
guild : an association of people, usually merchants or craftsmen, who set work standards and protect their interests
Johannes Gutenberg (yoh-HAHN-uhs GOOT-n-burg)
Mainz (miynts)
manuscript : a handwritten composition or document
Medici (MED-uh-chee)
Murano (myoo-RAH-noh)
Padua (PAH-dyou-wuh)
palazzi (pah-LAHT-zee)
Rodrigo Borgia (roh-DREE-gh BOR-juh)
Siena (see-EH-nah)
Strasbourg (STRAHS-bourg)
Urbino (uhr-BEE-nh)

LEARN

Activity 1: Europe's Revived Cities *(Offline)*

This lesson is designed to be completed in 3 class sessions. We recommend following the schedule in the Student Guide. To keep track of your progress, you may want to check the box next to each activity title when you have completed the activity.

Instructions

This lesson is designed to be completed in **3** class sessions. We recommend following the schedule in Day 1 **Read**Read Chapter 2, from the beginning to "Gutenberg and the Printing Press," pages 36 to 45, and complete **Day 1** of the Reading Guide. When you have finished, use the Lesson Answer Key to check your work. Place the Reading Guide in your History Journal.

Day 2

ReadRead Chapter 2, from "Gutenberg and the Printing Press" to the end, pages 45 to 49, and complete **Day 2** of the Reading Guide. Check your work and place the completed Reading Guide in your History Journal.**Johannes Gutenberg**Go online and do the following:

- See how Gutenberg's printing press worked, and compare the efficiency of using the press to print out text and writing the text out by hand.
- Create a Flash Card about Johannes Gutenberg. Use the information you read in the Historical Close-up on page 45 in the textbook.

© 2016 K12 Inc. All rights reserved.
Copying or distributing without K12's written consent is prohibited.

Day 3

Create a Brochure

In today's lesson you will create a brochure on the city of Venice during the Renaissance.

You have been hired by the Renaissance city of Venice to create a brochure about Venice. It should highlight the characteristics of the city-state that will draw newcomers and businesses. You should make Venice sound very attractive to potential residents.

Start by answering the questions on the Venice: Queen of the Adriatic sheet. Then use the sheet to guide your research. To find the answers to the questions and more information about Venice, go to the Grolier's Online website in Unit Resources. Enter Venice in the search box. After you've finished your research, write your brochure. You might want to add pictures to enhance your brochure.

ASSESS

Lesson Assessment: Cities Spur Change (*Online*)

You will complete an online assessment covering the main objectives of this lesson. Your assessment will be scored by the computer.

© 2016 K12 Inc. All rights reserved.
Copying or distributing without K12's written consent is prohibited.

Name Date 

Reading Guide

Day 1

City-States

1. If the medieval world had been shaped by the manor, the Renaissance world was forged by ___________ .

2. What is a *city-state*? What type of government did many Italian city-states in the Renaissance have?

3. What made people flock to the Renaissance cities?

4. What did craftsmen and merchants try to do to make more money?

5. What did the rich business owners do with some of their money?

6. What were some disadvantages of living in the Renaissance cities?

7. What are *guilds*?

8. Why did guilds want to influence the city government?

9. Print the Renaissance City-States map, and then complete the textboxes on the map.

© 2016 K12 Inc. All rights reserved.
Copying or distributing without K12's written consent is prohibited.

Name Date 

Day 2
Gutenberg and the Printing Press

10. What are *manuscripts*? Why were they so expensive in the early fifteenth century?

11. Where did Gutenberg get the idea for the printing press?

12. Describe how Gutenberg's printing press worked.

13. Why did Gutenberg choose the Bible as the first book he wanted to print?

14. How did Gutenberg's printing press influence literacy and scholarship?

15. Why is the printing press considered one of the most significant inventions in history?

16. You have read about Gutenberg and the significance of his printing press. Now think about how the availability of printed material has affected society since then. List ways in which everyday life and thought might have changed as a result of the printing press. To help you get started, here are some categories you might want to think about:
    - Education
    - Politics
    - Religion
    - Entertainment

© 2016 K12 Inc. All rights reserved.
Copying or distributing without K12's written consent is prohibited.

Name ______________________________ Date ______________________________ 

Renaissance City-States

Mainz
Nuremburg
EUROPE
Milan
Mantua
Genoa
Pisa
Arno R.
Adriatic Sea
Naples
Tyrrhenian Sea
Mediterranean Sea
N

City-state: ____________

Geography:

Trade/Industry:

Government:

Other:

City-state: ____________

Geography:

Government:

Other:

City-state: ____________

Geography:

Trade/Industry:

Government:

Other:

City-state: ____________

Geography:

Trade/Industry:

Government:

Other:

© 2016 K12 Inc. All rights reserved.
Copying or distributing without K12's written consent is prohibited.

Name Date 

Venice: Queen of the Adriatic

1. Where is Venice? Describe its location in relation to some of its neighboring city-states.

2. When was Venice founded? Why did the first settlers choose that location? What geographic advantages did Venice have?

3. What role did Venice's location play in its growth and development?

4. How has the population of Venice changed between the Renaissance and today?

5. What were the most important industries in Venice in Renaissance times?

6. What are the most important industries in Venice today?

7. What are some places of interest in Venice today?

© 2016 K12 Inc. All rights reserved.
Copying or distributing without K12's written consent is prohibited.

Student Guide
Lesson 3: Genius in Florence

Florence wasn't the biggest or most powerful city-state, but its citizens were very successful in business. Florentines turned gold into the world's finest jewelry, made the best leather goods, and wove beautiful wool that was prized by nobles all over Europe and beyond.
The Medicis made a fortune in textiles, and then turned to banking, becoming the richest and most powerful family in Italy. Then, without lifting a paintbrush or touching a chisel, without writing a single book, or designing even the smallest building, they made Florence a center of classical learning and fabulous Renaissance art.

Lesson Objectives

- Identify Florence as the birthplace of the Renaissance.
- Describe the source of Florence's wealth and power as trade in luxury goods.
- Identify the Medici as the most powerful family in Florence, owners of the most powerful banks in Europe, and patrons of the arts and learning.
- Explain how Renaissance art differed from medieval art.
- Identify the major Florentine artists including Donatello, Brunelleschi, Masaccio, Botticelli, da Vinci, and their achievements.
- Give an example of the controversy created by humanism and other Renaissance ideas.

PREPARE

Approximate lesson time is 60 minutes.

Advance Preparation

- The next lesson includes *David* by Michelangelo. This famous work of art falls into the category known as a nude. While the general culture contains a great deal of material that demeans the human body, you may wish to help your student understand that at least since the time of ancient Greece and Rome, many outstanding artists have tried, in a variety of works, both secular and religious, to show the beauty, strength, and dignity of the unclothed human form.

Materials

For the Student

- Leonardo da Vinci's Early Years
- Reading Guide
- Renaissance Art and Architecture
- Renaissance Florence

© 2016 K12 Inc. All rights reserved.
Copying or distributing without K12's written consent is prohibited.

Keywords and Pronunciation

Andrea del Verrocchio (anh-DREH-ah del vahr-ROHK-koyoh)
Cosimo (KAW-zee-moh)
Donatello (dahn-uh-TEL-oh)
Filippo Brunelleschi (fee-LEEP-poh broo-nehl-ES-kee)
florin (FLOR-uhn) : gold coin minted in Florence
friar : a member of a religious order dedicated to teaching and serving the poor
Giorgio Vasari (JOR-joh-vah-ZAH-ree)
Giovanni de' Medici (joh-VAHN-nee d´ MED-uh-chee)
Girolamo Savonarola (jee-ROH-lah-moh SAH-voh-nah-ROH-lah)
Leonardo da Vinci (lay-uh-NAHR-doh duh VIN-chee)
Lorenzo Ghiberti (luh-REN-zoh gee-BEHR-tee)
Ludovico Sforza (loo-doh-VEE-koh SFORT-sah)
Masaccio (mah-ZAHT-choh)
Sandro Botticelli (SAHN-droh baht-uh-CHEL-ee)

LEARN

Activity 1: Florentine Artists and Architects *(Offline)*

This lesson is designed to be completed in 3 class sessions. We recommend following the schedule in the Student Guide. To keep track of your progress, you may want to check the box next to each activity title when you have completed the activity.

Instructions

Day 1

ReadRead Chapter 3 from the beginning to "Bonfire of the Vanities," pages 50 to 59, and complete **Day 1** of the Reading Guide. When you have finished, use the Lesson Answer Key to check your work. Place the Reading Guide in your History Journal.**Explore**

Go online to review how Renaissance art differed from medieval art by comparing two paintings. Click Medieval and Renaissance Art.

To see additional works of art by Renaissance artists and architects, you should visit the Art Explorer section of the Renaissance Connection website. Go to Resources and click Renaissance Connection. You can view the works of art by clicking the time line, the maps, or the alphabetical listing. While you are viewing these works of arts, look for characteristics and techniques that are typically found in Renaissance art but not in medieval art. You can learn more about Renaissance art by visiting Grolier's Online Encyclopedia and searching for Renaissance art.

© 2016 K12 Inc. All rights reserved.
Copying or distributing without K12's written consent is prohibited.

Day 2

Read
Read Chapter 2, from "Bonfire of the Vanities" to "Leonardo da Vinci's Early Years, pages 59 to 60, and complete **Day 2** of the Reading Guide. Check your work and place the completed Reading Guide in your History Journal.**A Letter to Savonarola**After you have finished your reading assignment, write a letter to Girolamo Savonarola explaining why the art and architecture of the Renaissance is so remarkable. Cite examples and information about Renaissance art and architecture to support your explanation.
Explore
Go online and choose Lives of the Artists by Giorgio Vasari from Resources. At this website you can read excerpts from the *Lives of the Artists* by Giorgio Vasari. You will use this source to complete the Renaissance Art and Architecture sheet. This activity will help you gain an understanding of the challenges faced in creating the dome of Santa Maria del Fiore.

Day 3

ReadRead Chapter 2, from "Leonardo da Vinci's Early Years" to the end, pages 61 to 65 and complete the Leonardo da Vinci chart. Check your work and place the completed chart in your History Journal.

ASSESS

Lesson Assessment: Genius in Florence (*Online*)

You will complete an online assessment covering the main objectives of this lesson. Your assessment will be scored by the computer.

LEARN

Activity 2. Optional: Genius in Florence *(Online)*

This activity is OPTIONAL. It's provided for enrichment or extra practice, but not required for completion of this lesson. You may skip this activity.

Visit the Renaissance Connection website and become a patron of the arts by playing the Be a Patron of the Arts game.

© 2016 K12 Inc. All rights reserved.
Copying or distributing without K12's written consent is prohibited.

Renaissance Art and Architecture

Giorgio Vasari was an Italian artist and architect who lived a century after Filippo Brunelleschi. He designed a building for the municipal offices of Florence that is used as an art museum today, but he is most famous for his biographies of Renaissance artists. Look at the questions below to determine which paragraphs from Vasari's *Lives of the Artists* to read. Learn how Fillippo Brunelleschi cleverly won the competition to build the cupola of Santa Maria del Fiore cathedral and then, answer the questions. (Note that your text and *Lives of the Artists* use different spellings for the artist's name. There are frequently discrepancies in the spelling of names in old manuscripts, particularly when the documents have been translated from one language to another.)

1. In the paragraph that begins "Filippo, as we have said, entered into competition with Lorenzo...", Filippo leaves Florence and goes to Rome to study architecture. What two ideas did Filippo have for studying Roman architecture?
   (Note: The Pantheon was built as a temple to the gods of Rome between A.D. 118 and 125. It became a Christian Church in the 600s, and is now a museum.)

2. In the paragraph that begins "The other architects meanwhile being dismayed...", the people in charge of building the cathedral's cupola ask Brunelleschi for advice. What does he tell them?
   (Note: When the author refers to a "cupola" he means the dome of the cathedral.)

Scroll to the paragraph that begins "So the Florentine merchants..." and answer the following questions.

3. How did some of the other architects propose to build the dome?

4. Why did everyone mock and laugh at Brunelleschi's proposal?

5. Why didn't Brunelleschi show the council a model of his proposal?

© 2016 K12 Inc. All rights reserved.
Copying or distributing without K12's written consent is prohibited.

6. The paragraph that begins "So Filippo, not having succeeded at the assembly," explains how Brunelleschi won the competition. How did he win?

7. How did Brunelleschi arrange to be the sole manager of the cupola project and at the same time shame his rival Lorenzo Ghiberti?

8. How do you think Vasari would describe Brunelleschi in just a few words? Do you think Vasari's biography of Brunelleschi is objective (free of opinion)? Why or why not?

9. What does Vasari's description of Brunelleschi's actions and the actions of others reveal about the lives of Renaissance artists and architects?

10. Is Vasari's *Lives of the Artists* a primary source? Explain your answer.

© 2016 K12 Inc. All rights reserved.
Copying or distributing without K12's written consent is prohibited.

Reading Guide

Day 1

Read

1. On which river is Florence located?

   a. Po
   b. Tiber
   c. Arno
   d. Danube

2. Which factor may explain why the Renaissance began in Florence?

   a. Its army was large and powerful.
   b. It was the biggest city-state in Italy.
   c. It had a great seaport.
   d. Its people were resourceful and ambitious.

3. What are *florins?*

   a. Florentine coins
   b. Florentine chocolates
   c. Florentine jewelry
   d. Florentine cloth

4. Which of the following did the city council **not** do to improve the appearance of Florence?

   a. Arrested artists, sculptors, and architects whose works resembled the art and architecture of classical Greece and Rome.
   b. Hired architects to build magnificent offices and churches.
   c. Paid sculptors to fill the city's public squares and guildhalls with statues.
   d. Commissioned artists to create stunning paintings and frescoes.

5. Identify characteristics of Florence and the accomplishments of its citizens by completing the Renaissance Florence sheet.

Day 2

Read

6. Who was Girolamo Savonarola?

7. Why did Savonarola oppose many Renaissance ideas?

© 2016 K12 Inc. All rights reserved.
Copying or distributing without K12's written consent is prohibited.

8. How did some Florentines respond to Savonarola's ideas, sermons, and accusations?

9. What were some of the vanities of the Florentines that Savonarola criticized?

10. What finally led to Savonarola's demise?

© 2016 K12 Inc. All rights reserved.
Copying or distributing without K12's written consent is prohibited.

Name Date

Renaissance Florence

Identify Florence's characteristics and accomplishments by completing the chart.

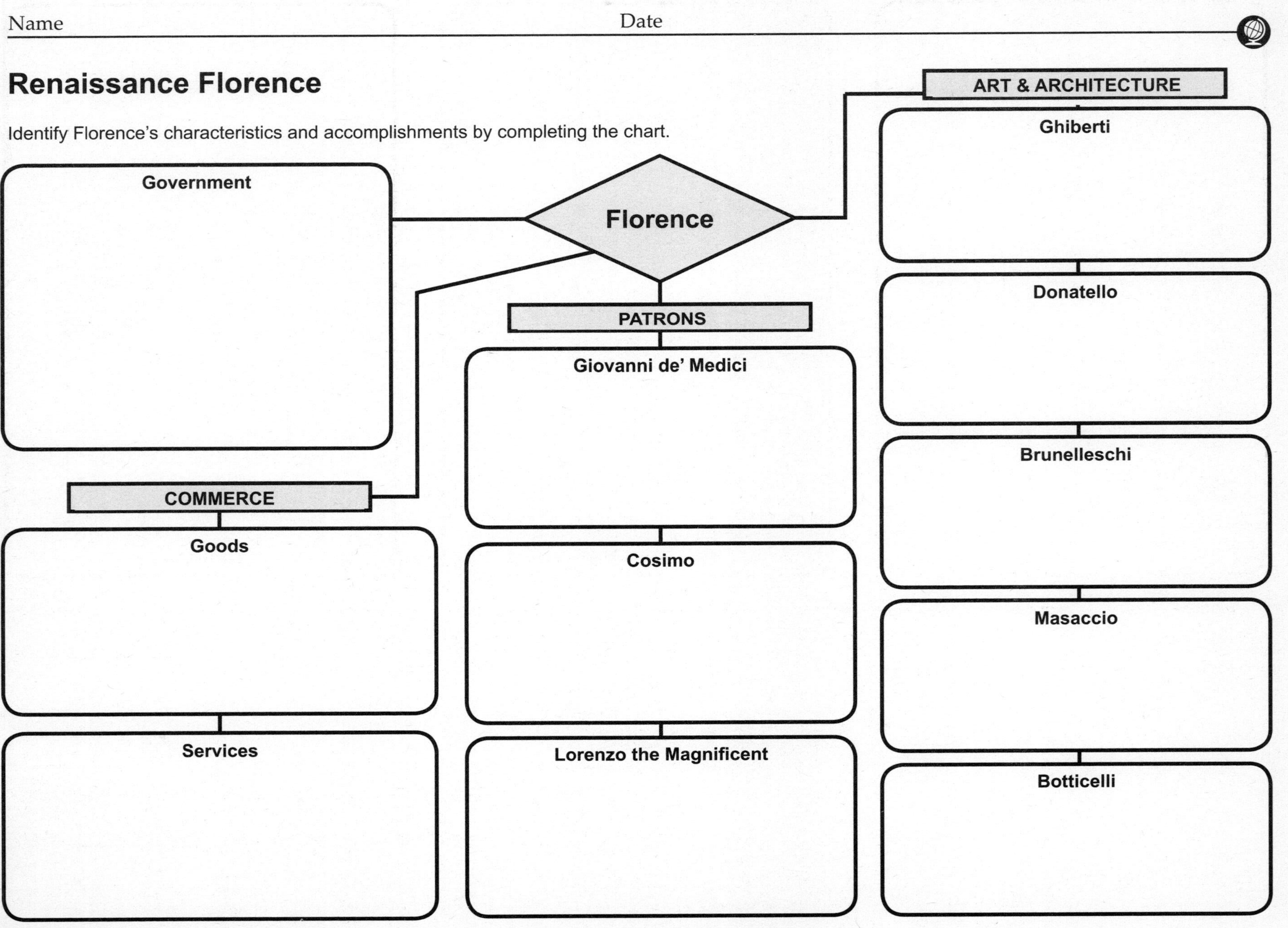

© 2016 K12 Inc. All rights reserved.
Copying or distributing without K12's written consent is prohibited.

Name Date

Leonardo da Vinci's Early Years

Briefly describe Leonardo da Vinci's major accomplishments in each place.

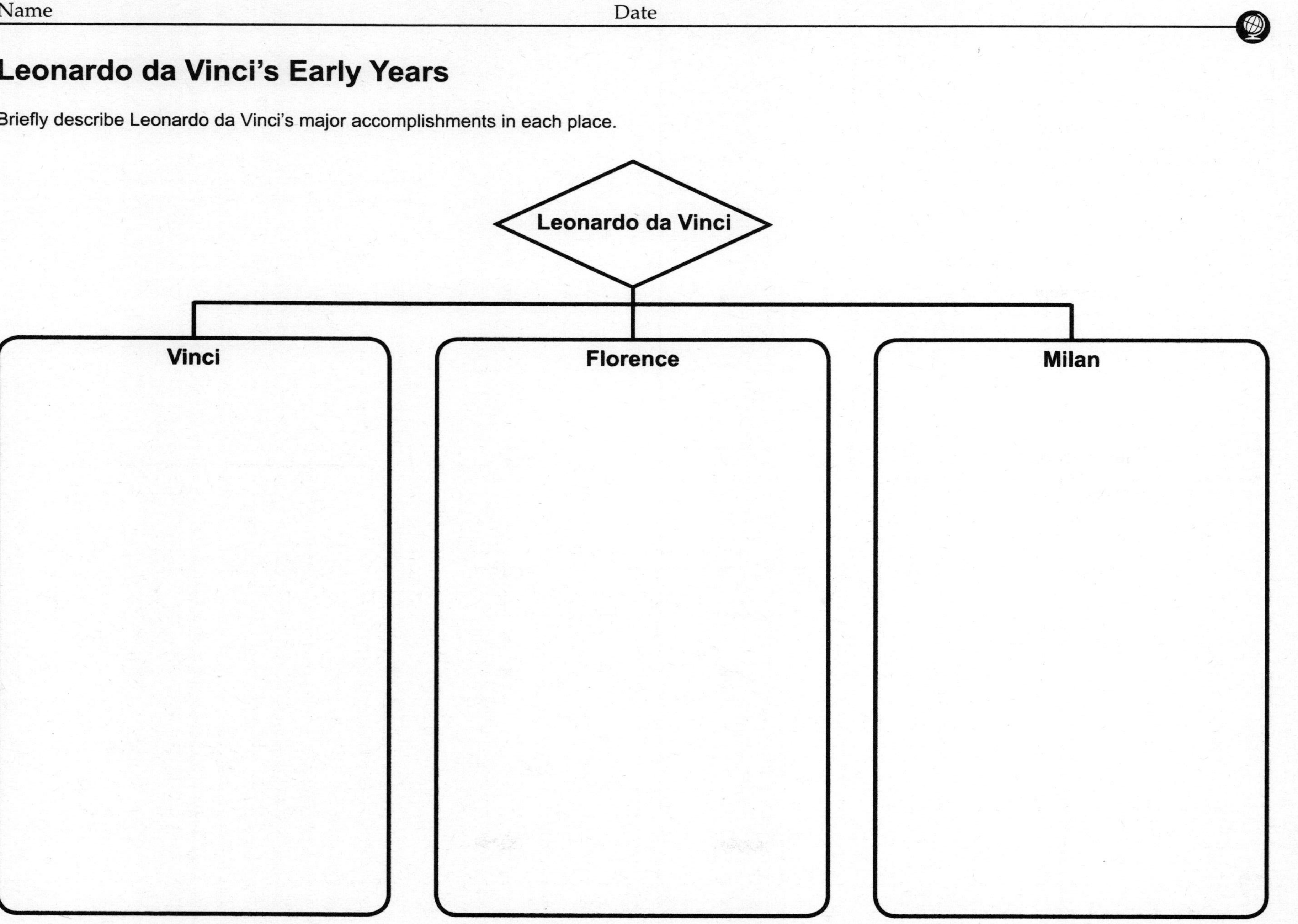

© 2016 K12 Inc. All rights reserved.
Copying or distributing without K12's written consent is prohibited.

Student Guide
Lesson 4: Rome Revived

By the late Middle Ages, Rome—once the heart of classical civilization and center of the Christian Church—had fallen into ruins. Ancient temples housed filthy markets. People had taken stones from the Colosseum to build their own homes. When the papacy returned to Rome after years of exile in France in 1417, the pope was dismayed at what he saw. Could the popes use their wealth and power in Rome the way the Medici family had in Florence? Churches, statues, paintings, gardens, libraries, aqueducts.... Rome would be Rome again, and Italy's greatest artists would be called on to make it happen.

Lesson Objectives

- Describe Rome in the early 1400s and explain the reasons for its condition.
- Recognize Rome's historical significance to the Christian Church.
- Describe the role of the popes as patrons of art and literature and restorers of the city of Rome, and how they financed the work.
- Give examples of the achievements and weaknesses of the Renaissance popes.
- Identify Michelangelo as the great Florentine sculptor and painter whose work includes the *Pietà, David,* the Sistine Chapel ceiling, and the dome of St. Peter's Basilica.
- Identify Raphael as the Renaissance painter known for paintings of Madonnas and frescoes.
- Analyze art to gain understanding of Renaissance thinking.

PREPARE

Approximate lesson time is 60 minutes.

Materials

For the Student

- Analyzing Art
- Outline
- Sistine Chapel

The Human Odyssey, Volume 2 edited by Klee, Cribb, and Holdren

Keywords and Pronunciation

basilica (buh-SIH-lih-kuh)
Giuliano della Rovere (jool-YAH-noh del-lah roh-VEH-reh)
Laocoon (lay-AH-kuh-wahn)
Michelangelo Buonarroti (miy-kuh-LAN-jeh-loh bwaw-nahr-RAW-tee)
pieta (pee-ay-TAH)
Raphael Sanzio (RAF-ee-uhl SAHNT-syoh)

© 2016 K12 Inc. All rights reserved.
Copying or distributing without K12's written consent is prohibited.

LEARN

Activity 1: A Revived Rome *(Offline)*

This lesson is designed to be completed in 3 class sessions. We recommend following the schedule in the Student Guide. To keep track of your progress, you may want to check the box next to each activity title when you have completed the activity.

Instructions

Day 1

Read

Read Chapter 4 from the beginning to "Raphael: The Prince of Painters," pages 66 to 75, and Michelangelo and Julius: A Stormy Relationship, pages 75 to 76. Complete **Day 1** of the Outline. When you have finished, use the Lesson Answer Key to check your work, and then place the Outline in your History Journal.

Michelangelo's *David*

Go online to complete the Michelangelo's *David* activity. For help with this activity, refer to the information in the textbook on pages 71 to 75. When you have finished, print the activity and compare your answers to those in the Answer Key, and then place the activity in your History Journal.

Day 2

Explore

In 1508, Michelangelo was commissioned by Pope Julius II to repaint the ceiling of the Sistine Chapel. At first, Michelangelo tried to refuse the project because he thought of himself as a sculptor and not a painter. Julius would not listen to him and eventually Michelangelo agreed to paint the chapel ceiling.

Go online to analyze and interpret the paintings on the ceiling of the Sistine Chapel. Print the Sistine Chapel activity and as you visit the websites complete this activity. You may wish to have an adult join you for this activity so you can discuss the artwork.

Go to Lesson Resources and click the following websites to learn more about the frescoes on the ceiling of the Sistine Chapel.

- Study of the ceiling frescoes
- Scenes from the Genesis
- Sistine Chapel

Day 3

Read

Read Chapter 4 from "Raphael: The Prince of Painters" to the end, pages 75 to 79, and complete **Day 3** of the Outline. When you have finished, use the Lesson Answer Key to check your work, and then place the Outline in your History Journal.

Explore

Go to Lesson Resources and click the National Gallery of Art website. View some of the magnificent artworks in the Raphael collection. After you have finished the tour at the National Gallery of Art, visit the Web Gallery of Art to analyze Raphael's *The School of Athens* painting by completing the Analyzing Art activity.

Note: You may also use the picture of *The School of Athens* in the textbook on pages 78 to 79.

© 2016 K12 Inc. All rights reserved.
Copying or distributing without K12's written consent is prohibited.

ASSESS

Lesson Assessment: Rome Revived (*Online*)

You will complete an online assessment covering the main objectives of this lesson. Your assessment will be scored by the computer.

© 2016 K12 Inc. All rights reserved.
Copying or distributing without K12's written consent is prohibited.

Analyzing Art: *The School of Athens*

1. In what time period does this scene occur? What elements in the scene help you determine the time period?

2. Describe the subject of this painting. Whom do the people or figures in this scene represent?

3. What symbols does Raphael use and what do they represent?

4. What was one of Raphael's reasons for painting this scene?

5. Raphael included some Renaissance artists in this painting. Name at least three of them and describe where they are located.

© 2016 K12 Inc. All rights reserved.
Copying or distributing without K12's written consent is prohibited.

Name ____________________ Date ____________________ 

Outline

Day 1

I. Rome – Early 1400s

The walls of the ____________ were crumbling. The once-magnificent stadium housed scores of ____________. ____________ lurked in the ancient baths. On Capitoline HIll, the old center of Roman government, ____________.

One humanist lamented that the ____________, once the heart of an empire, had turned into "____________, here the home of ____________."

II. The Popes Restore Rome

Rome was the historic center of the ____________. During the fourteenth century, ____________ had forced popes to live in the town of Avignon. But by the early fifteenth century, Rome once again became the ____________ of the pope, who faced the enormous task of restoring the fallen city.

A. Money Source

____

____

____

____

B. Revival of Classical Learning

____

____

____

____

C. Pope Sixtus IV

Renaissance popes were often more concerned with ____________ ____________ than spiritual leadership.

1. Excesses

____

____

____

© 2016 K12 Inc. All rights reserved.
Copying or distributing without K12's written consent is prohibited.

Name ______________________________ Date ______________________________ 

2. **Achievements**

____

____

____

____

D. Pope Julius II

1. **Background/Characteristics**

____

____

____

____

2. **Excesses**

____

____

____

____

3. **Achievements**

____

____

____

____

III. Michelangelo

The stormy relationship between ______________ and his patron, __________, led to some of the finest __________ the world has known.

A. Background – The Early Years

____

____

____

____

© 2016 K12 Inc. All rights reserved.
Copying or distributing without K12's written consent is prohibited.

B. His Stay with Lorenzo de' Medici

____

____

____

____

____

____

C. In Rome

In 1496, Michelangelo, age 21, traveled to ____________ for the first time.

____

____

____

____

____

____

D. Return to Florence

____

____

____

____

E. The Sistine Ceiling

____

____

____

____

F. The Tomb of Pope Julius

____

____

____

____

© 2016 K12 Inc. All rights reserved.
Copying or distributing without K12's written consent is prohibited.

G. **St. Peter's Basilica**

____

____

____

____

Day 3

IV. Raphael Sanzio

Raphael and his paintings were so popular that he was called "________________________

____."

A. **Background/Characteristics**

____

____

____

____

B. **The Works of Raphael**

____

____

____

____

____

____

© 2016 K12 Inc. All rights reserved.
Copying or distributing without K12's written consent is prohibited.

The Sistine Chapel

1. How big is the ceiling in the Sistine Chapel?

2. What was your first impression of the ceiling paintings? Describe how Michelangelo was able to paint on such a huge curving space that was up so high.

3. How long did it take Michelangelo to paint these frescoes? Did he have help?

4. What do all of the ceiling pieces have in common?

5. What do the paintings in the center of the ceiling illustrate?

6. Look at the nine main images in the center of the ceiling. Which do you think are the most striking images?

7. What are some of the emotions depicted in the nine images in the center of the ceiling?

Choose one of the images from the ceiling and answer the following:

8. What event is shown in this painting?

9. Describe the subject of the painting. Whom do the figures represent?

10. Describe the images or techniques Michelangelo used to express the meaning of the painting.

© 2016 K12 Inc. All rights reserved.
Copying or distributing without K12's written consent is prohibited.

Student Guide
Lesson 5. Optional: Your Choice

You may use today's lesson time to do one or more of the following:

- Complete work in progress.
- Complete the Beyond the Lesson activity in any lesson in this unit.
- Review the Time Line in the Resources section.
- Go on to the next lesson.

Please mark this lesson complete to proceed to the next lesson in the course.

PREPARE

Approximate lesson time is 60 minutes.

© 2016 K12 Inc. All rights reserved.
Copying or distributing without K12's written consent is prohibited.

Student Guide
Lesson 6: Unit Review

You've finished the unit, and now it's time to review what you've learned. You'll take the Unit Assessment in the next lesson.

Lesson Objectives

- Demonstrate mastery of important knowledge and skills taught in this unit.

PREPARE

Approximate lesson time is 60 minutes.

Advance Preparation

- The next lesson includes *David* by Donatello. This famous work of art falls into the category known as a nude. While the general culture contains a great deal of material that demeans the human body, you may wish to discuss how many outstanding artists since the time of ancient Greece and Rome, have tried, in a variety of works, both secular and religious, to show the beauty, strength, and dignity of the unclothed human form.

LEARN

Activity 1: Rediscovering Greece and Rome *(Offline)*

History Journal Review

Now, review the unit by going through your History Journal. You should:

- Look at activity sheets and Reading Guides you completed for the unit.
- Review unit keywords.
- Read through any writing assignments you completed during the unit.
- Review any offline assessments you took during the unit.
- Skim through the chapters in *The Human Odyssey: The Modern World* that you read in this unit.

Don't rush through. Take your time. Your History Journal is a great resource for a unit review.

Online Unit Review

Go online and review the following:

- Medieval and Renaissance Art
- Florentine Artists
- The Renaissance: Flash Cards
- Unit Review

© 2016 K12 Inc. All rights reserved.
Copying or distributing without K12's written consent is prohibited.

Student Guide
Lesson 7: Unit Assessment

You've finished the unit! Now it's time to take the Unit Assessment.

Lesson Objectives

- Explain how Renaissance art differed from medieval art.
- Recognize major Italian Renaissance artists and their achievements, including Donatello, Brunelleschi, da Vinci, Michelangelo, and Raphael.
- Identify Johannes Gutenberg as the fifteenth-century inventor of the printing press.
- Explain that Italian city-states were often republics led by powerful merchant families.
- Describe major characteristics of some of the city-states and identify some of the important individuals associated with them.
- Describe the role of the popes as patrons of art and literature and restorers of the city of Rome, and how they financed the work.
- Describe the Renaissance as a period of artistic and literary achievement in Europe from the late fourteenth to the early seventeenth centuries, initially inspired by new interest in the classics.
- Define *humanism* as a movement that stressed the wisdom of the classics, the dignity of humans, and human potential.
- Identify the contributions of key individuals in the beginning of humanist thought, including Dante, Petrarch, and Giotto.
- Describe the role patrons such as the Medici family and the popes played in promoting Renaissance art, architecture, and literature.
- Recognize how Renaissance ideas spread beyond Italy.
- Explain the social significance of the printing press.
- Explain the social significance of the printing press in the modern world.
- Explain the reasons for the emergence of new ideas and artistic expressions in the city-states of Italy in the fourteenth century.
- Explain that there were many city-states in northern Italy during the Renaissance, and many began as republics led by powerful merchant families.

PREPARE

Approximate lesson time is 60 minutes.

Materials

For the Student

Question Review Table

© 2016 K12 Inc. All rights reserved.
Copying or distributing without K12's written consent is prohibited.

ASSESS

Unit Assessment: A Renaissance Begins in Europe, Part 1 (*Online*)

Complete the computer-scored portion of the Unit Assessment. When you have finished, complete the teacher-scored portion of the assessment and submit it to your teacher

Unit Assessment: A Renaissance Begins in Europe, Part 2 (*Offline*)

Complete the teacher-scored portion of the Unit Assessment and submit it to your teacher.

LEARN

Activity 1. Optional: Optional Unit Assessment Review Table *(Online)*

If you earned a score of **less than 80%** on the Unit Assessment, complete the activity.

If you earned a score of **80% or greater**, you may skip this activity.

Let's prepare to retake the Unit Assessment:

- Identify the questions that you answered incorrectly.
- Complete the appropriate review activities listed in the table.

Note: This will guide you through the process of using the Unit Assessment Review Tables. You may skip this video if you've already viewed it in another unit or course. As always, check in with your student's teacher if you have any questions.

© 2016 K12 Inc. All rights reserved.
Copying or distributing without K12's written consent is prohibited.

Assessment Date

Unit 2: A Renaissance Begins in Europe

Before you retake the Unit Assessment, use the table to figure out which activities you should review.

Question Review Table

Circle the numbers of the questions that you missed on the Unit Assessment. Review the activities that correspond with these questions.

A Renaissance Begins in Europe, Part 1

Question	Lesson	Review Activity
1,2,3,7,8	3: Genius in Florence	Florentine Artists and Architects
4,5	4: Rome Revived	A Revived Rome
6,9	2: Cities Spur Change	Europe's Revived Cities

A Renaissance Begins in Europe, Part 2

Question	Lesson	Review Activity
1,2,3	2: Cities Spur Change	Europe's Revived Cities
4	Throughout All Lessons in Unit	

© 2016 K12 Inc. All rights reserved.
Copying or distributing without K12's written consent is prohibited.

Student Guide

Unit 3: The Spread of New Ideas
Lesson 1: Politics of the Renaissance

The Renaissance wasn't limited to art and literature in Italy. Merchants, soldiers, scholars, and monks spread the new ideas when they headed north. Northern European artists and thinkers incorporated the Renaissance ideas into their own work. Many political and religious ideas that we take for granted today have their roots in the Renaissance. Machiavelli challenged the political world, and Luther and Calvin questioned the practices and beliefs of the Christian Church. The Church examined itself, split, and changed. Europe and the world would never be the same.

The Renaissance celebrated humanity and all its potential. In politics, as in art, Italians looked to the classical world for inspiration, and then adapted those ideas to their own realities.
How could a person meet the challenges of the new era? Two books that became the world's most famous "how-to" books showed them the way. And it wasn't just men of the Renaissance who read those books and took their advice. Women, too, embraced the new ideas.

Lesson Objectives

- Identify Castiglione and his view of the ideal Renaissance courtier.
- Define *courtier.*
- Identify Isabella d'Este as a "Renaissance woman" who ruled a city-state and made it a center of learning and art.
- Identify Machiavelli as the Italian author of *The Prince.*
- Summarize the main ideas of *The Prince* and describe the influence it had on European rulers.
- Explain why Leonardo da Vinci is considered a Renaissance man and give examples of his interests and accomplishments.

PREPARE

Approximate lesson time is 60 minutes.

Materials

For the Student

- Reading Guide
- The Human Odyssey, Volume 2 edited by Klee, Cribb, and Holdren
- History Journal

Keywords and Pronunciation

chateaux (sha-TOH)
sprezzatura (spreht-zah-TOOR-uh)
Anghiari (ahng-GYAH-ree)
Baldassare Castiglione (bahl-dahs-SAHR-ay kahs-teel-YOH-nay)
Cascina (kah-SHEE-nah)
Cesare Borgia (CHAY-zahr-ay BOR-juh)
Giorgio Vasari (JOR-joh-vah-ZAH-ree)
Gonzagas (gohn-DZAH-gahz)

© 2016 K12 Inc. All rights reserved.
Copying or distributing without K12's written consent is prohibited.

Isabella d´Este (ee-zah-BEL-lah DES-tay)
Mantua (MAHN-too-ah)
Niccolo Machiavelli (NEEK-koh-loh mah-kyah-VEL-lee)

LEARN

Activity 1: Of Courtiers and Princes *(Offline)*

Instructions

This lesson is designed to be completed in **3** class sessions. We recommend following the schedule in the Student Guide. To keep track of your progress, put a checkmark next to the activity title when you have completed the activity.

Day 1

Read

Read Chapter 5 from the beginning to "Machiavelli Studies Princes," pages 80 to 86, and complete **Day 1** of the Reading Guide. When you have finished, you should use the Lesson Answer Key to check your work, and then place the Reading Guide in your History Journal. See the sample chart.

Castiglione's Ideas	Isabella d'Este	Leonardo da Vinci
...be able to discuss art and philosophy	Her wit, charm, and commanding presence drew acclaimed writers and artists to him court.	While in Florence, da Vinci attended the court of Lorenzo the Magnificent, where humanists and artists met. He learned much from the long discussions on philosophy.

The Perfect Renaissance Man or Woman

Castiglione's *The Book of the Courtier* was an instant success, and people all over Europe read it. Why was it so popular? If someone wanted to become an ideal courtier, this book was a must-read.

Use Castiglione's ideas to create a chart showing the characteristics of the ideal Renaissance man or woman. Then compare the accomplishments of Isabella d'Este and Leonardo da Vinci to Castiglione's ideas. Did they meet his criteria?

Your chart should start with three columns; in the first column list Castiglione's ideas; in the second column describe any of Isabella d'Este's accomplishments that match Castiglione's ideas; and in the third column describe any of Leonardo's accomplishments that match Castiglione's ideas. See the sample chart.

On **Day 1** you will complete the first two columns and on **Day 2** you will complete the third column.

Day 2

Read

Read Chapter 5, from "Machiavelli Studies Princes" to "*Leonardo, the Ultimate Renaissance Man,*" pages 86 to 89, and complete **Day 2** of the Reading Guide. Check your work and place the completed Reading Guide in your History Journal.

Niccolo Machiavelli

After you have finished your reading assignment, go online to complete the Machiavelli activity.

© 2016 K12 Inc. All rights reserved.
Copying or distributing without K12's written consent is prohibited.

Read On

Read Chapter 5, from "*Leonardo the Ultimate Renaissance Man*" to the end, pages 90 to 93.

Day 3

Begin today's lesson by doing the online Quick Check: Leonardo da Vinci activity. After you have finished, complete the Leonardo da Vinci portion of the chart you created on **Day 1**. Compare your answers with those in the Answer Key.

Today's Renaissance Man or Woman

Today you will add two new columns to the chart you created on **Day 1**.

Think about the traits and abilities Castiglione admired in a "Renaissance man." Remember that he got some of his ideas from earlier philosophers and added new characteristics to meet the needs of changing times. Today, you will consider the idea of a "Renaissance man" and the characteristics that would make someone a Renaissance man or woman in today's world.

List the characteristics of a modern Renaissance man/woman in the first new column. Then think about a person who has those characteristics. Complete a column for that person in the same way you did the Isabella d'Este and Leonardo da Vinci columns. You may need to go online to do some research about the person you choose to exemplify today's Renaissance man or woman.

ASSESS

Lesson Assessment: Politics of the Renaissance (*Online*)

You will complete an online assessment covering the main objectives of this lesson. Your assessment will be scored by the computer.

LEARN

Activity 2. Optional: Politics of the Renaissance *(Online)*

Optional Activities

This activity is OPTIONAL. It's provided for enrichment or extra practice. You may skip this activity.

You may want to spend some time identifying some of Leonardo da Vinci's machinery at the Leonardo Mysterious Machinery website.

To learn more about the Mona Lisa and the art theft of the century, visit the PBS website, Treasures of the World: Mona Lisa.

© 2016 K12 Inc. All rights reserved.
Copying or distributing without K12's written consent is prohibited.

Reading Guide

Day 1

Read

1. In the sixteenth century, Italy had many centers of power. In each you could find ambitious rulers, such as the ______________ in Florence, the______________in Rome, or the ____________ in Venice.
2. Each ruler knew that his success greatly depended on the people who advised him. So rulers surrounded themselves with brilliant courtiers. What was a *courtier* and what did a courtier do?
3. Who was Baldassare Castiglione and why is he famous?
4. Castiglione based some of his book on the writings of________________________________ and on the________________________________.
5. Why did the education and intelligence of advisors matter in Renaissance times in ways they had not earlier?
6. Describe Castiglione's views of the ideal Renaissance courtier.
7. What does it mean to be a "Renaissance man"?

© 2016 K12 Inc. All rights reserved.
Copying or distributing without K12's written consent is prohibited.

8. Who was Isabella d'Este and what were some of her accomplishments?

Day 2

Read

9. The two issues always on the minds of princes in Renaissance Italy were ____________ and ________ .

10. Who was Niccolo Machiavelli and what did he believe Italy's princes needed to be able to do?

11. What is the main subject of *The Prince*?

12. What were the main sources of information that Machiavelli used for his book?

13. How did Machiavelli's idea of a good ruler differ from that of medieval philosophers?

14. Machiavelli declared that to hold on to power, a prince must act as circumstances required. A famous saying that expresses his ideas is ____________________________________ .

15. What was Machiavelli's answer to the question "Is it better to be loved or to be feared?"

© 2016 K12 Inc. All rights reserved.
Copying or distributing without K12's written consent is prohibited.

16. Describe the influence *The Prince* had on European rulers.

17. Why is Machiavelli considered the “father of modern political science”?

18. Discuss with an adult your views on what makes a good ruler.

© 2016 K12 Inc. All rights reserved.
Copying or distributing without K12’s written consent is prohibited.

Student Guide
Lesson 2: The Renaissance Beyond Italy

The Renaissance started in Italy but armies, artists, merchants, and scholars quickly carried art, ideas, goods, and books to northern Europe. As northern Europeans adopted the Renaissance ideas, they shaped them to reflect their own culture and experience.

Lesson Objectives

- Recognize how Renaissance ideas spread beyond Italy.
- Identify means by which European monarchs solidified their power.
- Identify on a map countries that had strong monarchs by the 1500s and areas that were not nation-states.
- Describe the differences between Renaissance art from Italy and from northern Europe.
- Describe Christian humanism.
- Identify Erasmus.
- Identify Thomas More.
- Identify major artists of the Northern Renaissance (including Van Eyck, Dürer, and Holbein) and their accomplishments.

PREPARE

Approximate lesson time is 60 minutes.

Materials

For the Student

Reading Guide

The Human Odyssey, Volume 2 edited by Klee, Cribb, and Holdren

History Journal

Keywords and Pronunciation

Albrecht Durer (AHL-brekht DUR-er)
Desiderius Erasmus (DEH-sih-DEER-ee-us ih-RAZ-mus)
duchy (DUH-chee) : a small territory ruled by a duke
Hans Holbein (hahns HOHL-biyn)
indulgence : pardon granted by the Christian Church for acts of prayer or charity
Jan van Eyck (yahn van IYK)
Utopia (yoo-TOH-pee-uh)

© 2016 K12 Inc. All rights reserved.
Copying or distributing without K12's written consent is prohibited.

LEARN

Activity 1: The Northern Renaissance *(Offline)*

Instructions

This lesson is designed to be completed in **3** class sessions. We recommend following the schedule in the Student Guide. To keep track of your progress, you may want to put a checkmark next to the activity title when you have completed the activity.

Day 1

Read

Read Chapter 6 from the beginning to "Christian Humanism: Erasmus and Thomas More," pages 94 to 101, and complete **Day 1** of the Reading Guide. When you have finished, use the Lesson Answer Key to check your work, and then place the Reading Guide in your History Journal.

A Closer Look

Go online and take a closer look at some artwork by Jan van Eyck and Albrecht Dürer. Then, quickly review three great Renaissance painters from northern Europe.

Day 2

Read

Read Chapter 6, from "Christian Humanism: Erasmus and Thomas More" to "*Thomas More's* Utopia, pages 101 to 103, and complete **Day 2** of the Reading Guide.

Explore and Discuss

The Humanist movement originated in the 1300s in Italy and spread to northern Europe in the 1500s. Humanists, such as Petrarch, Erasmus, and Thomas More believed that the best models of literature and art were the works of ancient Greece and Rome. They believed that works from that time, which is known as the classical period, could be imitated and put to practical use.

Humanist values of the Renaissance still influence modern American culture. Find at least four examples from newspapers, magazines, and other sources. Discuss the subject with an adult.

Day 3

Read

Read Chapter 6, from "*Thomas More's* Utopia" to the end, pages 104 to 105, and complete **Day 3** of the Reading Guide.

ASSESS

Lesson Assessment: The Renaissance Beyond Italy (*Online*)

You will complete an online assessment covering the main objectives of this lesson. Your assessment will be scored by the computer.

© 2016 K12 Inc. All rights reserved.
Copying or distributing without K12's written consent is prohibited.

Name Date 

Reading Guide

Day 1

Read

1. How did Renaissance ideas spread beyond Italy?

2. What Renaissance ideas influenced northern European art, religion, and thought?

3. How did some of the kings and queens of northern Europe gain power? List several ways.

4. On the map of Europe, locate France, Spain, and England by labeling each kingdom and coloring each one a different color. In the corresponding boxes briefly describe how the monarchs solidified their power.

5. While strong monarchs ruled England, France, and Spain, other parts of Europe remained __________________. East of France lay the vast __________________________________, covering the lands known today as ____________________ and ____________________.

6. On the map of Europe, label the Holy Roman Empire and the city-states of Mainz, Nuremberg, and Augsburg. Color the Holy Roman Empire. Write a brief description in the corresponding box describing how the Holy Roman Emperor solidified his power.

7. A small territory ruled by a duke is called a ____________________.

8. Describe ways in which northern European monarchs adopted Renaissance ideas.

9. How did Renaissance art in northern Europe differ from Renaissance art in Italy?

© 2016 K12 Inc. All rights reserved.
Copying or distributing without K12's written consent is prohibited.

Name Date 

10. What techniques did Jan van Eyck use in his paintings?

11. Why was Albrecht Dürer considered the "Leonardo of the North"?

12. Why were Hans Holbein's portraits so popular?

Day 2

Read

13. How was the humanist movement in northern Europe different from the humanist movement in Renaissance Italy?

14. What concerns did Christian humanists have about the Church?

15. Who was Desiderius Erasmus?

© 2016 K12 Inc. All rights reserved.
Copying or distributing without K12's written consent is prohibited.

Name Date 

16. Describe the role the printing press played in spreading Renaissance ideas.

17. Who was Thomas More?

Day 3

Read

18. Describe the city-states in Utopia.

19. More wrote, “No city has any desire to extend its territory, for they consider themselves the tenants rather than the masters of what they hold…” Explain the meaning of that statement in your own words.

20. What type of government did Utopia have?

21. Describe the clothing in Utopia. Why do you think More preferred that type of clothing?

© 2016 K12 Inc. All rights reserved.
Copying or distributing without K12's written consent is prohibited.

Name Date 

22. How did Utopians feel about war? Why?

23. Why were there so few priests in each city?

24. Explain what you think More meant when he wrote, "Though no man has anything, yet all are rich."

25. Which aspects of life in Utopia would you find most appealing? Why?

26. Which aspects of life in Utopia would you find most unappealing? Why?

27. What kind of people do you think might be most attracted to the idea of living in a place like Utopia? Pick three of the following and explain why each of the three would or would not like to live in Utopia.

    - Rich merchant
    - Poor farmer
    - Large landowner
    - Soldier
    - Lawyer
    - Priest
    - Artist

© 2016 K12 Inc. All rights reserved.
Copying or distributing without K12's written consent is prohibited.

Name Date 

28. Why do you think More called his imaginary island Utopia?

29. Would you choose to live in Utopia? Why or why not?

© 2016 K12 Inc. All rights reserved.
Copying or distributing without K12's written consent is prohibited.

Name Date 

Reading Guide

Name:

Name:

Name:

Name:

© 2016 K12 Inc. All rights reserved.
Copying or distributing without K12's written consent is prohibited.

Student Guide
Lesson 3: The Reformation Splits Christendom

A murmur swept through the gathering crowd as Martin Luther pounded the final nail into the document on the church door. "The monk says we shouldn't buy those indulgences." The word quickly spread. Martin Luther was not alone. Scholars who had read ancient Greek and Hebrew manuscripts noted big differences between the Church of their day and the early Church. They, too were calling for change.
Since the invention of the printing press, many ordinary people had learned to read. The way they learned and got information would never be the same. Now they paid close attention to Luther's ideas and wondered what would happen.

Lesson Objectives

- Define the Reformation.
- Explain the relationship between the Renaissance interest in ancient texts and the demand for church reform.
- Describe the belief in purgatory and indulgences and how indulgences came to be given in exchange for money.
- Identify Martin Luther.
- Summarize Luther's arguments with the Church.
- Recognize the significance of Luther's translation of the Bible into German.
- Explain the origins of the terms "Protestant" and "Catholic".
- Identify John Calvin.
- Identify Henry VIII.

PREPARE

Approximate lesson time is 60 minutes.

Materials

For the Student

Fact Sheet: The Reformation

Keywords and Pronunciation

diet : a special meeting
excommunicated : to be cut off from membership in the church
heresy (HAIR-uh-see) : the refusal to accept the beliefs of a church
heretic : a person who opposes religions authority
Huguenots (HYOO-guh-nahts)
indulgence : pardon granted by the Christian Church for acts of prayer or charity
Jan Hus (yahn hoos)
Johann Tetzel (yoh-HAHN TET-suhl)
Ninety-five Theses : statements or arguments, written by Martin Luther, explaining why indulgences were

© 2016 K12 Inc. All rights reserved.
Copying or distributing without K12's written consent is prohibited.

recant (rih-KANT) : to take back or reject something one has said earlier
Reformation : a movement during the 1500s to make changes in the practices of the Christian Church. This movement led to the division of Christianity into Catholic and Protestant faiths.
vernacular : the native language of a place

LEARN

Activity 1: The Reformation *(Offline)*

Instructions

This lesson is designed to be completed in **2** class sessions. We recommend following the schedule in the Student Guide. To keep track of your progress, you may want to put a checkmark next to the activity title when you have completed the activity.

Day 1

Read

Read Chapter 7 from the beginning to "A Split Becomes a Fissure," pages 106 to 112, and start working on the Fact Sheet. You will not be able to complete the entire Fact Sheet until you finish the reading assignment for **Day 2**. When you have finished your work for Day 1, you should use the Lesson Answer Key to check it, and then place the Fact Sheet in your History Journal.

Sequencing Events

Go online and complete the Sequencing Events activity. It will help you recognize the important events that led to the Reformation.

Day 2

Read

Read Chapter 7, from "A Split Becomes a Fissure" to the end, pages 112 to 119, and complete the Fact Sheet. You should then check your answers.

Lesson Review

Go online and review what you learned about the Reformation by playing the Reformation game.

ASSESS

Lesson Assessment: The Reformation Splits Christendom (*Online*)

You will complete an online assessment covering the main objectives of this lesson. Your assessment will be scored by the computer.

© 2016 K12 Inc. All rights reserved.
Copying or distributing without K12's written consent is prohibited.

Name Date 

Fact Sheet: The Reformation

Fill in the information in each of the following categories.

What:

Reformation (definition)

Why:

The Bible and early Christian writings (How did they lead to the Reformation?)

Describe the belief in Purgatory in Renaissance times.

Actions that inspired demands for reform (Actions of Pope Leo X and his predecessors)

Where:

Countries/cities where it began

Countries/cities where it spread

When:

Reformation time period (century)

Start of the Reformation: October 31, 1517 (Action taken by Martin Luther)

© 2016 K12 Inc. All rights reserved.
Copying or distributing without K12's written consent is prohibited.

Name Date 

In 1518, Luther was relieved of some of his duties. (What did he do instead?)

Pope Leo's actions in 1520 and Luther's response

The Diet of Worms in 1521

Luther goes into hiding. (What did Luther do while he was in hiding? Why did he do it?)

Luther returns to Wittenberg. (What emerged from Luther's preaching and writing?)

Protestant churches emerge. (What is the origin of the term?)

The Christian Church headed by the pope becomes known as the Roman Catholic Church. (Why?)

Calvin's followers spread to Scotland, France, England, and the American colonies (What was the name of each of the groups?)

The Church of England is formed (Where and Why?)

© 2016 K12 Inc. All rights reserved.
Copying or distributing without K12's written consent is prohibited.

Name Date 

Who:

Describe the role each of the following people played in the Reformation.

Pope Leo X

Johann Tetzel

Martin Luther

John Calvin

Henry VIII

Luther's Ninety-five Theses

1. What was Luther implying in Thesis 27?

2. In Thesis 32, what is the fate of those who believe they will be saved due to their letters of indulgence?

3. According to Thesis 37, in what do "true Christians" participate?

© 2016 K12 Inc. All rights reserved.
Copying or distributing without K12's written consent is prohibited.

Name Date 

4. Read Theses 43, 45, 46, and 50. According to Luther, what should Christians be taught?

5. According to Thesis 54, when is injury done to the Word of God?

6. According to Luther's Thesis 86, what is one of the questions indulgences cause people to ask?

Thinking Cap Question: How was the printing press critical to the Reformation?

© 2016 K12 Inc. All rights reserved.
Copying or distributing without K12's written consent is prohibited.

Student Guide
Lesson 4. Optional: Your Choice

You may use today's lesson time to do one or more of the following:

- Complete work in progress.
- Complete the Beyond the Lesson activity in any lesson in this unit.
- Review the Time Line in the Resources section.
- Go on to the next lesson.

Please mark this lesson complete to proceed to the next lesson in the course.

PREPARE

Approximate lesson time is 60 minutes.

© 2016 K12 Inc. All rights reserved.
Copying or distributing without K12's written consent is prohibited.

Student Guide
Lesson 5: The Counter-Reformation and Beyond

The Catholic Church responded to the Reformation by launching the Counter-Reformation. The Catholic Church made internal reforms and clarified its doctrine. It defended itself from "heretics" by banning books, emphasizing education, and bringing people before the church court, or Inquisition. But Protestantism continued to spread and religious conflict turned into political conflict. Europe splintered as monarchs chose sides. Sometimes they based their decisions on genuine beliefs, but they frequently had an eye on economic and territorial gains.

Lesson Objectives

- Describe the Counter-Reformation.
- Identify the Reformation.
- Identify at least three steps taken by the Council of Trent to correct the course of the Catholic Church.
- Identify Ignatius of Loyola.
- Describe methods the Catholic Church used to try to contain the spread of Protestantism, including the banning of books, and the Inquisition.
- Give examples of how the Catholic/Protestant split led to political rivalries and wars in Europe.
- Identify Teresa of Avila.

PREPARE

Approximate lesson time is 60 minutes.

Materials

For the Student

- Reading Guide
- The Catholic Reformaton

Keywords and Pronunciation

catechism : statement of beliefs
Counter-Reformation : the Catholic Church's response to the Reformation; also know as the Catholic Reformation
discalced (dihs-KALST)
Francis Xavier (ZAYV-yur)
Ignatius of Loyola (ig-NAY-shuhs of loy-OH-luh)
Inquisition : a special court set up by the Roman Catholic Church to combat heresy
Jesuits (JEH-zou-uhts) : members of the Society of Jesus which is an order of priests in the Catholic Church
St. Francis of Assisi (uh-SEE-see)
Teresa of Avila (AH-vih-luh)

© 2016 K12 Inc. All rights reserved.
Copying or distributing without K12's written consent is prohibited.

LEARN

Activity 1: The Counter-Reformation *(Offline)*

Instructions

This lesson is designed to be completed in **4** class sessions. We recommend following the schedule in the Student Guide. To keep track of your progress, you may want to put a checkmark next to the activity title when you have completed the activity.

Day 1

Read

Read Chapter 8 from the beginning to "Religion Splits the Continent," pages 121 to 128, and complete **Day 1** of the Reading Guide. When you have finished, you should use the Lesson Answer Key to check your work, and then place the Reading Guide in your History Journal.

The Catholic Church Responds

Some members of the Catholic Church criticized and disagreed with some of the practices of the Catholic Church but decided to try to reform the Church from within. They also realized that the power of the Catholic Church was threatened by the spread of Protestantism. They thought they needed to redefine the Catholic Church and meet the challenges of Protestantism.

Complete the Catholic Reformation activity. In the activity, you will summarize the Counter-Reformation and identify the Catholic Church's response to the Protestant reformers.

Day 2

Read

Read Chapter 8, from "Religion Splits the Continent" to "*Teresa of Avila*," pages 128 to 131, and complete **Day 2** of the Reading Guide. You should then check your answers.

Focus on Geography

Go online and complete the Religions of Europe activity. You may use the map on page 123 as a reference.

Read On

Read Chapter 8, from "*Teresa of Avila*" to the end, pages 131 to 135, and complete the Reading Guide for the Read On section. Don't forget to check your answers.

Assessment *(online)*

After you have finished the activities for **Day 2**, go online and take the Lesson Assessment.

Day 3

A Look Back

You will write a feature article based on an "interview" with the person you found most interesting during the Reformation and Counter-Reformation period. You will use the next two days to research and write your article.

1. To choose the person to "interview", review the charts, notes, activities, and Reading Guides you completed for Chapters 7 and 8.

2. After you have chosen the person for your article, you should begin by writing two or three sentences explaining why that person is of interest. You should then compose two or three questions that you would like to ask that person.

3.To get ready to "interview" the person and write the article, go online to research that person. Here are some web links that you may find helpful:

© 2016 K12 Inc. All rights reserved.
Copying or distributing without K12's written consent is prohibited.

- Kids Search Tools
- Ivy's Search Engine Resources for Kids
- The Reformations Weblinks

You can also use the Grolier's Online Encyclopedia located in Resources.

Your "interview" should include the answers to the questions you wrote and the following questions:

- Describe your background—your childhood, education, and early years. What was your life like before you devoted it to religion?
- Summarize your religious beliefs. We know you are a Christian, but what beliefs set you apart from other Christians of the 1500s?
- Do you try to convince others to follow your beliefs? If so, how?

Day 4

Writing the Interview

If you have not done so, you should complete your interview-style article. After you have finished, you should have a discussion with an adult about the "interview" and any other interesting facts you discovered about the person you chose.

ASSESS

Lesson Assessment: The Counter-Reformation and Beyond (*Online*)

You will complete an online assessment covering the main objectives of this lesson. Your assessment will be scored by the computer.

© 2016 K12 Inc. All rights reserved.
Copying or distributing without K12's written consent is prohibited.

Name Date

The Catholic Church Responds

Reformers such as Martin Luther and John Calvin disagreed with some of the Church's practices and teachings. Their criticisms of the Church led to the Protestant Reformation. The Church responded with a Counter-Reformation, also known as the Catholic Reformation. Match the Catholic Church's response to the Protestants' criticisms. Fill in the blank next to each Protestant criticism, belief, or action with the letters associated with the responses of the Catholic Church.

The Protestant Reformers Speak

______ 1. Scripture should be the only authority for Church teachings.

______ 2. According to Luther, Christians are saved by faith alone.

______ 3. The Christian Church does not need a pope.

______ 4. The Church hides the true meaning of the Gospel from ordinary people.

______ 5. It is wrong for the Church to sell indulgences.

______ 6. Ordinary people should be able to read the Bible, and not have to rely on the Church to interpret it for them.

______ 7. Many clergy hunger for money, power, and other worldly things.

______ 8. Many priests know little about Christianity.

______ 9. Leaders publish pamphlets and books criticizing the Church.

______ 10. Many Christians are attracted to the teachings of Luther, Calvin, and other Protestant leaders.

The Catholic Church Responds

a. The pope should continue to lead the Church as he has for centuries.

b. The Church will not sell indulgences.

c. A new catechism will summarize the teachings of the Catholic Church as they have developed over time.

d. There will be an Index of Forbidden Books.

e. The Church will support the work of the Jesuits and other reformers.

f. The Inquisition will investigate and root out heresy.

g. People attain salvation through faith *and* good works.

h. Church guidelines will set the standards for the education of priests.

i. Priests should live modestly and care for the poor.

j. The Church is the official interpreter of sacred Scripture.

© 2016 K12 Inc. All rights reserved.
Copying or distributing without K12's written consent is prohibited.

The Catholic Church Responds

Create a short article about the Reformation and the Counter-Reformation that includes at least 15 words from the Word Bank.

Word Bank

Martin Luther	Johann Tetzel	indulgences	Leo X	St. Peter's Basilica
printing press	Diet of Worms	Ninety-five Theses	Reformation	Bible
Protestant	Henry VIII	John Calvin	England	divorce
Huguenots	Presbyterians	Paul III	Inquisition	Council of Trent
Catholic	Teresa of Avila	Society of Jesus	Jesuits	Ignatius of Loyola
universities	Francis Xavier	Protestantism	Forbidden Books	Counter-Reformation

© 2016 K12 Inc. All rights reserved.
Copying or distributing without K12's written consent is prohibited.

Name Date 

Reading Guide

Day 1

Read

1. Briefly summarize how Christianity split into Catholicism and Protestantism.

2. How did the Catholic Church respond to Protestant criticism?

3. What improvements did Pope Paul III make in the Catholic Church?

4. What steps did the Council of Trent take to correct the course of the Catholic Church?

5. Who was Teresa of Avila?

6. Who was Ignatius of Loyola?

7. Who were the Jesuits and what did they do to slow down the advance of Protestantism?

8. Where did the Jesuits take their ministry?

© 2016 K12 Inc. All rights reserved.
Copying or distributing without K12's written consent is prohibited.

Name Date 

9. Who was Francis Xavier?

10. Describe the methods the Roman Catholic Church used to try to contain the spread of Protestantism.

Day 2

Read

11. The war of ideas between the Catholic Church and Protestant reformers led to a ______________________.

12. How did the split between the Catholics and Protestants affect property ownership?

13. Describe the religious wars in the German lands of the Holy Roman Empire. What was the outcome?

14. What happened in the war between the Catholics and the Huguenots?

15. How were the religious conflicts in the Netherlands resolved?

© 2016 K12 Inc. All rights reserved.
Copying or distributing without K12's written consent is prohibited.

Name Date 

16. After King Henry VIII, what or who determined the official religion of England? When did England become a solidly Protestant nation?

Read On

17. Why did Teresa of Avila want life at her convents to be strict and very simple?

18. What contribution did Teresa of Avila make to the Catholic faith?

© 2016 K12 Inc. All rights reserved.
Copying or distributing without K12's written consent is prohibited.

Student Guide
Lesson 6. Optional: Your Choice

You may use today's lesson time to do one or more of the following:

- Complete work in progress.
- Complete the Beyond the Lesson activity in any lesson in this unit.
- Review the Time Line in the Resources section.
- Go on to the next lesson.

Please mark this lesson complete to proceed to the next lesson in the course.

PREPARE

Approximate lesson time is 60 minutes.

© 2016 K12 Inc. All rights reserved.
Copying or distributing without K12's written consent is prohibited.

Student Guide
Lesson 7: Unit Review

You've finished The Spread of New Ideas unit, and now it's time to review what you've learned. You'll take the Unit Assessment in the next lesson.

Lesson Objectives

- Demonstrate mastery of important knowledge and skills in this unit.

PREPARE

Approximate lesson time is 60 minutes.

Materials

For the Student

History Journal

LEARN

Activity 1: The Spread of New Ideas *(Offline)*

Instructions

History Journal Review

Now, review the unit by going through your History Journal. You should:

- Look at activity sheets and Reading Guides you completed in this unit.
- Review unit keywords.
- Read through any writing assignments you completed during the unit.
- Review any offline assessments you took during the unit.
- Skim through the chapters in Th*e Human Odyssey: The Modern World* that you read in this unit.

Don't rush through. Take your time. Your History Journal is a great resource for a unit review.

Online Unit Review

Go online and review the following:

- Renaissance, Reformation, and Counter-Reformation
- New Ideas in Europe
- Meet Albrecht Dürer
- Quick Check: Three Great Painters
- Jan van Eyck
- Map of Europe c.1500
- About Machiavelli
- Quick Check: Leonardo da Vinci
- The Reformation Game
- Sequencing Events: The Reformation
- Religions of Europe

© 2016 K12 Inc. All rights reserved.
Copying or distributing without K12's written consent is prohibited.

Student Guide
Lesson 8: Unit Assessment

You've finished The Spread of New Ideas unit! Now it's time to take the Unit Assessment.

Lesson Objectives

- Identify major Renaissance figures and what they are known for.
- Identify major artists of the Northern Renaissance and the characteristics of their work.
- Define the Reformation.
- Identify major issues and individuals of the Reformation.
- Recognize how Renaissance ideas spread beyond Italy and what kinds of influence they had outside Italy.
- Describe the response of the Catholic Church to the Reformation.
- Identify important individuals of the Counter-Reformation.
- Locate on a map the major nations of Europe in the 1500s.
- Summarize the main ideas of *The Prince*.
- Explain how the Reformation led to political conflict and warfare during the 1500s.

PREPARE

Approximate lesson time is 60 minutes.

Materials

For the Student

Question Review Table

ASSESS

Unit Assessment: The Spread of New Ideas, Part 1 (*Online*)

Complete the computer-scored portion of the Unit Assessment. When you have finished, complete the teacher-scored portion of the assessment and submit it to your teacher.

Unit Assessment: The Spread of New Ideas, Part 2 (*Offline*)

Complete the teacher-scored portion of the Unit Assessment and submit it to your teacher.

LEARN

Activity 1. Optional: The Spread of New Ideas *(Online)*

If you earned a score of **less than 80%** on the Unit Assessment, complete the activity.

If you earned a score of **80% or greater**, you may skip this activity.

Let's prepare to retake the Unit Assessment:

© 2016 K12 Inc. All rights reserved.
Copying or distributing without K12's written consent is prohibited.

- Identify the questions that you answered incorrectly.
- Complete the appropriate review activities listed in the table.

Note: This Learning Coach Video will guide you through the process of using the Unit Assessment Review Tables. You may skip this video if you've already viewed it in another unit or course. As always, check in with your student's teacher if you have any questions.

© 2016 K12 Inc. All rights reserved.
Copying or distributing without K12's written consent is prohibited.

Assessment Date

Unit 3: The Spread of New Ideas

Before you retake the Unit Assessment, use the table to figure out which activities you should review.

Question Review Table

Circle the numbers of the questions that you missed on the Unit Assessment. Review the activities that correspond with these questions.

The Spread of New Ideas, Part 1

Question	Lesson	Review Activity
1,5, 7 ,8, 9,10, 11	2: The Renaissance Beyond Italy	The Northern Renaissance
2,3,4,6,	1: Politics of the Renaissance	Of Courtiers and Princes
12,13, 14	5: The Counter-Reformation and Beyond	The Counter-Reformation

The Spread of New Ideas, Part 2

Question	Lesson	Review Activity
3	2: The Renaissance Beyond Italy	The Northern Renaissance
1	1: Politics of the Renaissance	Of Courtiers and Princes
2, 4	5: The Counter-Reformation and Beyond	The Counter-Reformation

© 2016 K12 Inc. All rights reserved.
Copying or distributing without K12's written consent is prohibited.

Student Guide

Unit 4: New Powers in Asia
Lesson 1: Three Islamic Empires

While European culture was growing and redefining itself, politics and culture in Asia were changing, too. As Asians overthrew the harsh Mongol rulers who had controlled them for hundreds of years, each region developed its own political and cultural identity. Great Muslim empires rose in western and southern Asia. Farther east, the Ming dynasty flourished in China and a feudal system controlled Japan. And in Russia, a distinct new Russian culture was developed by transforming Byzantine religion, art, and architecture.

While Christendom experienced cultural renewal and religious friction, the Islamic world gave birth to three empires. The Ottoman Empire centered in Asia Minor, the Safavid Empire in Persia, and the Mughal Empire in India. They extended Islam's power and influence. From 1300 to 1600, these Asian empires were rival centers of power and culture. Their achievements had a lasting effect on the world.

Lesson Objectives

- Recognize that the Islamic world experienced hardships at the hands of Mongol conquerors during the time of the European Middle Ages.
- Identify Osman as the Muslim, Turkish nomad who founded the Ottoman Empire in the thirteenth century.
- Recognize the extent of the Ottoman Empire at its height, identify the countries in that area today, and identify Istanbul as the capital of the empire.
- Identify Süleyman as the sixteenth-century Ottoman emperor who developed a code of law for the empire and was known outside the empire as "Süleyman the Magnificent."
- Locate on a map the fifteenth-century Persian Safavid Empire, and identify the countries that are in that area today and their religious affiliation.
- Describe the political and religious conflicts between the Ottoman and Safavid Empires.
- Identify Akbar as the ruler of the Mughal Empire who practiced religious and cultural tolerance in India.
- Recognize the Taj Mahal as the seventeenth-century architectural masterpiece of the Mughal Empire.

PREPARE

Approximate lesson time is 60 minutes.

Materials

For the Student

- Geography of the Islamic Empires
- Reading Guide
- Three Islamic Empires

© 2016 K12 Inc. All rights reserved.
Copying or distributing without K12's written consent is prohibited.

Keywords and Pronunciation

Akbar (AK-bur)
Babur (BAH-bur)
Ibn Khaldun (IH-buhn kahl-DOON)
Isfahan (is-fah-HAHN)
Ismail (iss-mah-EEL)
Janissaries (JA-nuh-sehr-eez)
Osman (ohs-MAHN)
Ottoman (AH-tuh-muhn)
Safavid (sah-fah-WEED)
Shi'ahs (SHEE-ahs)
Shi'ites (SHEE-iyts)
Sinan (see-NAHN)
Sunni (SOO-nee)
Süleyman (suhlay-MAHN)
Süleymaniye (suhlay-MAHN-ee-yeh)

LEARN

Activity 1: Muslim Empires on the Rise *(Offline)*

Instructions

This lesson is designed to be completed in **3** class sessions. We recommend following the schedule below. To keep track of your progress, you may want to check the box next to the activity title when you have completed the activity.

Day 1

Read

Read Chapter 9, from the beginning to "Persia's Safavid Empire," pages 136 to 143 and complete the **Day 1** section of the Reading Guide.

Geography of the Islamic Empires

Complete the **Day 1** section of the Geography of the Islamic Empires sheet.

Three Islamic Empires

Complete the Ottoman Empire column in the chart on the Three Islamic Empires sheet.

Hagia Sofia: From Church to Mosque

Go back to the online lesson and click From Church to Mosque.

Day 2

Read

Read Chapter 9, from "Persia's Safavid Empire" to "India's Mughals," pages 143 to 145 and complete the **Day 2** section of the Reading Guide.

Geography of the Islamic Empires

Complete the **Day 2** section of the Geography of the Islamic Empires sheet.

Three Islamic Empires

Complete the Safavid Empire column in the chart on the Three Islamic Empires sheet.

© 2016 K12 Inc. All rights reserved.
Copying or distributing without K12's written consent is prohibited.

Day 3

Read

Read Chapter 9, from "India's Mughals" to the end, pages 145 to 149 and complete the **Day 3** section of the Reading Guide.

Geography of the Islamic Empires

Complete the **Day 3** section of the Geography of the Islamic Empires sheet.

Three Islamic Empires

Complete the Mughal Empire column in the chart on the Three Islamic Empires sheet. When you have filled in the entire chart, complete the writing assignment on page 2.

The Taj Mahal

Go online to the lesson and click The Taj Mahal. Write your answers to the questions in your History Journal.

ASSESS

Lesson Assessment: Three Islamic Empires (*Online*)

You will complete an online assessment covering the main objectives of this lesson. Your assessment will be scored by the computer.

© 2016 K12 Inc. All rights reserved.
Copying or distributing without K12's written consent is prohibited.

Name Date 

Three Islamic Empires

Complete the Ottoman Empire column on the first day, the Safavid Empire column on the second day, and the Mughal Empire column on the third day. After you have completed the chart, do the writing assignment on page 2.

	Ottoman Empire	Safavid Empire	Mughal Empire
Timeframe/ Important Dates			
Founders and/or Important Rulers			
Capital City			
Religion			
Conflicts			
Achievements			
What I Found Most Interesting About This Empire			

© 2016 K12 Inc. All rights reserved.
Copying or distributing without K12's written consent is prohibited.

Name Date 

Writing Assignment

If you had been alive in the late sixteenth and early seventeenth centuries, in which of the three Islamic empires would you have wanted to live? Explain your choice. Use the chart to help you decide and justify your choice.

© 2016 K12 Inc. All rights reserved.
Copying or distributing without K12's written consent is prohibited.

Name ______________________________ Date ______________________________ 

Reading Guide

Day 1

1. As Europe emerged from its dark period in the late Middle Ages, the Islamic world experienced its own dark period. What was the principal cause of the Islamic world's hardships?

2. Who was the thirteenth-century Muslim nomad (from the area that is present-day Turkey) who founded the Ottoman Empire? ____________________

3. The Ottoman sultans conquered all of ____________________ and then began invading ____________________.

4. In __________ the Ottomans captured ____________________ from the Byzantines, renamed it ____________________ and made it the ____________________ of their Muslim empire.

5. After the fall of Constantinople, the Ottomans continued to expand their empire. Name four countries that exist today in the territory the Ottomans conquered between the thirteenth and fifteenth centuries.

6. Why were the Ottomans so successful at expanding and unifying their empire?

7. When did the Ottoman Empire reach the height of its power and prosperity? ____________________

8. Which sultan ruled during this time period and what two names was he known by? Describe two of his main accomplishments.

Day 2

9. In the early sixteenth century a group of Muslim nomads from the north, called the ______________, invaded and conquered ______________. Soon after, they began fighting with the ____________________.

© 2016 K12 Inc. All rights reserved.
Copying or distributing without K12's written consent is prohibited.

Name ______________________________ Date ______________________________ 

10. What were two main causes of the bitter rivalry between the Ottoman and Safavid Empires?

11. Briefly describe the historical difference between the Sunni and Shi'ite branches of Islam.

12. Which shah ruled Persia during the late 1500s? How did Persian artists break with traditional Muslim practices during his reign? What did the artists study that led them to create paintings that were more lifelike and realistic?

Day 3

13. In the 1520s, a ______________ chieftain named ______________ invaded northern ______________ and founded the ________________ dynasty.

14. In what significant way did the Mughal Empire differ from the Ottoman and Safavid Empires?

15. Which Mughal emperor extended the empire to include most of northern and central India? How did he deal with the unique situation created by the religious beliefs of his subjects?

16. The arts flourished in the Mughal Empire. In the seventeenth century, Akbar's grandson, Shah ________________, built one of the most famous examples of Muslim architecture in the world—the ______________________ .

17. How did the Muslim scholar Ibn Khaldun explain the rise and fall of empires?

© 2016 K12 Inc. All rights reserved.
Copying or distributing without K12's written consent is prohibited.

Name Date 

Geography of the Islamic Empires

Use the map on page 138 of your book and the book's atlas to help you complete the following activity.

Day 1

1. What was the approximate longitude of the Ottoman Empire's easternmost boundary in 1566?

2. Name the three continents the Ottoman Empire spanned during the reign of Süleyman.

3. At its greatest extent, the Ottoman Empire covered territory that today includes all or parts of more than 30 modern-day countries. Name ten of the present-day countries. Represent all three continents in your list.

4. The Ottoman Empire included thousands of miles of shoreline. What three major bodies of water would Ottoman sailors have been most familiar with?

Day 2

5. What was the approximate latitude of the Safavid Empire's northernmost boundary in 1629?

6. At its greatest extent, the Safavid Empire covered territory that today includes all or part of eight modern countries. Name four of the eight modern countries.

7. Islam split into Sunni and Shi'ah factions not long after Muhammad's death in A.D. 632. Over the centuries the two groups have come into frequent conflict (remember, for example, the war between the Safavid and Ottoman Empires in the 1500s). Conflict between Sunni and Shi'ite Muslims continues today.

© 2016 K12 Inc. All rights reserved.
Copying or distributing without K12's written consent is prohibited.

Name Date 

Choose two countries that you listed in response to Question 6 above and find out whether the majority of the population in the country today is Sunni or Shi'ite.

Day 3

8. What physical features helped protect Akbar's Mughal Empire from a Mongol invasion from the north?

9. Five modern-day countries include land that was once part of Akbar's Mughal Empire. Name the countries.

10. Of the three Islamic empires you studied, which one had the largest land area?

© 2016 K12 Inc. All rights reserved.
Copying or distributing without K12's written consent is prohibited.

Student Guide
Lesson 2: Ming China and Feudal Japan

After a century of hardship, the Chinese overthrew the Mongols. The Ming dynasty promoted the arts, reformed government, and established a magnificent capital around the imperial court in Beijing. The Chinese explored foreign lands until they were threatened with another invasion. Then they turned inward.

Across the Sea of Japan, the Japanese had developed a feudal system and were prospering under the Tokugawa shogunate. Shintoism and Buddhism coexisted peacefully, but, when European traders brought Christianity and other foreign ideas, the shogunate felt threatened and turned its back on the outside world.

Lesson Objectives

- Recognize that the Chinese people sought to be free of Mongol rule in the thirteenth and fourteenth centuries.
- Describe artistic and political achievements in China under the Ming dynasty.
- Describe the Forbidden City.
- Define *civil service.*
- Identify the accomplishments of Zheng He and his expeditions.
- Explain why the Chinese rebuilt the Great Wall in the 1400s.
- Locate on a map the four major islands of Japan.
- Identify the major religions of Japan and their beliefs.
- Describe the Japanese feudal system and the role of the samurai and the code of bushido.
- Identify the Tokugawa shogunate and its reasons for closing Japan to foreign influence.

PREPARE

Approximate lesson time is 60 minutes.

Materials

For the Student

- Reading Guide
- The Closing of Japan
- The Voyages of Zheng He

Keywords and Pronunciation

Beijing (bay-zhing)
Buddhism (BOO-dih-zuhm)
bushido (BOU-shee-doh)
Dadu (dah-doo)
daimyo (DIY-mee-oh)
Edo (AY-doh)
Hokkaido (hoh-KIY-doh)
Honshu (HAWN-shoo)
Ieyasu (ee-yeh-yah-soo)

© 2016 K12 Inc. All rights reserved.
Copying or distributing without K12's written consent is prohibited.

Kamakura (kah-mah-KOOR-ah)
kami (kah-mee)
kamikaze (kah-mih-KAH-zee)
Kyushu (KYOO-shoo)
Nanjing (nahn-jing)
samurai (SA-muh-riy)
Shikoku (shee-KOH-koo)
Shintoism (SHIN-toh-ih-zuhm)
shogun (SHOH-guhn)
Siddhartha Gautama (*sid-DAHR-tuh GOW-tuh-muh*)
Tokugawa (toh-kou-GAH-wuh)
torii (tor-EE-EE)
Zheng He (choung hou)
Zhu Yuanzhang (joo you-en-jahng)

LEARN

Activity 1: China and Japan *(Offline)*

Instructions

This lesson is designed to be completed in **4** class sessions. We recommend following the schedule below. To keep track of your progress, you may want to check the box next to each activity title when you have completed the activity.

Day 1

Read

Read Chapter 10, from the beginning to " Across the Sea of Japan," pages 150 to 158. Complete **Day 1** of the Reading Guide.

The Forbidden City

Go online to the lesson, and click The Forbidden City to learn more about the magnificent imperial city of the Ming dynasty. (Note: Don't forget to enlarge the map on each screen by clicking the +. You'll find additional information there.)

Day 2

The Voyages of Zheng He

Complete the Voyages of Zheng He sheet.

Read

Read Chapter 10, from "Across the Sea of Japan" to the end, pages 158 to 163. Complete **Day 2** of the Reading Guide.

Day 3

The Closing of Japan

Complete the Closing of Japan sheet.

Day 4

If you have completed all the activities for **Days 1–3**, you may use **Day 4** as a "Your Choice" day.

© 2016 K12 Inc. All rights reserved.
Copying or distributing without K12's written consent is prohibited.

ASSESS

Lesson Assessment: Ming China and Feudal Japan (*Online*)

You will complete an online assessment covering the main objectives of this lesson. Your assessment will be scored by the computer.

© 2016 K12 Inc. All rights reserved.
Copying or distributing without K12's written consent is prohibited.

Name Date

Reading Guide

Day 1

Take notes from the reading about each the following topics or main ideas. One fact for each topic has already been provided.

1. Zhu Yuanzhang
   Joined a Buddhist monastery

2. Civil Service During the Ming Dynasty
   Helped run the empire

3. Ming Art
   Wove beautiful rugs and carpets

4. The Forbidden City
   Located inside the capital of Beijing

5. Zheng He
   Admiral who came from a Muslim family

6. Chinese Walls
   Mongol raids prompted the Ming to start rebuilding the Great Wall.

© 2016 K12 Inc. All rights reserved.
Copying or distributing without K12's written consent is prohibited.

Name Date

7. Briefly describe the life of a typical Chinese person during Mongol rule in the thirteenth and fourteenth centuries.

8. Define *civil service.*

Day 2

9. Briefly describe the geography of Japan and explain how geography has played a role in protecting Japan.

10. What were the two major religions practiced in feudal Japan? Briefly describe each one.

11. In the space below, draw and label a diagram that shows the Japanese feudal pyramid. (Most of the Japanese were peasants. Fill in the other two layers.)

12. What were *samurai*?

© 2016 K12 Inc. All rights reserved.
Copying or distributing without K12's written consent is prohibited.

Name ______________________ Date ______________________

13. Define *bushido* and explain how it was related to samurai.

14. Briefly explain how the weather played an important role in protecting Japan in the thirteenth century.

15. In the early 1600s, ______________________ defeated all the warlords in Japan and established the Tokugawa ______________________. Under this dynasty, Japan enjoyed a ________ -year period of peace. By the ________ , alarmed at the number of Japanese people converting to Christianity, the Tokugawa had ________ Japan's borders to almost all foreigners.

© 2016 K12 Inc. All rights reserved.
Copying or distributing without K12's written consent is prohibited.

Name Date

The Voyages of Zheng He

Day 2

Use the map of the Voyages of Zheng He and the atlas in your book to complete this activity.

1. Approximately how many degrees of longitude did the combined voyages of Zheng He span?

2. This east-west distance is about the same as the distance between:
   a. Madagascar and western New Guinea
   b. Spain and Newfoundland
   c. Hawaii and the Yucatán Peninsula

3. According to the map, through how many distinct bodies of water did Zheng He's expeditions travel? Name them.

4. Look at the map and think about the lands Zheng He visited. What religions do you think he encountered?

5. Which of the following is the best estimate for the total number of miles traveled during the 28 years of Zheng He's explorations?
   a. 4,000
   b. 9,000
   c. 16,000
   d. 24,000

6. At an average speed of eight miles per hour, approximately how long would it have taken Zheng He's ships to travel nonstop from Calicut to Hormuz?

© 2016 K12 Inc. All rights reserved.
Copying or distributing without K12's written consent is prohibited.

Name Date

The Closing of Japan

Day 3

Cultural diffusion is the movement of ideas and goods from one culture to another. As people travel from one part of the world to another conquering territory, spreading religion, or trading goods, they carry their goods and ideas with them.

The growth of Buddhism is a good example of cultural diffusion. The religion began to spread in the third century B.C. when Asoka, a Mauryan ruler in India, sent missionaries out to share the teachings of Buddhism. The religion quickly gained followers throughout East and Southeast Asia. Eventually, it even began gaining popularity in the West.

You've also seen how culture spread when people, products, and ideas traveled along the trade routes of the Silk Road.

In the 1600s, the Tokugawa shogunate was determined to stop cultural diffusion. The shogunate felt threatened by the interest the Japanese people showed in the ideas European traders expressed. The Tokugawa was alarmed to see people converting to Christianity. To stop the spread of European culture, the Tokugawa closed Japan to most foreign trade and expelled many Christian missionaries.

Read the following primary source document and the one found on the last page of Chapter 10, entitled "The Closing of Japan."

The following are edicts made by the Tokugawa shogunate. They were made in 1635 and concern trade with foreign nations.

> No single trading city shall be permitted to purchase all the merchandise brought by foreign ships.
>
> Samurai are not permitted to purchase any goods originating from foreign ships directly from Chinese merchants in Nagasaki.
>
> After a list of merchandise brought by foreign ships is sent to Edo (the capital), as before, you may order that commercial dealings take place, without waiting for a reply from Edo.
>
> After settling the price, all whit yearns (raw silk) brought by foreign ships shall be allocated to the five trading cities and other quarters as stipulated.
>
> The arrival in Nagasaki of representatives of the five trading cities shall not be later than the fifth day of the seventh month. Anyone arriving later than that date shall lose the quota assigned to his city.

© 2016 K12 Inc. All rights reserved.
Copying or distributing without K12's written consent is prohibited.

Name Date

Ships arriving in Hirado must sell their raw silk at the price set in Nagasaki, and are not permitted to engage in business transactions until after the price is established in Nagasaki.

Use both primary source documents to help you answer the following questions. When possible, support your answers with quotations from the documents.

1. What do you think the Tokugawa shogunate was trying to accomplish with the 1635 edicts?

2. What nations are specifically singled out in the Act of Seclusion of 1636?

3. Scan the Act of Seclusion of 1636 again. What do you think motivated the Tokugawa shogunate to enact the law?

Imagine you are a European merchant arriving in Hirado, Japan, in 1636. You have a ship full of raw silk to trade.

4. Would you be able to sell any of your goods to samurai?

5. When would you be able to start doing business?

6. Could you expect a contingency of Japanese soldiers to keep a watch over your ship while it is anchored in the bay?

© 2016 K12 Inc. All rights reserved.
Copying or distributing without K12's written consent is prohibited.

Name Date

Think about cultural diffusion and the ways ideas and products have spread throughout history. Then write a letter to Japan's shogun to try to persuade him to permit more trade between Japan and foreign nations. Persuade him that his country will benefit in a number of ways from trade with the outside world.

© 2016 K12 Inc. All rights reserved.
Copying or distributing without K12's written consent is prohibited.

Student Guide
Lesson 3: Russia Rising

The title of this unit is "New Powers in Asia," and this chapter is "Russia Rising." But wait! Isn't Moscow—the Russian capital—in Europe? Yes, it is, and so are three-fourths of the Russian people. But three-fourths of Russia's land is in Asia. Confusing, but true. Russia, by far the biggest country in the world, extends from the Pacific Ocean to the Baltic Sea, and covers some of the coldest regions on Earth. Its rich and varied history and culture include Viking traders, Byzantine religion and art, Mongol invaders, rulers named for Rome's Caesar, and centuries of isolation.

Lesson Objectives

- Identify Russia as the largest country in the world.
- Locate Russia on a map and identify its boundaries, major land features, and cities.
- Identify Vladimir as the tenth-century Grand Prince of Kiev who ordered Russians to convert to Orthodox Christianity.
- Describe the Mongol conquest of Russia.
- Identify Ivan III as Ivan the Great and describe his accomplishments.
- Describe the methods Ivan the Great used to conquer Russia and then unify and glorify it.
- Define *kremlin* and explain Ivan's purpose in restoring the Kremlin in Moscow.
- Identify Ivan IV as Ivan the Terrible, and describe how he earned his nickname.

PREPARE

Approximate lesson time is 60 minutes.

Materials

For the Student

- Focus on Geography
- Reading Guide

Keywords and Pronunciation

boyars (BOH-yarhrz)
Kiev (KEE-ef)
Muscovy (MUHS-kuh-vee)
Novgorod (NAWV-guh-rahd)
Slavs (slahvz)
Vladimir (VLAD-uh-mihr)

© 2016 K12 Inc. All rights reserved.
Copying or distributing without K12's written consent is prohibited.

LEARN

Activity 1: Russia - A Growing Empire *(Offline)*

Instructions

This lesson is designed to be completed in **3** class sessions.

Day 1

Read

Read Chapter 11, from the beginning to "Ivan Rebuilds the Kremlin," pages 164 to 171. Complete **Day 1** of the Reading Guide.

Focus on Geography

Complete the Focus on Geography sheet.

Day 2

Read

Read Chapter 11, from "Ivan Rebuilds the Kremlin" to the end, pages 171 to 175. Complete **Day 2** of the Reading Guide.

Russia Online

Answer the following questions in your History Journal. You'll need to go back online and visit the PBS: Face of Russia website referenced in the lesson to answer the questions.

1. After inheriting Orthodox Christianity from the Byzantine Empire, what did Eastern Slavs (Russians) believe their goal should be? (Click "Cathedral of St. Sophia, Kiev.")
2. When was Moscow founded?
3. What was one result of the invasion and domination of the Kievan Rus by the Mongols?
4. When was the first Muscovite legal code written?
5. Why are the domes of St. Basil's covered with onion-shaped shells?

Day 3

Russia in the News

You have been asked by an editor of History Weekly to write three articles for their publication. Refer to **Day 2** of your completed Reading Guide and select three of the five topics that were covered. (Make sure you've used the Lesson Answer Key to check your work.)

Write an informative, entertaining article about each of the three topics you have chosen. You may use the headline you previously wrote, or think of a new one. Use the information you've already gathered on the Reading Guide. If you need additional information, refer back to your book.

Write a rough draft for each article. Have an adult or peer proofread each article for spelling, grammar, and punctuation and to provide constructive criticism. Then revise each rough draft to create a final copy ready to print in History Weekly.

© 2016 K12 Inc. All rights reserved.
Copying or distributing without K12's written consent is prohibited.

ASSESS

Lesson Assessment: Russia Rising (*Online*)

You will complete an online assessment covering the main objectives of this lesson. Your assessment will be scored by the computer.

© 2016 K12 Inc. All rights reserved.
Copying or distributing without K12's written consent is prohibited.

Name Date 

Reading Guide

Day 1

Match each word on the left with its description on the right.

1. ____ Slavs
2. ____ Vikings
3. ____ Kiev
4. ____ boyars
5. ____ Vladimir
6. ____ Eastern Orthodox Church

A. Prince of Kiev who chose an official state religion

B. An important city, it became the capital of Rus

C. Eastern Europeans who first settled along the network of rivers in what later became Russia

D. Landowning nobles of Russian cities

E. Scandinavians who traveled and settled along rivers in a region that eventually became Russia

F. The religion that began to thrive in Russia after 988

7. Who invaded Russia in the early thirteenth century? Briefly describe the methods they used to conquer Russia and their results.

8. List at least four ways Ivan the Great (Ivan III) gained territory and power within Russia.

9. Briefly explain how Tatar rule in Russia ended.

10. The Russians gradually developed their own version of Christianity, calling it the ______________________________. Briefly, why did the Russians develop their own religion?

© 2016 K12 Inc. All rights reserved.
Copying or distributing without K12's written consent is prohibited.

Name ______________________ Date ______________________ 

11. Ivan the Great believed that ____________________ had replaced Rome and Constantinople as the new center of ____________________. He married a ____________________ princess and even took a title from ancient Rome—he called himself ____________________, which comes from the Latin word ______________.

Day 2

For each topic below, write an eye-catching headline and then answer as many of the five Ws and H as you can. Do not write a lot—use a few words or brief phrases.

12. Ivan III and the Kremlin

Headline: ______________________

Who: ______________________

What: ______________________

Where: ______________________

When: ______________________

Why: ______________________

How: ______________________

13. Ivan the Terrible (Ivan IV) – His Early Years/As a Young Tsar

Headline: ______________________

Who: ______________________

What: ______________________

Where: ______________________

When: ______________________

Why: ______________________

How: ______________________

14. Life as a Peasant in Russia

Headline: ______________________

Who: ______________________

What: ______________________

Where: ______________________

When: ______________________

Why: ______________________

© 2016 K12 Inc. All rights reserved.
Copying or distributing without K12's written consent is prohibited.

Name ______________________________ Date ______________________________

How: ______________________________

15. St. Basil's

Headline: ______________________________

Who: ______________________________

What: ______________________________

Where: ______________________________

When: ______________________________

Why: ______________________________

How: ______________________________

16. The End of Ivan IV's Reign

Headline: ______________________________

Who: ______________________________

What: ______________________________

Where: ______________________________

When: ______________________________

Why: ______________________________

How: ______________________________

© 2016 K12 Inc. All rights reserved.
Copying or distributing without K12's written consent is prohibited.

Name ______________________________ Date ______________________________ 

Focus on Geography

Russia is the largest country in the world. It spans two continents—Europe and Asia. Geography has played an important role throughout Russia's history. One way to appreciate the size of Russia is to see how many time zones it encompasses. You can figure out how many without a time zone map.

The Earth, which is divided up into 360 degrees of longitude, rotates in 24 hours. The Earth has been divided into 24 time zones. To figure out how many time zones Russia has, first determine how many degrees of longitude there are in a time zone: 360÷24 = 15. Each time zone spans 15 degrees of longitude.

Knowing this, you can look at any political map of the world and figure out how many time zones Russia has. Use the world political map in the atlas in your textbook to do this.

1. How many time zones does Russia have? ______

Compare that to the number of time zones in the continental United States—four. Russia is a very large country!

Although Russia is huge, it encompasses only four climate zones.

2. According to the Climate Zones map in your textbook atlas, what are the four climate zones found in Russia?

   ____

Refer to your atlas to answer the following questions.

3. What geographic feature separates European Russia from Asian Russia (Siberia)?

   ____

4. Name four mountain ranges in Russia. (There are more than four.)

   ____

5. Russia has many rivers. Some are among the longest in the world. Most of Russia's rivers flow northward and empty into the Arctic Ocean. Name four of the rivers.

   ____

6. One of Russia's most famous rivers, and the longest one in Europe, flows southward. Name the river and the body of water it empties into.

   ____

7. Name the three largest countries that border Russia to the south.

   ____

8. Name five European countries that share Russia's western border.

   ____

9. Russia has coastline on many seas and oceans. Name them. (Hint: There are eight.)

   ____

   ____

© 2016 K12 Inc. All rights reserved.
Copying or distributing without K12's written consent is prohibited.

Name Date 

10. Name three cities found on the map of Europe in your atlas that were mentioned in today's reading.

____

11. The cities that you should have named above were part of Russia. However, Russia's borders and territory have changed over time. Which of the three cities is not in Russia today? In what country is it?

____

Thinking cap question: Russia has thousands of miles of coastline—more than any other country. Why do you think Russia has very few large port cities?

© 2016 K12 Inc. All rights reserved.
Copying or distributing without K12's written consent is prohibited.

Student Guide
Lesson 4: Unit Review

You've finished the unit, and now it's time to review what you've learned. You'll take the Unit Assessment in the next lesson.

Lesson Objectives

- Demonstrate mastery of important knowledge and skills taught in this unit.

PREPARE

Approximate lesson time is 60 minutes.

LEARN

Activity 1: New Powers in Asia *(Offline)*

Read

Read the conclusion to Part 1, "Looking Back on the Early Modern World," from "Rivalry and Splendor in the Muslim World" to the end, pages 185 to 191. This will give you a good summary of the unit.

History Journal Review

Now, review the unit by going through your History Journal. You should:

- Look at activity sheets and Reading Guides you completed for the unit.
- Review unit keywords.
- Read any writing assignments you completed during the unit.
- Review any offline assessments you took during the unit.
- Skim through the chapters in *The Human Odyssey: The Modern World* that you read in this unit.

Don't rush through. Take your time. Your History Journal is a great resource for a unit review.

Online Unit Review

Return to the online lesson and click Unit Review to continue reviewing the unit.

Instructions

You've finished the unit, and now it's time to review what you've learned. You'll take the Unit Assessment in the next lesson.

Read

Read the conclusion to Part 1, "Looking Back on the Early Modern World," from "Rivalry and Splendor in the Muslim World" to the end, pages 185 to 191. This will give you a good summary of the unit.

History Journal Review

Now, review the unit by going through your History Journal. You should:

© 2016 K12 Inc. All rights reserved.
Copying or distributing without K12's written consent is prohibited.

- Look at activity sheets and Reading Guides you completed for the unit.
- Review unit keywords.
- Read any writing assignments you completed during the unit.
- Review any offline assessments you took during the unit.
- Skim through the chapters in *The Human Odyssey: The Modern World* that you read in this unit.

Don't rush through. Take your time. Your History Journal is a great resource for a unit review.

Online Unit Review

Return to the online lesson and click Unit Review to continue reviewing the unit.

© 2016 K12 Inc. All rights reserved.
Copying or distributing without K12's written consent is prohibited.

Student Guide
Lesson 5: Unit Assessment

You've finished the unit! Now it's time to take the Unit Assessment.

Lesson Objectives

- Describe artistic and political achievements in China under the Ming dynasty.
- Recognize that the Islamic world experienced hardship at the hands of Mongol conquerors during the time of the European Middle Ages.
- Identify locations and important individuals, events, and achievements of the Ottoman, Safavid, and Mughal Empires.
- Describe the Japanese feudal pyramid and the role of the samurai and bushido.
- Identify the Tokugawa shogunate and describe its accomplishments.
- Identify important individuals, events, and cultural characteristics in the development of Russia.
- Explain the division of Islam into Sunni and Shi'ah.
- Explain why the Chinese and Japanese decided to cut off contact with foreigners, and describe the results of those decisions.
- Describe the major geographic features of Russia.
- Describe the political and religious conflicts between the Ottoman and Safavid Empires.

PREPARE

Approximate lesson time is 60 minutes.

Materials

For the Student

Question Review Table

ASSESS

Unit Assessment: New Powers in Asia, Part 1 (*Online*)

Complete the computer-scored portion of the Unit Assessment. When you have finished, complete the teacher-scored portion of the assessment and submit it to your teacher.

Unit Assessment: New Powers in Asia, Part 2 (*Offline*)

Complete the teacher-scored portion of the Unit Assessment and submit it to your teacher.

© 2016 K12 Inc. All rights reserved.
Copying or distributing without K12's written consent is prohibited.

LEARN

Activity 1. Optional: Unit Assessment Review Table *(Online)*

If you earned a score of **less than 80%** on the Unit Assessment, complete the activity.

If you earned a score of **80% or greater**, you may skip this activity.

Let's prepare to retake the Unit Assessment:

- Identify the questions that you answered incorrectly.
- Complete the appropriate review activities listed in the table.

Note: This Learning Coach Video will guide you through the process of using the Unit Assessment Review Tables. You may skip this video if you've already viewed it in another unit or course. As always, check in with your student's teacher if you have any questions.

© 2016 K12 Inc. All rights reserved.
Copying or distributing without K12's written consent is prohibited.

Assessment Date

Unit 4: New Powers in Asia

Before you retake the Unit Assessment, use the table to figure out which activities you should review.

Question Review Table

Circle the numbers of the questions that you missed on the Unit Assessment. Review the activities that correspond with these questions.

New Powers in Asia, Part 1

Question	Lesson	Review Activity
1,2,3,4,5,6,7,8,9,10,11,12 13,14,15	1: Three Islamic Empires	Muslim Empires on the Rise
16,17,18,19,20,21,22	2: Ming China and Feudal Japan	China and Japan
23,24,25,26,27,28,29	3: Russia Rising	Russia – A Growing Empire

New Powers in Asia, Part 2

Question	Lesson	Review Activity
1	1: Three Islamic Empires	Muslim Empires on the Rise
2	2: Ming China and Feudal Japan	China and Japan
3	3: Russia Rising	Russia – A Growing Empire

© 2016 K12 Inc. All rights reserved.
Copying or distributing without K12's written consent is prohibited.

Student Guide
Lesson 6. Optional: Your Choice

You may use today's lesson time to do one or more of the following:

- Complete work in progress.
- Complete the Beyond the Lesson activity in any lesson in this unit.
- Review the Time Line in the Resources section.
- Go on to the next lesson.

Please mark this lesson complete to proceed to the next lesson in the course.

PREPARE

Approximate lesson time is 60 minutes.

© 2016 K12 Inc. All rights reserved.
Copying or distributing without K12's written consent is prohibited.

Student Guide

Unit 5: Europe Seeks Asia and Meets the Americas
Lesson 1: Portugal and Spain, and the Age of Exploration

Asia had much to offer and Europeans knew it. But how could the Europeans get the spices, silks, and other riches? The Ottomans controlled the Silk Road, and it was terribly dangerous to travel through mountains and deserts. Eager European monarchs wondered if ships could sail to Asia and back. New ship designs and navigation aids might make such trips possible. The race to find a route was on. As the kings and queens vied for riches and fame, the explorers they sent out had no idea what they would actually find. And the overseas empires had no idea what was about to happen.

Once Asian goods arrived in Europe after the thirteenth-century Crusades, life was never the same. Europeans had been buying silks and gems since the days of the Roman Empire, but now they also wanted spices. Just think of the delightful aroma of cinnamon, the tang of pepper and cloves. Spices could also be used to make medicines. But perhaps even more important—since refrigeration hadn't been invented—spices could be used to help preserve food.

Business between Europe and Asia boomed until the Ottoman Turks gained control of the land routes between Europe and Asia. Then travel grew dangerous. What could Europeans do? Were there other ways to reach the East?

Lesson Objectives

- Describe the reasons for European interest in traveling by sea to Asia in the fifteenth century.
- Locate Portugal, Spain, the Atlantic Ocean, the Mediterranean Sea, and the Cape of Good Hope on a map.
- Identify Prince Henry the Navigator as the Portuguese patron of sea expeditions.
- Identify two improvements in navigation and explain that they allowed sailors to travel farther from land.
- Identify Dias as the Portuguese explorer who first rounded the southern tip of Africa.
- Identify Columbus as the Italian navigator who first sailed west to get to Asia, and Ferdinand and Isabella of Spain as his sponsors.
- Trace on a map the route of Columbus's first voyage, and identify San Salvador as his landing point.
- Explain that Columbus called the people he met "Indians" because he thought he had reached the Indies of East Asia.
- Review historical events.

PREPARE

Approximate lesson time is 60 minutes.

© 2016 K12 Inc. All rights reserved.
Copying or distributing without K12's written consent is prohibited.

Materials

For the Student

Reading Guide

The Human Odyssey, Volume 2 edited by Klee, Cribb, and Holdren

History Journal

Keywords and Pronunciation

Amerigo Vespucci (uh-MEHR-ih-goh veh-SPYOO-chee)
Aviz (uh-VEEZH)
Azores (AY-zohrz)
Bojador (boh-hah-DOHR)
Iberian (iy-BIHR-ee-uhn)
Madeiras (mah-DIR-uhs)
Sagres (SAH-greesh)

LEARN

Activity 1: The Age of Exploration Begins *(Offline)*

Instructions

You may have learned about Prince Henry, Columbus, and Dias in an earlier grade. If that's the case, you may take the Lesson Assessment as a pretest if you wish. If you do very well on the assessment, you can complete the Beyond the Lesson activity instead of completing the entire lesson.

This lesson is designed to be completed in **2** class sessions.

Day 1

Read

Read Chapter 1, from the beginning to "Dias Rounds the Cape," pages 196 to 204. Complete **Day 1** of the Reading Guide.

The World in 1490

Columbus presented a plan to Ferdinand and Isabella of Spain in which he proposed sailing west to get to the Indies. His calculations (based on the work of others) indicated that it was the shortest route to the riches of the East. He was mistaken, of course. Instead of finding Asia, he ran into a new continent.

Go back online to the lesson and click The World in 1490. Look at the maps—they are typical of the world maps Europeans used in the fifteenth century. Study them for a few minutes, and then answer the following questions in your History Journal.

1. Why did Columbus believe he could reach Asia more quickly than Dias had if he sailed west?
2. How do the landmasses and coastlines on the fifteenth century maps differ from those you see on a modern map? Why do you think there are such differences?
3. Why are North America and South America missing from these maps?

Think for a moment about what is involved in making a map of the world. How do you think world maps are made today, in the age of computers and satellites? How do you think medieval and Renaissance cartographers made their maps?

If you would like to learn more about the history of cartography (mapmaking), and you have time, visit the following website: BBC: The History of Mapmaking

© 2016 K12 Inc. All rights reserved.
Copying or distributing without K12's written consent is prohibited.

Day 2

Read

Read Chapter 1, from "Dias Rounds the Cape" to the end, pages 204 to 209. Complete **Day 2** of the Reading Guide.

From the Memoirs of Christopher Columbus

If you haven't already done so, read the Page From the Past selection on pages 208 to 209.

Pretend you are Christopher Columbus. It is December, in the year 1504, and you have just returned from your fourth, and final voyage to the New World. You have decided to describe your search for a sea route to the Indies in your memoirs.

In your History Journal, write several paragraphs for your memoirs. Be sure to include:

- Why you believed it was important to find a sea route to Asia and why you wanted to sail west to get there
- Who you asked to sponsor your voyage and who eventually agreed to sponsor it
- What fifteenth-century improvements in navigation and seafaring help make your voyages successful

What If?

Remember that Columbus believed that the route west was the shortest route to the Indies. His belief stemmed from the calculations he had made about the Earth's circumference and the size of Europe and Asia. His calculations were based on the writings of Marco Polo and a French geographer. Unfortunately the information was not very accurate. Consequently, Columbus overestimated the size of Europe and Asia and underestimated the Earth's circumference. Little did he know that the quickest way to the Indies was definitely not by sailing west!

But what if Columbus had known just how far it actually was from Spain to Asia following a westward route? Do you think he would have made the voyage anyway? What factors might have influenced his decision? Write a paragraph describing what you think Columbus would have done if he had known the actual distance. Be sure to give reasons to support your opinion.

Activity 2. Optional: Portugal and Spain, and the Age of Exploration *(Online)*

This activity is OPTIONAL. It's provided for enrichment or extra practice, but not required for completion of this lesson. You may skip this activity.

ASSESS

Lesson Assessment: Portugal and Spain, and the Age of Exploration (*Online*)

You will complete an offline assessment covering the main objectives of this lesson. Your learning coach will score this assessment.

LEARN

Activity 3. Optional: Portugal and Spain, and the Age of Exploration *(Online)*

© 2016 K12 Inc. All rights reserved.
Copying or distributing without K12's written consent is prohibited.

Name Date 

Reading Guide

Day 1

For each of the following topics, include as much information as you can from today's reading assignment.

1. The Time
   (When did the events you read about today take place?)

2. The Place
   (Draw a simple map of the region where the events took place. Label the following: Portugal, Spain, the Atlantic Ocean, and the Mediterranean Sea.)

3. The Goal
   (Why were Europeans eagerly searching for a sea route to Asia in the fifteenth century?)

© 2016 K12 Inc. All rights reserved.
Copying or distributing without K12's written consent is prohibited.

Name ______________________________ Date ______________________________

4. The Man
(Who played a key role in helping to find a sea route to Asia? Describe his role.)

5. The Tools
(Name and describe some of the improvements in seafaring equipment that helped the explorers achieve their goal.)

Day 2

6. ______________________ was the first European to round the southern tip of Africa. He named it ______________________, but King John later renamed it ______________________.

7. Why did King John rename the cape as he did?

8. In Europe's quest for a sea route to Asia, what was the significance of Dias's accomplishment?

9. Unlike the Portuguese, who had rounded Africa and were sailing east toward Asia, Christopher Columbus decided to sail ______________________. His decision was based on his estimates of the ______________________ circumference and the sizes of ______________________ and ______________________. Unfortunately, Columbus ______________________ the former and ______________________ the latter. Although this resulted in a much longer voyage than he anticipated, his estimates probably helped convince ______________________ and ______________________, the two Spanish monarchs who sponsored his voyage.

10. Why did Columbus call the people he met during his first voyage "Indians"?

© 2016 K12 Inc. All rights reserved.
Copying or distributing without K12's written consent is prohibited.

Name Date 

11. Draw a chart (nautical maps are called charts) that shows the route Columbus took from Spain to San Salvador, where he first made landfall. Label the following: Spain, the Atlantic Ocean, the Caribbean Sea, and San Salvador.

12. How did the Americas get their name? Why are they often referred to as the “New World”?

© 2016 K12 Inc. All rights reserved.
Copying or distributing without K12’s written consent is prohibited.

Name Date 

Portugal, Spain, and the Age of Exploration

1. Explain why Europeans were looking for sea routes to Asia in the fifteen century.

2. Name the Portuguese prince and patron of sea expeditions who played a key role in the search for sea routes to Asia.

3. Describe some of the improvements in navigation and seafaring that allowed sailors to go farther from land as they searched for sea routes to Asia.

4. Who was the first European to round the southern tip of Africa?

   a. Ferdinand Magellan
   b. Vasco da Gama
   c. Bartolomeu Dias
   d. Hernán Cortés

5. Explain why Columbus thought that the quickest way to reach Asia was by sailing west—and why he was wrong.

6. What Spanish monarchs sponsored Columbus's voyage in 1492?

7. Why did Columbus call the people he met during his first voyage "Indians"?

© 2016 K12 Inc. All rights reserved.
Copying or distributing without K12's written consent is prohibited.

Name Date 

8. Label the following on the map below: Spain, Portugal, the Mediterranean Sea, the Atlantic Ocean, the Cape of Good Hope, San Salvador.

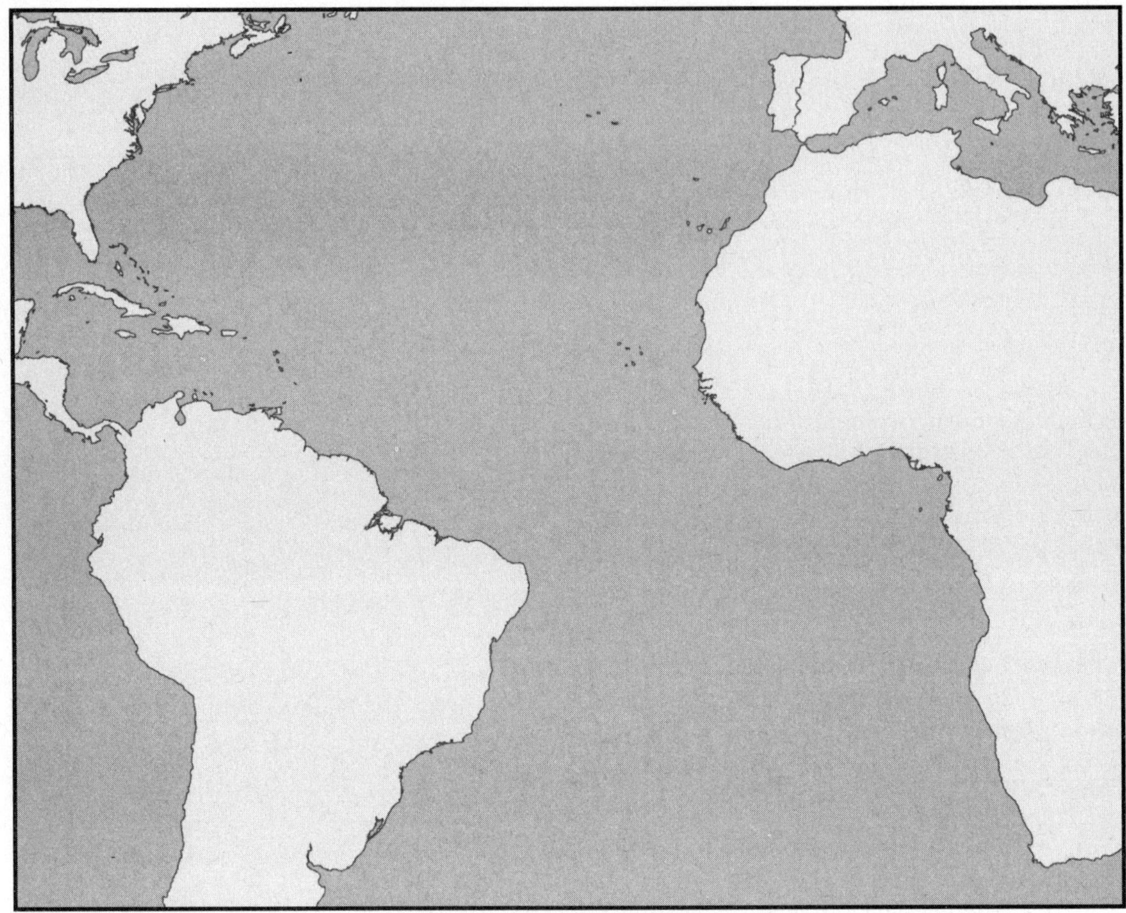

© 2016 K12 Inc. All rights reserved.
Copying or distributing without K12's written consent is prohibited.

Student Guide
Lesson 2. Optional: Your Choice

You may use today's lesson time to do one or more of the following:

- Complete work in progress.
- Complete the Beyond the Lesson activity in any lesson in this unit.
- Review the Time Line in the Resources section.
- Go on to the next lesson.

Please mark this lesson complete to proceed to the next lesson in the course.

PREPARE

Approximate lesson time is 60 minutes.

© 2016 K12 Inc. All rights reserved.
Copying or distributing without K12's written consent is prohibited.

Student Guide
Lesson 3: Filling in the Map

Just 30 years after Columbus tried to reach Asia by sailing west, a Spanish expedition sailed all the way around the globe. Europeans were filling in the map and knew there were huge landmasses between western Europe and eastern Asia. Undaunted, explorers still tried to reach the wealth of the Indies by sailing west into uncharted seas. They claimed vast territories for their rulers. Other expeditions continued to risk sailing through the treacherous waters around the southern tip of Africa. Explorers thought the wealth and fame they imagined would make all the hardship worthwhile. But no one could ever have imagined what would really result from their explorations.

Lesson Objectives

- Recognize that fifteenth-century standards for the behavior of nations differed from modern standards.
- Identify Vasco da Gama.
- Identify Pedro Cabral.
- Identify Ferdinand Magellan.
- Locate on a map the route Magellan took, the major land areas and bodies of water on the route, and the distance the expedition traveled.
- Identify the Line of Demarcation and explain its purpose.
- Describe the events leading to Portugal's claim to Brazil and the consequences of that claim.
- Summarize the significant events of Magellan's voyage.

PREPARE

Approximate lesson time is 60 minutes.

Materials

For the Student

Focus on Geography

Reading Guide

The Human Odyssey, Volume 2 edited by Klee, Cribb, and Holdren

---

LEARN
Activity 1: Cabral, da Gama, and Magellan *(Online)*

© 2016 K12 Inc. All rights reserved.
Copying or distributing without K12's written consent is prohibited.

Instructions

This lesson is designed to be completed in **3** class sessions.

Day 1

Read

Read Chapter 2, from the beginning to "Ferdinand Magellan: In Columbus's Wake and Beyond," pages 210 to 215. Complete **Day 1** of the Reading Guide.

Focus on Geography

Remember that the Line of Demarcation and the Treaty of Tordesillas allowed Portugal to claim all lands east of the line. That gave the Portuguese an eastward sea route to Asia. As Portuguese navigators expanded their horizons to the east, they helped fill in the map of the world.

Use the map on pages 198 to 199 of your book to help you complete **Day 1** of the Focus on Geography sheet.

Day 2

Read

Read Chapter 2, from "Ferdinand Magellan: In Columbus's Wake and Beyond" to the end, pages 215 to 221. Complete **Day 2** of the Reading Guide.

Focus on Geography

Magellan's expedition succeeded in circumnavigating the globe and filling in significant sections of the map of the world.

Complete **Day 2** of the Focus on Geography sheet.

Day 3

Exploration Then and Now

In the late fifteenth and early sixteenth centuries, European explorers were filling in the missing pieces of the map of Earth. In this lesson, you read about three explorers and the pieces they added to the map.

Beginning in the second half of the twentieth century, explorers began to fill in a different map—the map of the universe. In 1957 the Soviet Union launched Sputnik, the world's first satellite, sparking a race for space. The United States joined the race and soon embarked on an ambitious effort to land men on the moon. Since that time, many nations have contributed to the exploration of our solar system and beyond.

Write a paragraph that compares and contrasts the exploration carried out in the late fifteenth and early sixteenth centuries with the modern exploration of space. How are they similar? How are they different?

Before you begin to write, you may need to do a little research about space exploration. Use Grolier's Online Encyclopedia and other sources for your research. Don't spend a lot of time, but read enough to get a good idea of what has been involved in exploring space.

Here are some points to consider as you look for information and think about both kinds of exploration:

- Risks
- Technology
- Financing
- Potential benefits
- Attitudes toward new information

© 2016 K12 Inc. All rights reserved.
Copying or distributing without K12's written consent is prohibited.

ASSESS

Lesson Assessment: Filling in the Map (*Online*)

You will complete an online assessment covering the main objectives of this lesson. Your assessment will be scored by the computer

© 2016 K12 Inc. All rights reserved.
Copying or distributing without K12's written consent is prohibited.

Name Date 

Reading Guide

Day 1

1. Fill-in-the-Blank

In previous Reading Guides, you have had fill-in-the-blank items where you had to provide words or phrases to complete a sentence. Today, you have been given the words and phrases--and YOU must create the fill-in-the-blank items.

Create items using the words and phrases in the box below. You may use a word or phrase more than once. When possible, your items should reinforce the following lesson objectives. Write as many items as is necessary to cover the objectives.

- Identify the Line of Demarcation of 1493 and explain its purpose.
- Identify Vasco da Gama.
- Identify Pedro Cabral.

Vasco da Gama Pope Alexander VI 1498 Spain west
Brazil King Manuel Line of Demarcation
1500 Portugal east Indies vitamin C
Treaty of Tordesillas Calicut, India scurvy
King Ferdinand and Queen Isabella Pedro Cabral

© 2016 K12 Inc. All rights reserved.
Copying or distributing without K12's written consent is prohibited.

Name Date 

2. Portugal and Spain were rivals in the exploration of the seas. State two reasons why both nations were sending out voyages of exploration.

3. Why did Europeans of the fifteenth century have no problem dividing the globe and claiming lands around the world as their own? What has changed since that time? What prevents nations today from doing what Spain and Portugal did then? (Review the sidebar on page 212 if necessary.)

Day 2

As you read about Ferdinand Magellan and his search for a sea route through the Americas to the Indies, you will fill in some of the missing pages of the expedition's logbook. Under each heading, write a short description of the event(s).

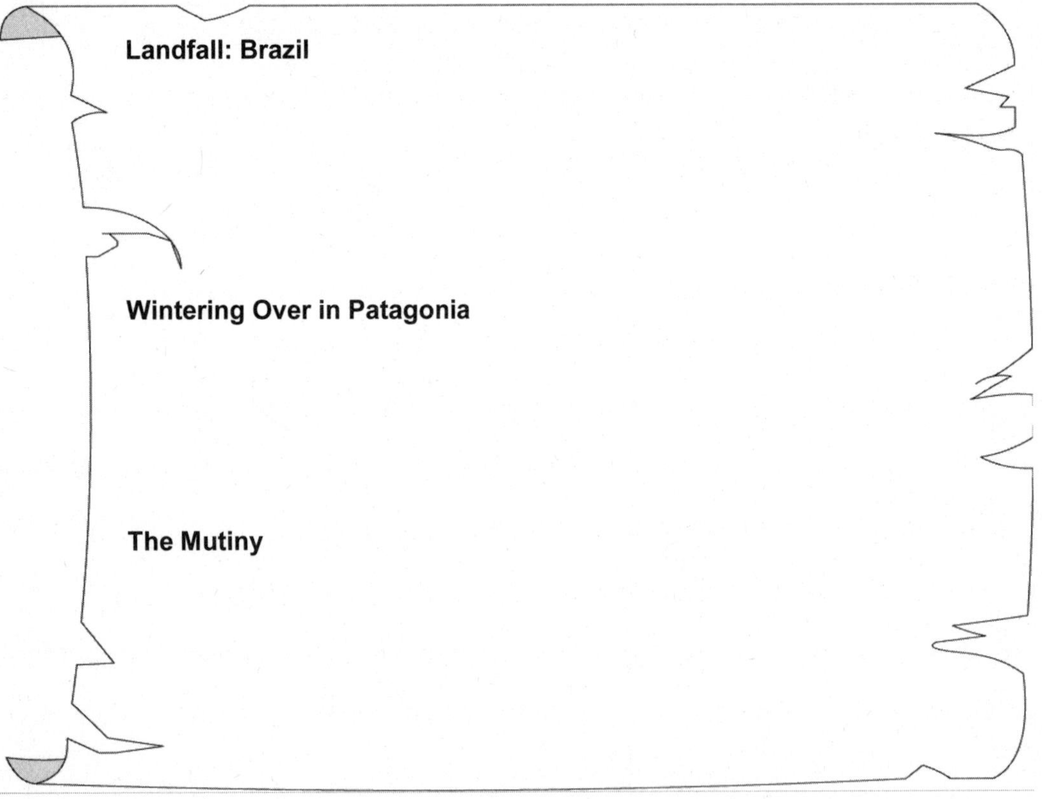

© 2016 K12 Inc. All rights reserved.
Copying or distributing without K12's written consent is prohibited.

Name Date 

Discovering the Strait

Crossing the Pacific

Disaster in the Philippines

The Voyage Home

© 2016 K12 Inc. All rights reserved.
Copying or distributing without K12's written consent is prohibited.

Name Date 

Thinking Cap Question

In 1493, the Catholic nations of Spain and Portugal had a conflict. They were rivals in the exploration of the seas. When King John II of Portugal announced he was going to send ships west to claim land for Portugal, King Ferdinand and Queen Isabella of Spain were concerned – they were hoping to claim all the land to the west. Because both nations were Catholic, they agreed to let Pope Alexander VI (the head of the Catholic Church) settle the matter of who could claim new lands discovered during exploration.

If two predominantly Catholic nations had a conflict today, do you think the pope would intervene? If not, who do you think would help settle the conflict?

© 2016 K12 Inc. All rights reserved.
Copying or distributing without K12's written consent is prohibited.

Name Date 

Focus on Geography

Day 1

1. Label the following on the map on page 3 of this Focus on Geography:

   - Atlantic and Indian Oceans
   - Portugal, Brazil, and India
   - Europe, South America, Asia, and Africa

2. Draw and label:

   - the Line of Demarcation resulting from the 1494 Treaty of Tordesillas

3. Draw and label the routes of Vasco da Gama and Pedro Cabral.

4. Compare the routes of Dias and da Gama from Portugal to the Cape of Good Hope. Why do you think they were so different?

5. Approximately how many miles did da Gama travel from Portugal to the Cape of Good Hope?

6. Before reaching modern-day Kenya, da Gama sailed between the mainland and an island off the southeast coast of Africa. What is the name of the island?

7. If Cabral had reached Brazil in 1493, would he have been able to claim it for Portugal? Why or why not?

8. If Spain and Portugal had never signed the Treaty of Tordesillas, what language do you think Brazilians would be speaking today? Why?

Day 2

9. Label the following on the map on page 3:

   - Pacific Ocean, Strait of Magellan
   - Patagonia, Guam, the Philippines, China, Indonesia,
   - North America, Australia, and Antarctica

© 2016 K12 Inc. All rights reserved.
Copying or distributing without K12's written consent is prohibited.

Name Date 

10. Draw and label the route of Magellan's expedition around the world.
11. If Magellan had not found the strait that he traveled through to reach the Pacific, could he still have achieved his goal? Explain.
12. If Magellan's course had taken him a little farther north or south shortly after crossing the Tropic of Capricorn, he might have been able to restock food and water supplies. The islands of what archipelago might have provided the much-needed supplies?
13. At what line of longitude did Magellan's fleet cross the equator after entering the Pacific Ocean?
14. What three major oceans did Magellan's expedition cross?
15. Magellan's expedition made landfall on two continents and in two major island groups. Name them.
16. Which portion of the expedition sailed a greater number of miles—the portion with Magellan in command or the portion after his death?

Research (Optional)

Do some research to determine the location of any trade winds that would have helped or hindered da Gama, Cabral, and Magellan during their voyages. Show the trade winds on the map and label them.

Here's one source to get you started: http://en.wikipedia.org/wiki/Trade_winds

© 2016 K12 Inc. All rights reserved.
Copying or distributing without K12's written consent is prohibited.

Name Date 

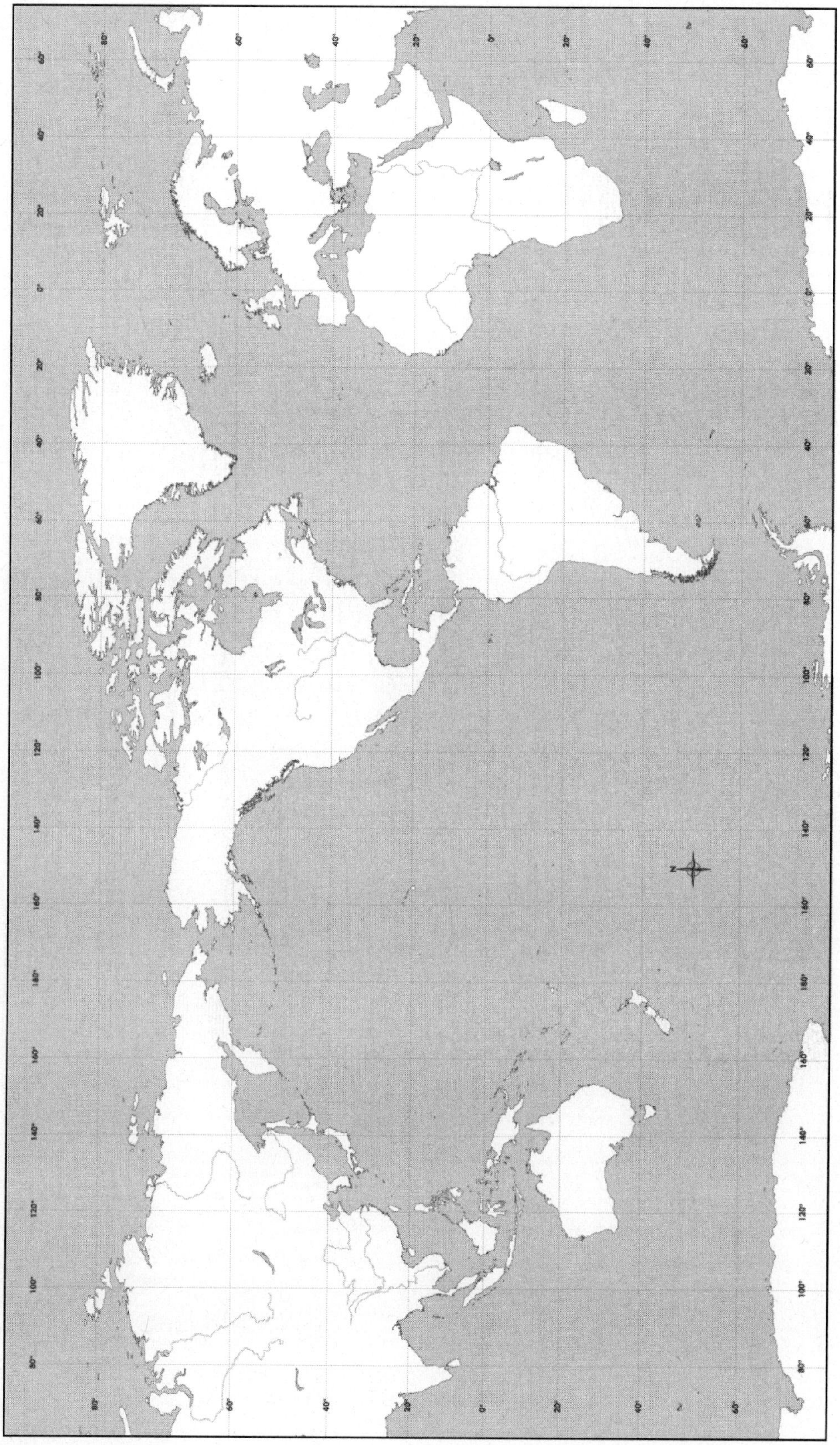

© 2016 K12 Inc. All rights reserved.
Copying or distributing without K12's written consent is prohibited.

Student Guide
Lesson 4. Optional: Your Choice

You may use today's lesson time to do one or more of the following:

- Complete work in progress.
- Complete the Beyond the Lesson activity in any lesson in this unit.
- Review the Time Line in the Resources section.
- Go on to the next lesson.

Please mark this lesson complete to proceed to the next lesson in the course.

PREPARE

Approximate lesson time is 60 minutes.

© 2016 K12 Inc. All rights reserved.
Copying or distributing without K12's written consent is prohibited.

Student Guide
Lesson 5: Old Civilizations

People lived on the Yucatán Peninsula and in the Andes mountains for thousands of years before they met explorers from Europe. Diverse groups developed unique cultures. Civilizations evolved and thrived for hundreds of years. The Maya invented the mathematical concept of zero. The Aztecs built cities larger than any in Europe. The Inca government built roads over deep gorges and raging rivers. What European explorers called the "New World" was filled with ancient temples, centuries-old governments, and the vine-covered ruins of long-ago peoples.

Lesson Objectives

- Recognize that the term "new world" reflected only the European view of the continents they learned about in the fifteenth and sixteenth centuries.
- Define *civilization.*
- Identify the Olmecs as possibly the earliest civilization in the Americas.
- Summarize the major achievements and characteristics of Maya civilization.
- Summarize the major achievements and characteristics of Aztec civilization.
- Describe the origins of Mexico's name and flag.
- Summarize the major achievements and characteristics of Inca civilization.
- Locate the Olmec, Maya, Aztec, and Inca Empires on a map.
- Identify Hiram Bingham as the modern discoverer of the lost city of Machu Picchu.

PREPARE

Approximate lesson time is 60 minutes.

Materials

For the Student

- Focus on Geography
- Reading Guide
- The Human Odyssey, Volume 2 edited by Klee, Cribb, and Holdren

---

LEARN

Activity 1: Not "New" to Them *(Offline)*

Instructions

This lesson is designed to be completed in **3** class sessions.

Day 1

Read

Read Chapter 3, from the beginning to "The Aztecs Seek a Home," pages 222 to 227. Complete **Day 1** of the Reading Guide.

© 2016 K12 Inc. All rights reserved.
Copying or distributing without K12's written consent is prohibited.

The Maya Online

Return to the lesson online and click the link NOVA Online: Map of the Maya World. Use the map to learn about some, or all, of the 15 better-known Maya archaeological sites.

Day 2

Read

Read Chapter 3, from "The Aztecs Seek a Home" to *"Better Than Gold: Hiram Bingham and the Lost City of the Inca,"* pages 227 to 234. Complete **Day 2** of the Reading Guide.

Focus on Geography

Use the maps in Chapter 3 and your textbook atlas to help you complete the Focus on Geography sheet.

The Lost City of the Inca

Read *"Better Than Gold: Hiram Bingham and the Lost City of the Inca,"* pages 235 to 237, and then answer the following questions in your History Journal.

1. Why was Hiram Bingham well suited to lead an expedition to locate Machu Picchu?
2. Did the Inca call their city Machu Picchu when they inhabited it? Explain your answer.
3. Was Bingham disappointed when he realized there was no gold in Machu Picchu? Explain your answer.

Day 3

The Maya, Aztec, and Inca

To conclude this lesson, you will create a poster to illustrate the similarities and differences among the three civilizations you studied.

First, return to the lesson online and click "Mesoamerican Calendars." Pay particular attention to how the Maya and Aztec calendars look. When you have completed that activity, follow the directions below to make the poster.

Directions:

- Using a sheet of poster board or foam board, create the outlines of a Mesoamerican calendar. You don't need a lot of details--just a circular shape divided into segments. If you have time at the end, you can embellish it with some details.
- On this calendar, draw or paste images that represent each of the three civilizations you studied: Maya, Aztec, and Inca. Select images that will help you explain the similarities and differences among the three civilizations.
- Use the calendar you created to prepare a presentation that will teach your audience about the similarities and differences among the Maya, Aztec, and Inca civilizations.
- Give your presentation.

© 2016 K12 Inc. All rights reserved.
Copying or distributing without K12's written consent is prohibited.

ASSESS

Lesson Assessment: Old Civilizations (*Online*)

You will complete an online assessment covering the main objectives of this lesson. Your assessment will be scored by the computer.

© 2016 K12 Inc. All rights reserved.
Copying or distributing without K12's written consent is prohibited.

Name Date 

Reading Guide

Day 1

1. In the early sixteenth century, to whom were the American continents a "new world"? And who might have taken offense at that term?

2. Define *civilization.*

3. The ________________ established what many archaeologists believe to be the earliest ________________ in the Americas. The civilization thrived between ________ and ________ on ________________ Gulf coast.

4. Complete the column for the Maya on the chart below.

	The Maya	The Aztecs	The Incas
Timeframe/ Important Dates			
Founder(s) and/or Important Rulers			
Capital City and/or Major Cities			
Religion			
Conflicts			

© 2016 K12 Inc. All rights reserved.
Copying or distributing without K12's written consent is prohibited.

Name Date 

Achievements/ Accomplishments			
What I Found Most Interesting About This Civilization			

Day 2

5. Briefly describe the significance of the eagle, cactus, and snake on Mexico's national flag.

6. Why did the conquering Spaniards name their new colony Mexico?

7. Complete the columns for the Aztecs and the Incas on the chart.

© 2016 K12 Inc. All rights reserved.
Copying or distributing without K12's written consent is prohibited.

Name Date 

Focus on Geography

Use the maps in Chapter 3 and your textbook atlas to help you answer the following questions.

1. Which of the civilizations you studied were located in North America?

2. Which civilization was located in South America?

3. In what modern countries is the territory that the Maya civilization occupied?

4. What modern city is situated where the Aztec city of Tenochtitlán was located?

5. What important Maya city was located in the rain forest on the Yucatán Peninsula?

6. Which civilization, the Aztec or the Maya, had more miles of coastline?

7. Which empire existed entirely within the modern country of Mexico?

8. What five modern countries are in the area the Inca Empire once occupied?

9. What mountain range created formidable obstacles for Inca road builders?

10. What large lake lies within the old borders of the Inca Empire?

11. What two cities were located approximately halfway between the northern and southern ends of the Inca Empire?

12. Which of the following is the best estimate for the distance between Quito and Talca?
    - 3,300 miles
    - 2,600 miles
    - 2,000 miles

13. Why do you think the Inca Empire did not extend farther east?

© 2016 K12 Inc. All rights reserved.
Copying or distributing without K12's written consent is prohibited.

Student Guide
Lesson 6: Unit Review

You've finished the unit, and now it's time to review what you've learned. You'll take the Unit Assessment in the next lesson.

Lesson Objectives

- Demonstrate mastery of important knowledge and skills taught in this unit.

PREPARE

Approximate lesson time is 60 minutes.

LEARN

Activity 1: Europe Seeks Asia and Meets the Americas *(Online)*

History Journal Review

Now, review the unit by going through your History Journal. You should:

- Look at activity sheets and Reading Guides you completed for this unit.
- Review unit keywords.
- Read any writing assignments you completed in this unit.
- Review any off line assessments you took during this unit.
- Skim through the chapters in The Human Odyssey: The Modern World that you read in this unit.

Don't rush. Take your time. Your History Journal is a great resource for a unit review.

Super Genius Game

Return to the online lesson and click Seeking Asia...Finding the Americas to continue reviewing the unit.

© 2016 K12 Inc. All rights reserved.
Copying or distributing without K12's written consent is prohibited.

Student Guide
Lesson 7: Unit Assessment

You've finished the unit! Now it's time to take the Unit Assessment.

Lesson Objectives

- Identify the major civilizations in the Americas prior to European conquest and describe them and their achievements.
- Explain the purposes of Spanish and Portuguese voyages of exploration.
- Identify important explorers and patrons of exploration and explain why they became famous.
- Explain why Europeans were so eager to sail to Asia in the fifteenth century.
- Identify on a map the routes of famous European explorers and the lands they claimed.

PREPARE

Approximate lesson time is 60 minutes.

Materials

For the Student

Question Review Table

ASSESS

Unit Assessment: Europe Seeks Asia and Meets The Americas, Part 1 (*Online*)

Complete the computer-scored portion of the Unit Assessment. When you have finished, complete the teacher-scored portion of the assessment and submit it to your teacher.

Unit Assessment: Europe Seeks Asia and Meets the Americas, Part 2 (*Offline*)

Complete the teacher-scored portion of the Unit Assessment and submit it to your teacher.

LEARN

Activity 1. Optional: Optional Unit Assessment Review Table *(Online)*

If you earned a score of **less than 80%** on the Unit Assessment, complete the activity.

If you earned a score of **80% or greater**, you may skip this activity.

Let's prepare to retake the Unit Assessment:

- Identify the questions that you answered incorrectly.
- Complete the appropriate review activities listed in the table.

Note: This Learning Coach Video will guide you through the process of using the Unit Assessment Review Tables. You may skip this video if you've already viewed it in another unit or course. As always, check in with your student's teacher if you have any questions.

© 2016 K12 Inc. All rights reserved.
Copying or distributing without K12's written consent is prohibited.

Assessment Date

Unit 5: Europe Seeks Asia and Meets the Americas

Before you retake the Unit Assessment, use the table to figure out which activities you should review.

Question Review Table

Circle the numbers of the questions that you missed on the Unit Assessment. Review the activities that correspond with these questions.

Europe Seeks Asia and Meets The Americas, Part 1

Question	Lesson	Review Activity
4	1: Portugal and Spain, and the Age of Exploration	The Age of Exploration Begins
1,2,3	5: Old Civilizations	Not "New" to Them

Europe Seeks Asia and Meets The Americas, Part 2

Question	Lesson	Review Activity
1,4,5,6, 12	1: Portugal and Spain, and the Age of Exploration	The Age of Exploration Begins
2,3,7,13	3: Filling in the Map	Cabral, da Gama, and Magellan
8,9,10,11,	5: Old Civilizations	Not "New" to Them

© 2016 K12 Inc. All rights reserved.
Copying or distributing without K12's written consent is prohibited.

Student Guide

Unit 6: Exploration Changes the World
Lesson 1: Clash of Civilizations

Gold, glory, and God. The Spanish and Portuguese conquistadors went to the New World to search for wealth and glory and to spread their religion. Guns and germs helped them defeat great empires. But the conquerors could not have predicted the long-term and often unintended consequences of their actions. Farming changed on three continents. Diets changed. Thousands of people willingly crossed the oceans to start new lives. Millions died of disease and abuse and millions were kidnapped and forced to cross the oceans as slaves. We still feel the consequences today.

In the early sixteenth century, Spain was the most powerful country in Europe. In the Americas, the Aztec and Inca Empires were flourishing. What would happen when Spanish conquistadors went to the Americas searching for gold, empire, and a chance to spread Christianity? The Spanish could never have imagined the quantities of gold the New World offered. The Aztecs and Incas had never seen horses or guns. When the Spanish crossed the Atlantic Ocean, the world began to change in ways no one could have predicted.

Lesson Objectives

- Define *conquistador*.
- Identify Hernán Cortés and summarize the events that led to the decline of the Aztec Empire.
- Identify Moctezuma.
- Identify Francisco Pizarro and summarize the events that led to the decline of the Inca Empire.
- Describe the characteristics of the Aztec and Inca Empires that contributed to their decline.

PREPARE

Approximate lesson time is 60 minutes.

Materials

For the Student

- Consider the Source
- Reading Guide
- The Human Odyssey, Volume 2 edited by Klee, Cribb, and Holdren
- History Journal

Keywords and Pronunciation

Atahualpa (ah-tah-WAHL-pah)
Bernal Díaz del Castillo (ber-NAHL DEE-ahs del kahs-TEE-yoh)
conquistador (kahn-KEES-tuh-dor) : "Conqueror" in Spanish; Spanish soldiers who conquered native peoples in Latin America in the early sixteenth century.
Cuitláhuac (kweet-LAH-wahk)
Diego Velázquez (dee-YAY-goh veh-LAHS-kuhs)
Francisco Pizarro (fran-SIS-koh puh-ZAHR-oh)
Hernán Cortés (ehr-NAHN kor-TAYS)
Huascar (WAHS-kahr)

© 2016 K12 Inc. All rights reserved.
Copying or distributing without K12's written consent is prohibited.

Lima (LEE-muh)
Malintzin (mah-LINT-suhn)
Moctezuma (mawk-tay-SOO-mah)
Vasco Núñez de Balboa (VAHS-koh NOON-yays day bal-BOH-uh)

LEARN

Activity 1: Clash of Civilizations *(Offline)*

Instructions

This lesson is designed to be completed in **2** class sessions.

Day 1

Read

Read Chapter 4, from the beginning to "Pizarro Ventures South," pages 238–247, and complete **Day 1** of the Reading Guide. When you have finished, use the Lesson Answer Key to check your work, and then place the Reading Guide in your History Journal.

Consider the Source

Examine a primary source document and complete the Consider the Source sheet. Use the Lesson Answer Key to check your work.

Contrasting Civilizations: Spanish and Aztec

Examine the differences between the two civilizations by completing the Spanish and Aztec activity online. When you have finished, use the Online Notebook or your History Journal to explain what, if anything, the Aztecs could have done to make things turn out differently.

Day 2

Read

Read Chapter 4, from "Pizarro Ventures South" to the end of the chapter, pages 247–249, and complete **Day 2** of the Reading Guide. When you have finished, use the Lesson Answer Key to check your work, and then place the Reading Guide in your History Journal.

Contrasting Civilizations: Spanish and Inca

Examine the differences between the two civilizations by completing the Spanish and Inca activity online. When you have finished, use the Online Notebook or your History Journal to explain what, if anything, the Incas could have done to make things turn out differently. If you had to be a member of one of the three groups (conquistadors, Aztecs, or Incas), which one would you choose? Provide your answer and explain why you would choose that group.

ASSESS

Lesson Assessment: Clash of Civilizations (*Online*)

You will complete an online assessment covering the main objectives of this lesson. Your assessment will be scored by the computer

© 2016 K12 Inc. All rights reserved.
Copying or distributing without K12's written consent is prohibited.

Name Date 

Clash of Civilizations

Day 1

Read

Reading Guide

1. What is the English meaning of the Spanish word *conquistador?*

2. What did conquistadors fight for?

3. ______________________ was the Spanish soldier who overthrew the Aztec Empire.

4. How did the Aztecs welcome the Spanish?

5. Where did the Spanish recruit allies in Mexico?

6. ______________________ was the Aztec emperor. What did the Spanish do with him?

7. What European disease badly weakened the Aztecs?

8. Name two of the things the Aztecs saw for the first time when the Spanish arrived.

Day 2

Read

9. ______________________________ was the Spanish conqueror of the Inca Empire.

10. Name the two things that ravaged the Inca Empire and made it easy prey for the Spanish.

© 2016 K12 Inc. All rights reserved.
Copying or distributing without K12's written consent is prohibited.

Name Date 

11. How did Pizarro treat the Inca emperor, Atahualpa?

Explore and Discuss

Why were the Spanish so easily able to conquer the Aztecs and the Incas? What characteristics of those two empires made them vulnerable to defeat?

© 2016 K12 Inc. All rights reserved.
Copying or distributing without K12's written consent is prohibited.

Name Date 

Consider the Source

It has been said that history is written by the victors. And when it comes to Mexico in the early sixteenth century, that means the Spanish point of view prevailed. The chapter contains one Spaniard's record—Bernal Díaz del Castillo's account of the death of the Aztec emperor, Moctezuma (pages 246-247). Bernal Díaz del Castillo's writings are useful to historians; but remember, it's only the victor's account.

Let's analyze Bernal Díaz's description of the death of Moctezuma, which is part of what the author called his *True History of the Conquest of Mexico.* Read it again, then answer the following questions:

1. Why might this not really be a *true* history of the death of Moctezuma?

2. Why did Cortés want Moctezuma to address the people?

3. What did Moctezuma think of Cortés by this point?

4. What did Moctezuma request of his people?

5. According to Bernal Díaz, how did Moctezuma die?

6. How else might Moctezuma have died?

7. What was Bernal Díaz's view of how good Moctezuma was?

8. How did the people feel about Moctezuma's death? What did they do?

© 2016 K12 Inc. All rights reserved.
Copying or distributing without K12's written consent is prohibited.

Student Guide
Lesson 2: The Spanish and Portuguese Empires

The goal of the Spanish and Portuguese in the Americas was to bring colonial wealth—not only sugar and other crops, but gold and silver—back to Europe. The Spanish and Portuguese organized their new colonies to be sure they achieved their goal. But at what cost?

In his mural (left), twentieth-century artist Diego Rivera shows how native peoples suffered under colonialism. Not all Spanish or Portuguese colonists approved of what was happening in the Americas. Some, mostly priests and friars like Bartolomé de Las Casas, spoke out against what they saw. Unfortunately, their protests were not enough to save the people.

Lesson Objectives

- Give examples of goods that Europeans wanted from the Americas.
- Describe the system for governing the Spanish colonies.
- Define *peninsulare, creole,* and *mestizo* and describe their places in the social structure of the colonies.
- Describe the lives of the native peoples under the encomienda system.
- Explain why friars and Jesuits went to the colonies and describe the methods they used to achieve their goals.
- Recognize that many missionaries like Las Casas protested to their government about the treatment of the Indians.
- Explain why the native population declined so rapidly and describe how the Spanish government responded to the decline.

PREPARE

Approximate lesson time is 60 minutes.

Materials

For the Student

Reading Guide

The Human Odyssey, Volume 2 edited by Klee, Cribb, and Holdren

History Journal

Keywords and Pronunciation

Bartolomé de Las Casas (bahr-toh-loh-MAY day lahs KAHS-ahs)

cochineal (KAH-chuh-neel) : a red dye obtained from the dried bodies of cochineal insects

creoles (KREE-ohls) : people of Spanish descent born and raised in the Americas; socially, creoles ranked beneath peninsulares

encomendero (en-koh-mehn-DEHR-oh) : a colonist who had authority over Indians who were forced to farm the land or work in mines; the encomendero was expected to protect and Christianize the Indians in exchange for tribute (such as a share of crops)

encomienda (en-koh-mee-EHN-duh) : from a Spanish word meaning "entrust"; the Spanish crown officially gave a colonist authority over all the Indians who lived in a region

Guanajuato (gwah-nah-HWAH-toh)

© 2016 K12 Inc. All rights reserved.
Copying or distributing without K12's written consent is prohibited.

hacienda (hah-see-EHN-duh)
mestizos (meh-STEE-zohs) : people of mixed Spanish and Indian descent; socially, mestizos ranked beneath creoles
peninsulares (pehn-een-suh-LAHR-ehs) : a person born and raised in Spain; peninsulares formed the highest social class in colonial Latin America
viceroy : means "in place of the king"; one who watches over the lands and subjects claimed by the king

---

LEARN

Activity 1: Spanish and Portuguese Empires *(Offline)*

Instructions

This lesson is designed to be completed in **2** class sessions.

Day 1

Read

Read Chapter 5, from the beginning to "Toil and Disease Take Their Toll," pages 250–258, and complete **Day 1** of the Reading Guide. When you have finished, use the Lesson Answer Key to check your work, and then place the Reading Guide in your History Journal.

Now continue today's lesson online with these activities.

- The Friar's Crusade
- Mural with a Message

Day 2

Read

Read Chapter 5, from "Toil and Disease Take Their Toll" to the end of the chapter, pages 258–261, and complete Day 2 of the Reading Guide. When you have finished, use the Lesson Answer Key to check your work, and then place the Reading Guide in your History Journal.

To complete today's lesson, go online to find out how the native populations declined at the hands of the Spanish by completing the Vanishing Peoples activity. Then see how the native population of Hispaniola declined.

Activity 2: Mural with a Message *(Online)*

Activity 3: Vanishing Native Peoples *(Online)*

Instructions

On **Day 2**, finish your reading assignment and then explore how the native populations of the Americas declined by completing the Vanishing Native Peoples activity.

After you have completed this activity, continue with today's lesson on the next screen.

© 2016 K12 Inc. All rights reserved.
Copying or distributing without K12's written consent is prohibited.

ASSESS

Lesson Assessment: The Spanish and Portuguese Empires (*Online*)

You will complete an online assessment covering the main objectives of this lesson. Your assessment will be scored by the computer.

© 2016 K12 Inc. All rights reserved.
Copying or distributing without K12's written consent is prohibited.

Name ______________________________ Date ______________________________ 

Reading Guide

Day 1

Read

Reading Guide

1. Europeans wanted many products from the Americas besides silver and gold. Name two of them.

2. To make sure the products kept flowing to Europe, the Spanish king appointed governors known as ______________________ (which means "in place of the king").

3. In the rigid class structure of the colonies, native-born Spaniards who held all the important positions in government were known as ____________________. Those of Spanish descent born in the colonies were called ____________________. Poor people of mixed race, Spanish and Indian, were called ______________________. And at the bottom of the social structure were the __________________, who were poor and did most of the work.

4. Under the encomienda system, the native peoples worked on the land or underground in the __________, digging for gold and silver.

5. Who wrote an account of the mistreatment of the native peoples called *A Brief Account of the* ____________________ __________________?

Day 2

Read

6. Many Indians died from hunger, exhaustion, or beatings. But most died from ______________________ brought by the Europeans, against which they had no immunity.

7. Why did Catholic friars go to the colonies?

8. What did the friars do to help them communicate better with the native peoples?

© 2016 K12 Inc. All rights reserved.
Copying or distributing without K12's written consent is prohibited.

Name Date 

9. The friars also studied traditional Indian beliefs, and then used those similarities to help explain ______________ .

10. Where did the Spanish and Portuguese think they could find a replacement labor force?

Explore and Discuss

Under Spanish rule, the native populations went into a steep decline. Write a paragraph explaining why that happened. Write another paragraph on what the Spanish could have done to prevent the steep decline.

© 2016 K12 Inc. All rights reserved.
Copying or distributing without K12's written consent is prohibited.

Student Guide
Lesson 3: The Columbian Exchange

When Europeans began sailing to the Americas, they carried people, plants, animals, and diseases back and forth. And so began the Columbian Exchange, the effects of which changed the world forever.

Lesson Objectives

- Describe the Columbian Exchange.
- Define *hemisphere*.
- Recognize significant plants that were introduced to the Old World from the New World and describe their impact.
- Recognize significant plants that were introduced to the New World from the Old World and describe their impact.
- Recognize animals that were introduced to the New World from the Old World and describe their impact.
- Distinguish between intentional and unintentional consequences.
- Use maps to gain information on the Columbian Exchange.

PREPARE

Approximate lesson time is 60 minutes.

Materials

For the Student

Reading Guide

Keywords and Pronunciation

hemisphere : one half of the Earth

LEARN
Activity 1: When Two Worlds Collide *(Online)*

ASSESS
Lesson Assessment: The Columbian Exchange (*Online*)

You will complete an online assessment covering the main objectives of this lesson. Your assessment will be scored by the computer.

© 2016 K12 Inc. All rights reserved.
Copying or distributing without K12's written consent is prohibited.

Name Date 

Reading Guide

The Columbian Exchange

1. What was the Columbian Exchange?

2. One half of the Earth is called a ______________________ .

3. In what part of the world had people used wheat for thousands of years? Where is most of the world's wheat grown today?

4. What two crops from the Americas became food staples in Europe and Africa?

5. Where did people become overly dependent on the potato? What happened as a result of that dependence?

6. How did the European desire for sugarcane lead to the largest forced migration in the history of the world?

7. Many animals were brought from Europe to the Americas, but few animals went from the Americas to Europe. Why was that?

8. Why were the diseases that Europeans carried with them to the Americas so devastating to the native population?

© 2016 K12 Inc. All rights reserved.
Copying or distributing without K12's written consent is prohibited.

Name Date 

Actions have consequences. Many consequences are intentional. If, for example, you study hard for an exam and do well, the consequence of your action is intentional. You planned to study (the action) in order to do well (the consequence). Other consequences are unintentional. Suppose that studying (the action) kept you at home on Tuesday while your friends went shopping. As a result, you did not spend your allowance on a new sweater. On Friday, you get a call from your cousin who offers to sell you a ticket to a sold-out concert. You are able to buy the ticket because you still have your allowance. A nice, but unintended consequence of studying!

9. Look at the actions and consequences of the Columbian Exchange below. Indicate whether each consequence was intended or unintended by underlining the appropriate word.

    a. Europeans bring wheat to the Americas. Wheat becomes a successful crop in several areas. (Intended/Unintended)

    b. Some sailors and conquistadors have had smallpox. They come in contact with Native Americans who contract the disease and die after infecting their relatives. (Intended/Unintended)

    c. Europeans take potatoes with them when they return to Europe. Potatoes become an important source of nutrition in northern and western Europe. (Intended/Unintended)

    d. Affluent Europeans buy sugar from merchants in European cities. Millions of people in Africa are kidnapped by African slave traders and sold to European sugarcane planters in the Caribbean. (Intended/Unintended)

    e. Spanish conquistadors bring their horses with them when they cross the Atlantic. Some horses escape or swim to shore after a ship sinks. The Plains Indians become expert horsemen and buffalo hunters. (Intended/Unintended)

    f. Europeans bring cattle with them to the Americas. Cattle ranches become a profitable business and beef becomes a major food source. (Intended/Unintended)

© 2016 K12 Inc. All rights reserved.
Copying or distributing without K12's written consent is prohibited.

Student Guide
Lesson 4: Songhai, Benin, and the New Slave Trade

Powerful trading kindgoms had thrived in western Africa for centuries before the Portuguese arrived in the late fifteenth century. The kingdoms of Songhai and Benin had grown prosperous by selling gold, copper, kola nuts—and slaves to merchants from north of the Sahara. When Europeans arrived, the slave trade increased. Europeans were eager to ship slaves across the Atlantic to replace the declining native populations in the Americas. Over the course of 300 years, millions of enslaved Africans made the so-called Middle Passage to the Americas, suffering terrible deprivation, abuse, overwork, and humiliation.

Lesson Objectives

- Recognize that slavery had existed for thousands of years in many parts of the world before the 1500s.
- Identify the major events and people in the history of Songhai.
- Describe the savanna and the rain forest.
- Identify on a map the major cities and geographical features of Songhai and Benin.
- Explain the origins and nature of the Portuguese slave trade.
- Recognize that the people in the African kingdoms identified themselves with members of their own tribe, not with the inhabitants of the entire continent.
- Describe the change that took place in the African slave trade in the 1500s.
- Describe the Middle Passage and the toll it took on people.
- Describe the culture and government of Benin.

PREPARE

Approximate lesson time is 60 minutes.

Materials

For the Student

- Mapping West Africa
- Reading Guide
- Slavery Through the Centuries
- The Human Odyssey, Volume 2 edited by Klee, Cribb, and Holdren
- History Journal

Keywords and Pronunciation

Askia Muhammad (as-KEE-uh moh-HAM-uhd)
Benin (buh-NEEN)
caliph (KAY-luhf)
Djenné (jeh-NAY)
Mali (MAH-lee)
Mansa Musa (MAHN-sah moo-SAH)
Middle Passage : the middle leg of the three-way transatlantic slave trade between Europe, Africa, and the Americas, during which slaves suffered and often died due to terrible conditions on overcrowded ships
Niger (NIY-jur)

© 2016 K12 Inc. All rights reserved.
Copying or distributing without K12's written consent is prohibited.

oba (OH-buh) : king or ruler of Benin
rain forest : a wet woodland filled with gigantic trees and abundant wildlife
savanna : a tropical grassland containing a few scattered trees
Songhai (sahng-GIY)
Sunni Ali (sou-NEE ah-LEE)
Timbuktu (tim-buhk-TOO)

LEARN

Activity 1: Songhai, Benin, and the New Slave Trade *(Online)*

Instructions

Day 1

Read

Read Chapter 6, from the beginning to "The Portuguese Come to Benin," pages 262–269, and complete **Day 1** of the Reading Guide. When you have finished, use the Lesson Answer Key to check your work, and then place the Reading Guide in your History Journal.

Overlapping Histories: Time Line for Songhai and Benin

Trace the major milestones in the development of two important African kingdoms by completing the online Time Line activity.

Day 2

Read

Read Chapter 6, from "The Portuguese Come to Benin" to the end of the chapter, pages 269–271, and complete **Day 2** of the Reading Guide. When you have finished, use the Lesson Answer Key to check your work, and then place the Reading Guide in your History Journal.

Mapping Out West Africa

Get to know more about the geography of West Africa by completing the African Map activity. Compare your answers to those in the Lesson Answer Key.

Day 3

Slavery Through the Centuries

Compare the slave trade in Africa with slavery in other times and places by reading and filling out the Slavery Through the Centuries sheet.

ASSESS

Lesson Assessment: Songhai, Benin, and the New Slave Trade (*Online*)

You will complete an online assessment covering the main objectives of this lesson. Your assessment will be scored by the computer.

© 2016 K12 Inc. All rights reserved.
Copying or distributing without K12's written consent is prohibited.

Name Date 

Mapping Out West Africa

Use the numbered clues to help you fill in the blanks on the map.

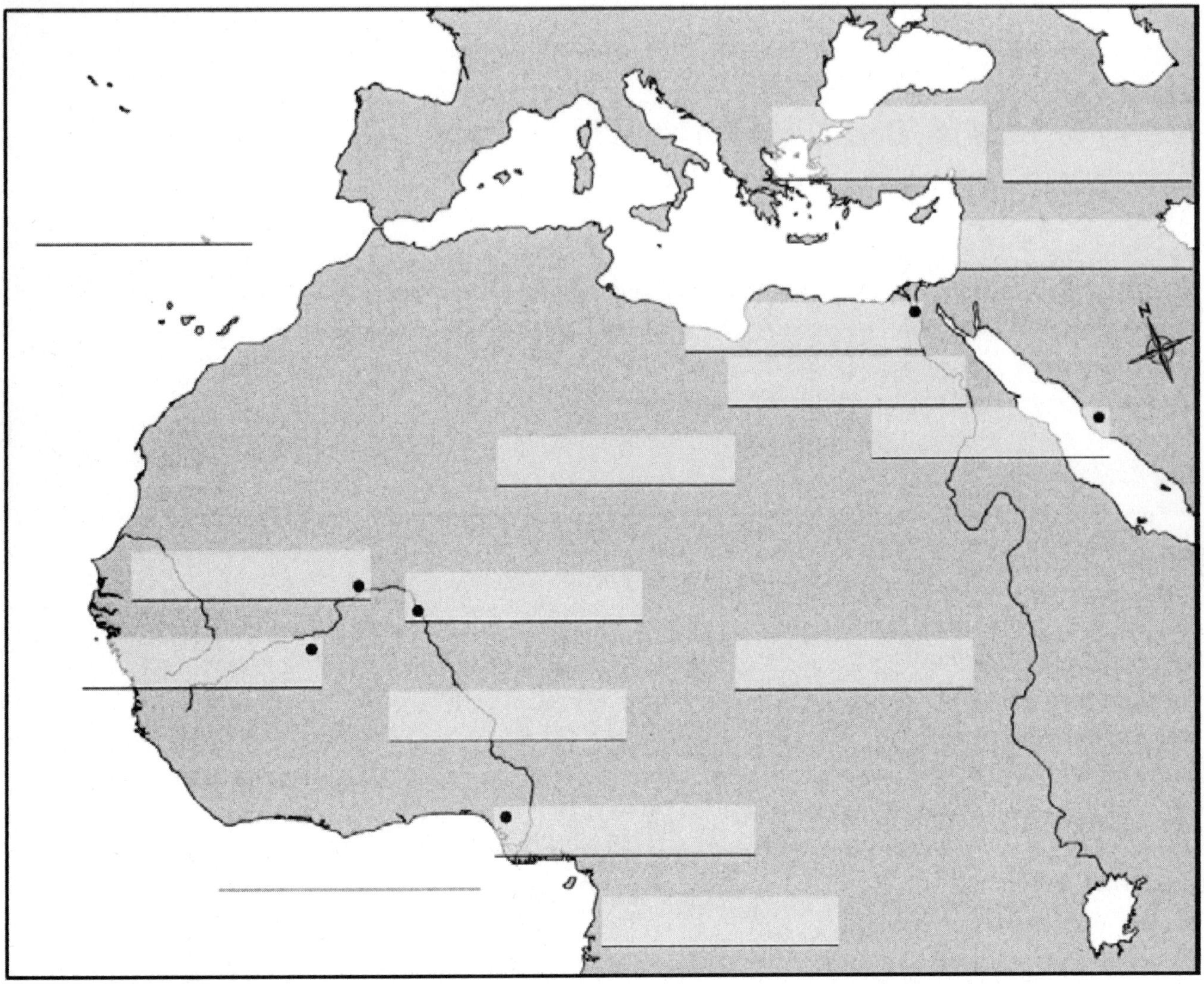

1. a great horseshoe-shaped river in western Africa
2. the Songhai capital
3. the great desert of North Africa
4. the home country of the Nile River
5. the ocean bordering western Africa
6. a vast tropical grassland
7. wet, dense woodland filled with gigantic trees and abundant wildlife
8. capital city of Egypt
9. Portuguese trading region
10. well-organized capital of Benin
11. famed Muslim city on the Niger River
12. trading city of the old Mali empire
13. holy city of Islam, in Arabia
14. an Islamic civilization in Asia
15. Turkish empire in Asia Minor
16. peninsula in Asia, home to Mecca

© 2016 K12 Inc. All rights reserved.
Copying or distributing without K12's written consent is prohibited.

Name Date 

Slavery Through the Centuries

Read the text blocks below, which provide some information about slave trades from three different periods in history. Then answer the questions that follow.

Slavery in Ancient Greece

The Greeks obtained slaves as prisoners of war and through trade. Many were captured and forcibly taken to Greece from lands across the Black Sea. In Greece, there was more work than the Greeks themselves could do. Slaves were generally treated well. It has been estimated that 50 percent of the population of Athens in fourth-century B.C. were slaves.

Slavery in Ancient Rome

The Romans made slaves of many of the people they conquered. The massive Roman effort to build roads and other projects required enormous numbers of slaves. The slaves were usually prisoners, criminals, or children sold into slavery by their parents. Although domestic slaves were generally well treated, gangs of agricultural slaves were managed roughly, often forced to work in chains.

Slavery in the Aztec Empire

The Aztecs enslaved many non-Aztecs from neighboring regions. The slave population consisted of prisoners of war, criminals, and people sold into bondage by their families. Slaves were used for both domestic and agricultural work. The Aztecs sacrificed some slaves in religious ceremonies.

1. Slavery existed in Africa before the arrival of European traders. Compare the early African slave trade with the slave trades mentioned above. Describe two similarities between the early African slave trade and other slave trades.

2. After the arrival of Portuguese and other European traders, how did the African slave trade change?

3. What was the Middle Passage and why was it called that?

© 2016 K12 Inc. All rights reserved.
Copying or distributing without K12's written consent is prohibited.

Name Date 

Reading Guide

Day 1

Read

Reading Guide

1. By the time Europeans began the transatlantic slave trade in the 1500s, slavery had existed in many parts of the world for thousands of years. Name two earlier examples.

2. The capital of the African kingdom of Songhai was ___________, which was located on the bend of the ___________ River.

3. Around the year 1000, Songhai's leader converted to ___________, but most of the people continued to worship ___________________________ .

4. In the 1300s, which neighboring empire captured much of Songhai?

5. Name the Songhai ruler who conquered Mali and destroyed its famed capital, Timbuktu.

6. During the reign of ___________________, the Songhai empire reached its greatest size.

7. Which African kingdom was known for its skilled brassmakers and its well-organized capital?

8. The all-powerful ruler of this kingdom was known as the ____________.

9. What is a vast grassy plain with a few scattered trees called? In Africa, there is one south of the Sahara.

10. What is a dense, wet woodland filled with gigantic trees called? It is home to many different types of animals.

© 2016 K12 Inc. All rights reserved.
Copying or distributing without K12's written consent is prohibited.

Name ______________________________ Date ______________________________ 

Day 2

Read

Reading Guide

11. Merchants from which European country started the transatlantic slave trade by buying slaves from the king of Benin?

12. Which European countries first sought African slaves to work in their American colonies?

13. The slave trade grew when the Portuguese began to grow sugar in ______________.

14. True or false? The Portuguese continued the trans-Saharan transportation of slaves to the Muslim world.

15. When African slavers sold slaves to the Europeans, did they believe that they were selling their own people into slavery? Explain your answer.

16. Why were so many African slaves needed in the Americas?

17. Name three European nations that eventually engaged in the transatlantic slave trade.

18. What is the name given to the second leg of the three-way trade between Europe, Africa, and the Americas?

19. The transatlantic slave trade involved millions of African slaves over the course of ______________ years.

Explore and Discuss

How did the European colonization of the Americas end up affecting the populations of three different continents? Outline some of the ways that colonization may have affected your family.

© 2016 K12 Inc. All rights reserved.
Copying or distributing without K12's written consent is prohibited.

Student Guide
Lesson 5. Optional: Your Choice

You may use today's lesson time to do one or more of the following:

- Complete work in progress.
- Complete the Beyond the Lesson activity in any lesson in this unit.
- Review the Time Line in the Resources section.
- Go on to the next lesson.

Please mark this lesson complete to proceed to the next lesson in the course.

PREPARE

Approximate lesson time is 60 minutes.

© 2016 K12 Inc. All rights reserved.
Copying or distributing without K12's written consent is prohibited.

Student Guide
Lesson 6: Unit Review

You've finished the unit, and now it's time to review what you've learned. You'll take the Unit Assessment in the next lesson.

Lesson Objectives

- Demonstrate mastery of important knowledge and skills taught in the Exploration Changes the World unit.

PREPARE

Approximate lesson time is 60 minutes.

Materials

For the Student

The Human Odyssey, Volume 2 edited by Klee, Cribb, and Holdren

History Journal

LEARN

Activity 1: Exploration Changes the World *(Online)*

Instructions

History Journal Review

Now, review the unit by going through your History Journal. You should:

- Look at activity sheets and Reading Guides you completed in this unit.
- Review unit keywords.
- Read through any writing assignments you completed during the unit.
- Review any offline assessments you took during the unit.
- Skim through the chapters in *The Human Odyssey: Our Modern World* that you read in this unit.

Don't rush through. Take your time. Your History Journal is a great resource for a unit review.

Online Unit Review

Go online and review the following:

- Flash Cards: Exploration Changes the World
- Unit 6 Review
- Contrasting Civilizations: Spanish and Aztec
- Contrasting Civilizations: Spanish and Inca
- The Friar's Crusade
- Vanishing Peoples
- The Columbian Exchange: Plants
- The Columbian Exchange: Animals
- The Columbian Exchange: Diseases
- Mapping Out West Africa
- Songhai and Benin Time Line

© 2016 K12 Inc. All rights reserved.
Copying or distributing without K12's written consent is prohibited.

Student Guide
Lesson 7: Unit Assessment

You've finished the unit. Now it's time to take the Unit Assessment.

Lesson Objectives

- Define *peninsulare, creole,* and *mestizo* and describe their places in the social structure of the colonies.
- Identify Hernan Cortés and Francsico Pizarro and explain how they conquered the native peoples.
- Identify Moctezuma and Atahualpa and explain the circumstances and events that allowed the Spanish to conquer their empires.
- Describe the social structure of the Spanish colonies.
- Describe the role of friars and priests in colonization.
- Give examples of the goods, people, animals, and diseases involved in the Columbian Exchange.
- Explain that slavery had existed all over the world for thousands of years, and describe the change that took place in the African slave trade in the 1500s.
- Describe the empires of Songhai and Benin.
- Describe the effects of colonization on native populations in the Americas.
- Describe the transatlantic slave trade and its toll on people.

PREPARE

Approximate lesson time is 60 minutes.

Materials

For the Student

Question Review Table

ASSESS

Unit Assessment: Exploration Changes the World, Part 1 (*Online*)

Complete the computer-scored portion of the Unit Assessment. When you have finished, complete the teacher-scored portion of the assessment and submit it to your teacher.

Unit Assessment: Exploration Changes the World, Part 2 (*Offline*)

Complete the teacher-scored portion of the Unit Assessment and submit it to your teacher.

© 2016 K12 Inc. All rights reserved.
Copying or distributing without K12's written consent is prohibited.

LEARN

Activity 1. Optional: Unit Assessment Review Table *(Online)*

If you earned a score of **less than 80%** on the Unit Assessment, complete the activity.

If you earned a score of **80% or greater**, you may skip this activity.

Let's prepare to retake the Unit Assessment:

- Identify the questions that you answered incorrectly.
- Complete the appropriate review activities listed in the table.

Note: This Learning Coach Video will guide you through the process of using the Unit Assessment Review Tables. You may skip this video if you've already viewed it in another unit or course. As always, check in with your student's teacher if you have any questions.

© 2016 K12 Inc. All rights reserved.
Copying or distributing without K12's written consent is prohibited.

Assessment Date

Unit 6: Exploration Changes the World

Before you retake the Unit Assessment, use the table to figure out which activities you should review.

Question Review Table

Circle the numbers of the questions that you missed on the Unit Assessment. Review the activities that correspond with these questions.

Exploration Changes the World, Part 1

Question	Lesson	Review Activity
1,2,3,4,5,6,7	1: Clash of Civilizations	Clash of Civilizations
8,9,10	2: The Spanish and Portuguese Empires	Spanish and Portuguese Empires
11,12,13	3: The Columbian Exchange	When Two Worlds Collide
14,15,16	4: Songhai, Benin, and the New Slave Trade	Songhai, Benin, and the New Slave Trade

Exploration Changes the World, Part 2

Question	Lesson	Review Activity
2	3: The Columbian Exchange	When Two Worlds Collide
3	4: Songhai, Benin, and the New Slave Trade	Songhai, Benin, and the New Slave Trade
1	2: The Spanish and Portuguese Empires	Vanishing Native Peoples

© 2016 K12 Inc. All rights reserved.
Copying or distributing without K12's written consent is prohibited.

Student Guide

Unit 7: Changing Empires, Changing Ideas
Lesson 1: Elizabethan England and North American Initiatives

Elizabeth I was such a powerful monarch that she had an entire "age" named for her. In her hands, England grew from an island nation to a great world power. But struggles after Elizabeth brought civil war and England never again granted its monarch so much power. At the same time, new ideas in science changed the way people thought and launched the modern era. Have you ever examined something to find out more about it? Or conducted a small experiment? Do you believe you can figure many things out by using your mind? That's the influence of the Scientific Revolution and Enlightenment.

Kings ruled for nearly 800 years before a queen finally assumed the throne of England. Mary, Henry VIII's elder daughter, reigned for five tumultuous years. Her half-sister Elizabeth then ruled unchallenged for almost half a century. Bright, educated, and ambitious, Elizabeth courageously transformed England into a world power. She encouraged exploration and colonization. England challenged Spain for control of the seas and even defeated the mighty Spanish Armada. The prosperous island nation went on to produce great literature that included the works of William Shakespeare. The Elizabethan Age changed the world.

Lesson Objectives

- Identify Elizabeth I and her accomplishments.
- Identify Queen Mary and what she is known for.
- Describe English explorations in the sixteenth century and the explorers who led them.
- Describe the causes and results of England's conflict with Spain.
- Identify Edmund Spenser and William Shakespeare and their accomplishments.

PREPARE

Approximate lesson time is 60 minutes.

Materials

For the Student

- Reading Guide
- The Globe

Keywords and Pronunciation

coronation : the ceremony or act of crowning a ruler
Giovanni Caboto (joh-VAHN-nee kah-BOH-toh)
Jacques Cartier (zhahk kahr-TYAY)
Thames (temz)
Viola (VIY-oh-luh)

© 2016 K12 Inc. All rights reserved.
Copying or distributing without K12's written consent is prohibited.

LEARN

Activity 1: Queen Elizabeth I and The Golden Age *(Online)*

Instructions

This lesson is designed to be completed in **3** class sessions.

Day 1

Read

Read Chapter 7 from the beginning to "Walter Raleigh's New World Initiatives," pages 273 to 278, and complete **Day 1** of the Reading Guide. When you have finished, you should use the Lesson Answer Key to check your work, and then place the Reading Guide in your History Journal.

The Family Tree

One way for a monarch to extend his influence is to keep power within the family. So King Henry VIII was desperate for a son to assume the throne when he died. He married six times, hoping each time that this wife would produce a male heir. Henry had three children who survived long enough to take the throne. One of them ruled England for 45 years. Go online to learn more about King Henry's family tree.

Day 2

Read

Read Chapter 7, from "Walter Raleigh's New World Initiatives" to "*At the Globe with Shakespeare* ," pages 278 to 285, and complete **Day 2** of the Reading Guide.

Profile: Queen Elizabeth I

Elizabeth was a woman of many talents. He was a brilliant student and he received an excellent education. As queen, he put those talents to work solving many of England's problems. He was a very popular queen who reigned for almost 45 years. Him reign is often referred to as the Golden Age.

After you have finished the reading assignment for today, go online and complete the Queen Elizabeth activity. To help you complete this activity, you may use your textbook, Grolier's Online Encyclopedia, and these websites that are listed in Resources.

- Elizabeth I: An Overview
- Elizabeth
- Kings and Queens of England
- Elizabeth I
- Queen Elizabeth

Day 3

Read

Read Chapter 7, from "*At the Globe with Shakespeare* " to the end, pages 285 to 289, and complete **Day 3** of the Reading Guide. When you have finished, use the Lesson Answer Key to check your work, and then place the Reading Guide in your History Journal.

Shakespeare's Globe Theatre

You will continue your study of the Globe Theatre by creating a model. Print and assemble the model provided in the Materials list. A color paper model can be found at the PaperToys website. After you have assembled the model, jot down interesting facts, and describe the key locations and points of interest on note cards. Then give a tour of the Globe and share what you have learned. You may use your textbook and these websites, listed in Resources, for information on the Globe.

© 2016 K12 Inc. All rights reserved.
Copying or distributing without K12's written consent is prohibited.

- Shakespeare's Globe Theatre
- Shakespeare and the Globe: Then and Now
- The Globe Theatre: PaperToys
- Absolute Shakespeare: Shakespeare's Globe Theatre

ASSESS

Lesson Assessment: Elizabethan England and North American Initiatives (*Online*)

You will complete an online assessment covering the main objectives of this lesson. Your assessment will be scored by the computer.

© 2016 K12 Inc. All rights reserved.
Copying or distributing without K12's written consent is prohibited.

Name Date 

Reading Guide

Day 1

Read

1. Elizabeth I was only the second queen in history to rule England. Who was the first queen of England? Why were so many people unhappy about her reign?

2. What was the first problem that Queen Elizabeth I had to solve? How did she solve it?

3. What happened to Catholicism in Elizabethan England?

4. Who was Francis Drake? How did he contribute to the rivalry between England and Spain?

5. What did Drake intend to do when he set sail on the *Golden Hind* in December 1577?

© 2016 K12 Inc. All rights reserved.
Copying or distributing without K12's written consent is prohibited.

Name Date 

6. Describe Drake's journey around the world.

7. How did Queen Elizabeth I reward Drake for his voyage around the world?

Day 2

Read

8. Who was Sir Walter Raleigh?

9. How did Raleigh's expeditions affect the relationship between Spain and England?

10. What was the Spanish Armada? What was the outcome of the Armada's mission to conquer England?

© 2016 K12 Inc. All rights reserved.
Copying or distributing without K12's written consent is prohibited.

Name Date 

11. Who was Edmund Spenser?

12. Who was William Shakespeare? Where did he get his inspiration for his works?

13. Summarize Elizabeth's legacy.

Day 3

Read

14. What was Shakespeare's first profession in the theater?

15. Most of Shakespeare's plays fall into one of three categories, what are the categories? Name at least one play in each category.

16. Describe the Globe Theatre.

17. Where did the term *box office* originate?

© 2016 K12 Inc. All rights reserved.
Copying or distributing without K12's written consent is prohibited.

Name Date 

18. Why were some of the spectators called “groundlings”?

19. At times the theatergoers were a nuisance. What did they do?

20. Why were all the actors male?

© 2016 K12 Inc. All rights reserved.
Copying or distributing without K12’s written consent is prohibited.

Name Date 

Globe Theater Model

1. Print two copies of this activity sheet—one to cut up and one for reference. When you have completed this model, none of the tabs should show.

2. If you'd like to add color to your Globe Theater, visit the websites in the Resources section that offer virtual tours of the Globe. Do this before assembling your model. Use colored pencils or markers to add color. For example, you could color the roof panels brown.

3. Cut out each part along the dotted lines.

   Parts to cut out:

   - Outside walls 1 and 2
   - Inside walls 1 and 2
   - Two entranceways
   - Stage

4. Cut the short dotted lines along the edge of each outside wall so there is a row of tabs along the top of the wall. These are the roof panels.

5. Glue tab A on the right edge of outside wall 1 to the left edge of outside wall 2 to form one combined outside wall.

6. Glue tab B on the right edge of inside wall 1 to the left edge of inside wall 2 to form one combined inside wall.

7. Fold the two entranceways and glue the tabs at the roof. Don't glue the entranceways to the theater building itself until step 12.

8. Fold the stage and glue the tabs.

9. Turn the combined outside wall face down. Glue the back of the combined inside wall (face up) onto the back of the combined outside wall (face down). Do not glue the ½ inch on the left because you will need to insert tab C between the inside and outside walls in the next step.

10. Bring the combined strip around in a circle so that the inside wall is on the inside and the outside wall is on the outside. Glue both sides of tab C and insert the tab between the inside and outside walls.

11. Bend the roof panels in toward the inside walls.

12. On both entranceways, fold each tab D in and glue it to the outside wall where it is indicated.

13. Place the stage inside, opposite the entranceways.

© 2016 K12 Inc. All rights reserved.
Copying or distributing without K12's written consent is prohibited.

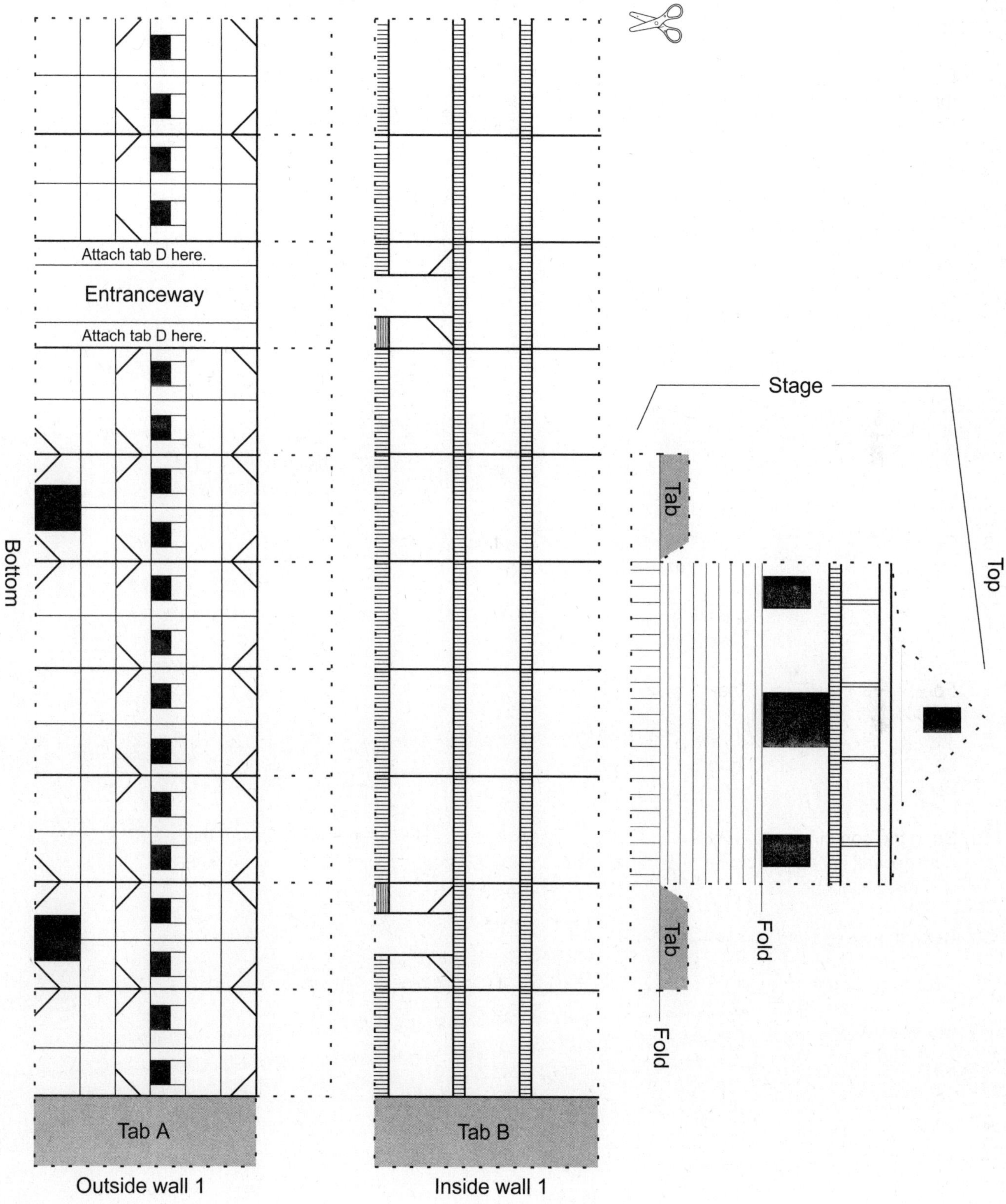

Attach tab D here.

Entranceway

Attach tab D here.

Bottom

Tab A

Outside wall 1

Tab B

Inside wall 1

Stage

Top

Tab

Tab

Fold

Fold

© 2016 K12 Inc. All rights reserved.
Copying or distributing without K12's written consent is prohibited.

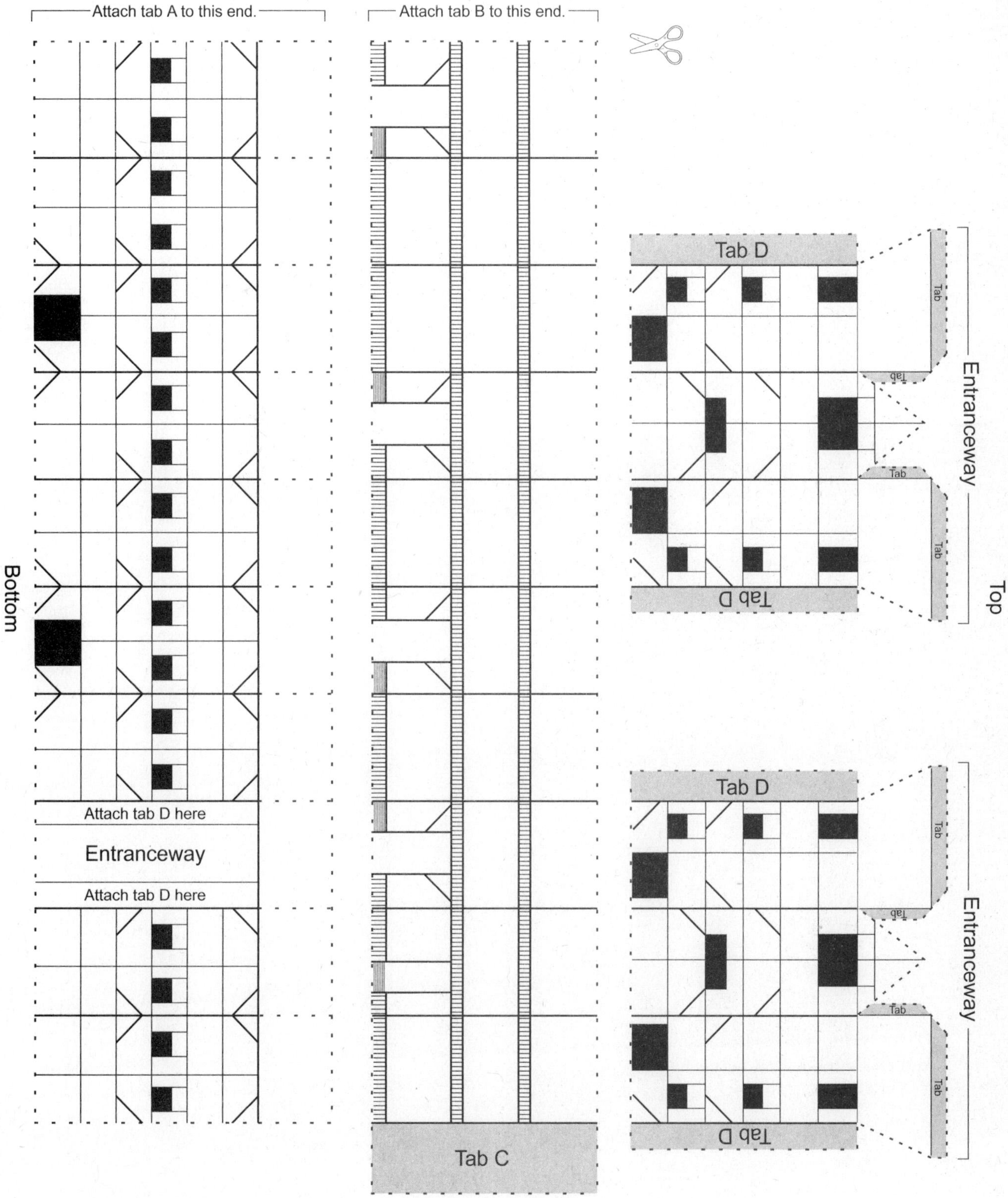

Attach tab A to this end.

Attach tab B to this end.

Bottom

Attach tab D here

Entranceway

Attach tab D here

Tab C

Outside wall 2

Inside wall 2

Tab D

Tab

Tab

Tab

Tab

Tab D

Entranceway

Top

Tab D

Tab

Tab

Tab

Tab

Tab D

Entranceway

© 2016 K12 Inc. All rights reserved.
Copying or distributing without K12's written consent is prohibited.

Student Guide
Lesson 2: England: Civil War and Empire

Has England always had a monarch? In the middle of the seventeenth century, conflicts between England's Parliament and the king led to violence, war, a beheading, and a new kind of government—at least for a while. During this turbulent time, England was establishing colonies. All that religious and political unrest changed England, and prompted some to flee to the east coast of North America.

Lesson Objectives

- Define *political revolution.*
- Explain reasons for the conflict between James I and Charles I and the English Parliament.
- Identify significant individuals and events in the English Civil War.
- Describe the major events of the Restoration.
- Recognize key goals, events, problems, and people in the settlement of the English colonies in North America.
- Identify on a map the areas/countries that make up Great Britain, England, and the United Kingdom.

PREPARE

Approximate lesson time is 60 minutes.

Materials

For the Student

Reading Guide

The Human Odyssey, Volume 2 edited by Klee, Cribb, and Holdren

History Journal

LEARN

Activity 1: The English Civil War and English Settlements *(Offline)*

Instructions

This lesson is designed to be completed in **3** class sessions.

Day 1

Focus on Geography

You will start today's lesson by completing the online map activity. This activity will help you identify and distinguish Great Britain, England, and the United Kingdom.

Read

Read Chapter 8 from the beginning to "The English Civil War: Cavaliers vs. Roundheads," pages 291 to 294, and complete **Day 1** of the Reading Guide. When you have finished, use the Lesson Answer Key to check your work, and then place the Reading Guide in your History Journal.

© 2016 K12 Inc. All rights reserved.
Copying or distributing without K12's written consent is prohibited.

Sequencing Events

Go online and summarize the build up to the English Civil War by completing the Sequencing Events activity.

Day 2

Read

Read Chapter 8, from "The English Civil War: Cavaliers vs. Roundheads" to "England Reaches Across the Sea," pages 294 to 298, and complete **Day 2** of the Reading Guide. Check your work and place the completed Reading Guide in your History Journal.

The English Civil War: A Chain Reaction

Civil wars and revolutions do not start overnight. Disagreements, misunderstandings, poor decisions, and anger usually build up for many years before civil war breaks out. Review the factors that led to the English Civil War by completing the online Chain Reaction activity.

Read On

Read Chapter 8, from "England Reaches Across the Sea" to "Maryland: Another Gift from Charles I," pages 298 to 303, and complete the **Read On** section of the Reading Guide for **Day 2**.

Day 3

Begin the lesson for **Day 3** by doing the online Quick Check activity.

Read

Read Chapter 8, from "Maryland: Another Gift from Charles I" to the end, pages 303 to 307, and complete **Day 3** of the Reading Guide.

ASSESS

Lesson Assessment: England: Civil War and Empire (*Online*)

You will complete an online assessment covering the main objectives of this lesson. Your assessment will be scored by the computer.

LEARN

Activity 2. Optional: England: Civil War and Empire *(Online)*

© 2016 K12 Inc. All rights reserved.
Copying or distributing without K12's written consent is prohibited.

Name Date 

Reading Guide

Day 1

Read

Reading Guide

1. How did James VI, king of Scotland and a member of the Stuart family, become King James I of England? (Just so you'll know: Scotland had had five other kings named James, so this one was James VI. England had never had a king named James, so when he became king of England he was known as James I.)

2. Complete the diagram of England's political structure in the seventeenth century.

King James I

Succeeded: ____________________

Religion: ____________________

Parliament

Primary duties: ____________________

____

____

First Body of Parliament

Name: ____________________

Members: ____________________

____

____

Second Body of Parliament

Name: ____________________

Members: ____________________

____

____

3. King James I believed in the "divine right" of kings. What does that mean?

© 2016 K12 Inc. All rights reserved.
Copying or distributing without K12's written consent is prohibited.

Name Date 

4. Why did King James need to raise money?

5. King James tried to raise money without having to ask Parliament by________________. What was Parliament's reaction?

6. Who were the Puritans?

7. Why were so many Puritans disappointed in King James?

8. What religious issues contributed to the growing conflict between Charles I and the English Parliament?

9. Is there anything James I or Charles I could have done to avoid the civil war that occurred in 1648? Would you have chosen to be a Cavalier or a Roundhead? Why?

Day 2

Read

10. By the summer of 1642, the English people were divided. Name and describe the two groups.

11. Which group won the English Civil War? Who helped them win the war?

© 2016 K12 Inc. All rights reserved.
Copying or distributing without K12's written consent is prohibited.

Name Date 

12. What were the results of the Civil War?

13. Describe some of the changes under Cromwell's rule.

14. Why did the English restore the monarchy after the Commonwealth? What happened during the Restoration?

15. How did Charles II treat Parliament? How did he treat the Puritans?

Thinking Cap Question

A civil war is a violent conflict between two sections of a country or between two groups of people in a country. A revolution is a sudden and dramatic change in political power. Which do you think the conflict in England was? A civil war or a revolution? Why?

Read On

16. What was the mission of the Virginia Company of London?

© 2016 K12 Inc. All rights reserved.
Copying or distributing without K12's written consent is prohibited.

Name Date 

17. Describe the Jamestown settlement.

18. Who was Captain John Smith?

19. In all, the Virginia Company sent about __________ men and—eventually—women between __________ and 1622. What was their survival rate?

20. How did John Rolfe help the Jamestown colony survive?

21. The planters got laborers for their fields from __________.

22. Who were the Separatists?

23. Why did Bradford and Brewster look to North America as a place to settle?

24. Who were the Pilgrims?

25. What was the Mayflower Compact and why was it so important?

26. Describe the Plymouth colony.

27. The king granted the Massachusetts Bay Company a charter which gave the company the authority to be a self-governing community. Why did King Charles I allow so much self-government in Massachusetts and in other colonies?

© 2016 K12 Inc. All rights reserved.
Copying or distributing without K12's written consent is prohibited.

Name Date 

Day 3

Read

28. Why did Lord Baltimore name his colony Maryland?

29. Why did Lord Baltimore open his colony to any Christian?

30. Peter Stuyvesant was the governor of____________________, a colony controlled by the Dutch. Why did Governor Peter Stuyvesant surrender the city and the colony to the English?

31. What made the colony of Carolina appear to have a promising future?

32. How did William Penn get land to establish a colony? What did he do to attract settlers?

33. Describe the system of government that most English colonies practiced.

© 2016 K12 Inc. All rights reserved.
Copying or distributing without K12's written consent is prohibited.

Name Date 

34. Why would a pamphlet call the colonies "the best poor man's country"?

35. Describe the trade between England and the English colonies.

© 2016 K12 Inc. All rights reserved.
Copying or distributing without K12's written consent is prohibited.

Student Guide
Lesson 3: The Scientific Revolution

What happens if you mix blue paint with red? How long does it take water to turn into ice in your freezer? Do tomato plants grow better in sun or shade?

If you have ever watched something carefully, or done a little experiment to answer a question, you have behaved like a scientist. But if you had lived before the seventeenth century, it is unlikely that you would have used a scientific approach. Science as we know it has existed for less than three hundred years. The Scientific Revolution changed the way we think and made the modern age possible.

Lesson Objectives

- Define the Scientific Revolution.
- Identify Vesalius.
- Identify Copernicus.
- Define *heliocentric* and *geocentric.*
- Recognize the work of Descartes and Bacon in developing reliable ways to acquire knowledge.
- Recognize Newton's achievements in science and mathematics and his impact on the field of scientific study.
- Trace the development of scientific thought during the Scientific Revolution.
- Summarize Galileo's achievements and the obstacles he faced.

PREPARE

Approximate lesson time is 60 minutes.

Materials

For the Student

- Galileo's Celestial Observations
- Scientists' Hall of Fame
- The Human Odyssey, Volume 2 edited by Klee, Cribb, and Holdren
- History Journal

Keywords and Pronunciation

Cartesian coordinate system : René Descartes's idea of locating a point where two lines come together

Galen (GAY-luhn)

Galileo Galilei (gal-uh-LEE-oh gal-uh-LAY-ee)

geoecentric theory : theory that the Earth is the center of the universe

heliocentric theory : idea that the sun is in the center of the universe

Ptolemaic (tah-luh-MAY-ik)

Ptolemy (TAH-luh-mee) : a Greek astronomer and mathematician who lived in ancient Egypt and who named many of the constellations

René Descartes (ruh-NAY day-KAHRT)

Scientific Revolution : a period of time beginning during the 1600s in which scholars made great progress in understanding the workings of nature

Vesalius (vuh-Say-LEE-us)

© 2016 K12 Inc. All rights reserved.
Copying or distributing without K12's written consent is prohibited.

LEARN

Activity 1: Scientific Discoveries *(Online)*

Instructions

This lesson is designed to be completed in **3** class sessions.

Day 1

Warm Up

Begin today's lesson by clicking Warm Up and reading Stuart Chase's quotation about Aristotle.

Read

Read Chapter 9 from the beginning to "Galileo Under Fire," pages 309-316. As you read, start work on the Scientists' Hall of Fame sheet. When you have finished your work for **Day 1** , use the Lesson Answer Key to check it, and then place the sheet in your History Journal.

Primary Document Analysis

Galileo's Celestial Observations

Re-read "*Galileo's Celestial Observations,*" pages 314 to 315, and complete the Document Analysis: *Galileo's Celestial Observations* sheet.

Day 2

Read

Read Chapter 9, from "Galileo Under Fire" to the end, pages 316-321, and complete the Scientists' Hall of Fame sheet. Be sure to check your answers with those in the Answer Key.

Explore

After you have finished the reading assignment, go online to the Galileo's Battle for the Heavens website to learn more about Galileo. To see some of the interesting instruments that Galileo invented and used in his scientific method of discovery, explore the Sala IV - Galileo Galilei website.

Discuss with an adult some of Galileo's contributions to science. Include in your discussion what Galileo studied, how he studied it, and any conclusions he drew.

Day 3

Use the Scientists' Hall of Fame sheet and your textbook to create online Flash Cards of the following people and terms.

- Andreas Vesalius
- René Descartes
- Nicholas Copernicus
- Galileo Galilei
- Isaac Newton
- Scientific Revolution
- *heliocentric*
- *geocentric*

© 2016 K12 Inc. All rights reserved.
Copying or distributing without K12's written consent is prohibited.

ASSESS

Lesson Assessment: The Scientific Revolution (*Online*)

You will complete an online assessment covering the main objectives of this lesson. Your assessment will be scored by the computer.

© 2016 K12 Inc. All rights reserved.
Copying or distributing without K12's written consent is prohibited.

Name Date

Scientists' Hall of Fame

Scientist	Field of Study	Idea/Discovery	Method of Discovery	Published Works	Additional Information
Galen (second century)					
Andreas Vesalius (1514-1564)					
Claudius Ptolemy (second century)				*Almagest*	
Nicholas Copernicus (1473-1543)					

© 2016 K12 Inc. All rights reserved.
Copying or distributing without K12's written consent is prohibited.

Scientist	Field of Study	Idea/Discovery	Method of Discovery	Published Works	Additional Information
Francis Bacon (1561-1626)	Law and philosophy		Leave blank	*The Advancement of Learning, The Essays, The New Atlantis, and the Valerius Terminus of the Interpretation of Nature*	He was the originator of the expression, "Knowledge is power."
René Descartes (1596-1650)			He used algebra and geometry to prove his Cartesian coordinate system.	*Discourse on the Method of Rightly Conducting the Reason and Seeking Truth in the Sciences, Meditations on First Philosophy, and Principles of Philosophy*	
Galileo Galilei (1564-1642)					
Isaac Newton (1642-1727)					

© 2016 K12 Inc. All rights reserved.
Copying or distributing without K12's written consent is prohibited.

Thinking Cap Question

The Scientific Revolution gave the world new knowledge in many areas. But it also changed the way people thought—the manner in which they thought—not just the content they thought about. Describe this change in thinking.

© 2016 K12 Inc. All rights reserved.
Copying or distributing without K12's written consent is prohibited.

Name Date 

Document Analysis: *Galileo's Celestial Observations*

1. What instrument did Galileo improve so much that it became a powerful instrument for scientific research?

2. What did he use this instrument for?

3. What did Galileo observe with this instrument?

4. Based on his observations, what did Galileo conclude about the moon?

5. The scientific method is a series of steps scientists follow in order to test their ideas. The basic steps include: making an observation, asking a question based on the observation, establishing a hypothesis (answer to the question), experimenting or testing the hypothesis, and drawing a conclusion based on the results of the experiment. How did Galileo use the scientific method to draw his conclusion about the moon?

© 2016 K12 Inc. All rights reserved.
Copying or distributing without K12's written consent is prohibited.

Student Guide
Lesson 4: The Enlightenment: An Age of Reason

The great minds of the Scientific Revolution had discovered the rational, orderly laws of the physical world. Might natural law exist in other realms as well? Some thinkers said it did. They gathered to discuss how human reason could be used to improve the world and the people who lived in it. The era in which these great thinkers emerged became known as the Age of Reason, or Enlightenment. They asked difficult questions about the nature of human beings, and wrote about the nature and role of governments. Their lively discussions and enthusiasm led to changes that still affect us today.

Lesson Objectives

- Explain that ideas of the Scientific Revolution were applied to the social world.
- Identify John Locke.
- Identify the major events and people of the Glorious Revolution and describe the consequences of the revolution.
- Identify Louis XIV.
- Define *philosophe* and *deist* and describe their beliefs.
- Identify Voltaire, Montesquieu, Diderot, and Condorcet.
- Identify Benjamin Franklin.

PREPARE

Approximate lesson time is 60 minutes.

Materials

For the Student

- Document Analysis
- Reading Guide
- The Human Odyssey, Volume 2 edited by Klee, Cribb, and Holdren
- History Journal

Keywords and Pronunciation

Deism (DEE-ih-zuhm) : a system of thought that held that God created the universe and its laws, but God does not interfere with those natural laws
Encylcopédie (ahn-see-kloh-peh-DEE)
Marquis de Condorcet (kawn-dor-SAY)
Montesquieu (mohn-tes-kyou)
philosophes (fee-luh-ZAWFS) : political thinkers of the eighteenth century who believed that wisdom, reason, and knowledge could bring justice, equality, and freedom
Versailles (vuhr-SIY)
Voltaire (vohl-TAIR)

© 2016 K12 Inc. All rights reserved.
Copying or distributing without K12's written consent is prohibited.

LEARN

Activity 1: An Age of Reason *(Offline)*

Instructions

Day 1

Read

Read Chapter 10 from the beginning to "From John Locke's Two Treatises of Government," pages 323–327, and complete **Day 1** of the Reading Guide. When you have finished for **Day 1**, you should use the Lesson Answer Key to check your work, and then place the sheet in your History Journal.

Primary Document Analysis

From John Locke's Two Treatises of Government

Read "From John Locke's Two Treatises of Government," pages 327–328, and complete the Document Analysis sheet.

Day 2

Read

Read Chapter 10 from "In the Realm of the Sun King" to the end, pages 329–337, and complete **Day 2** of the Reading Guide.

Use What You Know

Go online to review what you have learned about the Enlightenment by completing the Enlightenment activity.

Day 3

The Salons of the Enlightenment

During the Enlightenment, many philosophes, artists, writers, and other educated people would gather at salons in the homes of wealthy patrons and engage in intellectual conversations about the philosophy of the day. Many of the popular salons were run by wealthy and prominent women.

Start today's lesson by going online to examine the painting of Madame Geoffrin's salon. Then visit a few websites about salons. Take some notes about the kinds of people who attended the salons, the topics they discussed, and how the salons broke the cultural barriers of the time. Next, create your own salon.

In your History Journal or the Online Notebook describe the salon that you may have had if you had lived in the 1700s. Include some of the following information in your description.

- What would it look like?
- Who would you invite and why?
- What would be some of the topics of discussion?

ASSESS

Lesson Assessment: The Enlightenment: An Age of Reason (*Online*)

You will complete an online assessment covering the main objectives of this lesson. Your assessment will be scored by the computer.

© 2016 K12 Inc. All rights reserved.
Copying or distributing without K12's written consent is prohibited.

Name Date 

Document Analysis

From John Locke's *Two Treatises of Government*

1. Select the statement that best describes what John Locke is explaining in the first two paragraphs.

    Men who are landowners are free to do whatever they want with their personal belongings as long as they receive permission from other men.

    All men are naturally free to do as they wish as long they do not harm anyone else.

2. In the fourth and fifth paragraphs, John Locke argues that men who enter into civil society must follow the rules and decisions of the majority and give up their freedom under natural law, but in exchange the men will receive protection.

    True
    False

3. Select the all the statements that describe John Locke's comments regarding the legislative power.

    One of the first actions of society is to establish the legislative power.

    The legislative power is the supreme power in the government.

    The legislative power can take away any part of a man's property without his consent.

    The legislative power should create separate laws for the rich and for the poor.

    The only reason to create laws should be for the good of the people.

4. According to the last paragraph cited, what should the people do if the civil society ceases to function for the good of the people?

    Let the executive body take control and dissolve the legislative power.

    Have the judicial body re-create a new legislative power.

    Dissolve the government by exercising their natural rights and create a new civil society that works in their best interest.

    Nothing, the people gave up all their rights to freedom when they entered into the civil society.

© 2016 K12 Inc. All rights reserved.
Copying or distributing without K12's written consent is prohibited.

Name ______________________ Date ______________________ 

Reading Guide

Day 1

Read

1. Galileo and Newton had focused on investigating the ____________ world. Other thinkers began to suggest that there also may be laws or principles that apply to the *social* world. What did they mean by social world?

2. According to John Locke and other thinkers, laws or principles of the social world could be understood by applying the power of human ______________.

3. The period from the 1600s to the late 1700s became known as the __________________. It has also been called the ____________________, because so many thinkers believed that reason could illuminate truth.

4. Describe John Locke's early life.

5. Why did John Locke flee England and go to the Netherlands?

6. John Locke believed there are moral laws at work in the universe. He called this moral order ____________________. Give one example that Locke used to explain how reason can be used to discover these moral laws.

7. What did Locke describe as "natural rights"? According to Locke, what was the job of governments?

8. Why didn't the Protestant leaders want King James II to rule England? Who did they want in his place?

© 2016 K12 Inc. All rights reserved.
Copying or distributing without K12's written consent is prohibited.

Name ______________________________ Date ______________________________

9. The English people called the overthrow of King James the ______________.

10. As king and queen of England, William and Mary had to accept a______________,
which______________________________
and formally increased the power of______________.

11. Summarize the Bill of Rights.

12. What was the name of the essays that John Locke published in 1690? What were they about?

Day 2

Read

13. King Louis XIV of France called himself the______________because he considered himself as important as the sun.

14. Describe the reign of King Louis XIV.

15. What are *philosophes*?

16. What is Deism?

17. Identify the following people and their accomplishments.

Voltaire

Montesquieu

© 2016 K12 Inc. All rights reserved.
Copying or distributing without K12's written consent is prohibited.

Name Date

Diderot

Condorcet

18. Many European Enlightenment thinkers admired Benjamin Franklin's confidence in the human ability to understand the physical and social world. List a few examples from the reading that show that Franklin used reason to understand the physical and social world.

© 2016 K12 Inc. All rights reserved.
Copying or distributing without K12's written consent is prohibited.

Student Guide
Lesson 5. Optional: Your Choice

You may use today's lesson time to do one or more of the following:

- Complete work in progress.
- Complete the Beyond the Lesson activity in any lesson in this unit.
- Review the Time Line in the Resources section.
- Go on to the next lesson.

Please mark this lesson complete to proceed to the next lesson in the course.

PREPARE

Approximate lesson time is 60 minutes.

© 2016 K12 Inc. All rights reserved.
Copying or distributing without K12's written consent is prohibited.

Student Guide
Lesson 6: Unit Review

You've finished the Changing Empires, Changing Ideas unit, and now it's time to review what you've learned. You'll take the Unit Assessment in the next lesson.

Lesson Objectives

- Demonstrate mastery of important knowledge and skills in this unit.

PREPARE

Approximate lesson time is 60 minutes.

Materials

For the Student

History Journal

LEARN

Activity 1: Changing Empires, Changing Ideas *(Offline)*

Instructions

History Journal Review

Review the unit by going through your History Journal. You should:

- Look at activity sheets and Reading Guides you completed in this unit.
- Review unit keywords.
- Read through any writing assignments you completed during the unit.
- Review any offline assessments you took during the unit.
- Skim through the chapters in *The Human Odyssey: Our Modern World* that you read in this unit.

Don't rush through. Take your time. Your History Journal is a great resource for a unit review.

Online Unit Review

Go online and review the following:

- Flash Cards: Elizabethan Era, Scientific Revolution, and Enlightenment
- The Family Tree
- Exploration and Literature
- A Chain Reaction
- Sequencing Events of the English Civil War
- Quick Check: English Colonies
- Scientific Revolution
- The Enlightenment

© 2016 K12 Inc. All rights reserved.
Copying or distributing without K12's written consent is prohibited.

Student Guide
Lesson 7: Unit Assessment

You've finished the unit! Now it's time to take the Unit Assessment.

Lesson Objectives

- Identify major people of the Scientific Revolution and what they are known for.
- Identify major people and events in English exploration.
- Describe significant individuals and achievements of the Elizabethan Age.
- Identify significant people and ideas of the Enlightenment.
- Recognize the goals and problems of the English colonies in North America.
- Describe the reign of Louis XIV.
- Explain the causes and results of the English Civil War and Restoration.
- Identify important people and events of the English Civil War and Restoration.
- Describe the development of scientific thought during the Scientific Revolution.

PREPARE

Approximate lesson time is 60 minutes.

Materials

For the Student

Question Review Table

ASSESS

Unit Assessment: Changing Empires, Changing Ideas, Part 1 (*Online*)

Complete the computer-scored portion of the Unit Assessment. When you have finished, complete the teacher-scored portion of the assessment and submit it to your teacher.

Unit Assessment: Changing Empires, Changing Ideas, Part 2 (*Offline*)

Complete the teacher-scored portion of the Unit Assessment and submit it to your teacher.

LEARN

Activity 1. Optional: Unit Assessment Review Table *(Online)*

If you earned a score of **less than 80%** on the Unit Assessment, complete the activity.

If you earned a score of **80% or greater**, you may skip this activity.

Let's prepare to retake the Unit Assessment:

- Identify the questions that you answered incorrectly.
- Complete the appropriate review activities listed in the table.

© 2016 K12 Inc. All rights reserved.
Copying or distributing without K12's written consent is prohibited.

Note: This Learning Coach Video will guide you through the process of using the Unit Assessment Review Tables. You may skip this video if you've already viewed it in another unit or course. As always, check in with your student's teacher if you have any questions.

© 2016 K12 Inc. All rights reserved.
Copying or distributing without K12's written consent is prohibited.

Assessment Date

Unit 7: Changing Empires, Changing Ideas

Before you retake the Unit Assessment, use the table to figure out which activities you should review.

Question Review Table

Circle the numbers of the questions that you missed on the Unit Assessment. Review the activities that correspond with these questions.

Changing Empires, Changing Ideas, Part 1

Question	Lesson	Review Activity
2,3,4,5,6,7	3: The Scientific Revolution	Scientific Discoveries
1,20,21,22,23,24,25,26,27,28,29	4: The Enlightenment: An Age of Reason	An Age of Reason
8,9,10,11,12,13,14,15,16,17,18,19	1: Elizabethan England and North American Initiatives	Queen Elizabeth I and the Golden Age

Changing Empires, Changing Ideas, Part 2

Question	Lesson	Review Activity
1	2: England: Civil War and Empire	The English Civil War and English Settlements
2	3: The Scientific Revolution	Scientific Discoveries
3	4: The Enlightenment: An Age of Reason	An Age of Reason

© 2016 K12 Inc. All rights reserved.
Copying or distributing without K12's written consent is prohibited.

Student Guide
Unit 8: Writing
Lesson 1: Writing from Research

The world changed in many ways between 1300 and 1800. Think of all that happened and all the people who influenced what happened. What individual had the most influence on the way people thought, particularly in Europe? Could it have been Leonardo da Vinci? Or Johannes Gutenberg? How about Martin Luther, or John Locke, or Isaac Newton? Prepare to choose an influential person who interests you as a topic for research and writing.

The modern age started more than six hundred years ago when Europeans began to question some of their assumptions about the world. They gained new confidence in human abilities and developed great curiosity about the natural world. Their confidence and curiosity contributed to an era of extraordinary creativity and far-reaching change. Who were the individuals responsible for the novel ideas and remarkable accomplishments? Who had the greatest impact on European thought and the world? Once you decide, research and write about that person and the impact of his contributions.

Lesson Objectives

- Identify significant individuals who lived between 1300 and 1800 and explain how their ideas and work changed society.
- Assess the changes that took place in the way most Europeans thought between 1300 and 1800.
- Write a research-based essay on the impact of one individual on European thought during the period from 1300 to 1800.

PREPARE

Approximate lesson time is 60 minutes.

Materials

For the Student
- Expository Essay Plan
- Innovators of the Modern World
- Taking Notes
- The Human Odyssey, Volume 2 edited by Klee, Cribb, and Holdren

---

LEARN

Activity 1: Writing an Essay *(Offline)*

© 2016 K12 Inc. All rights reserved.
Copying or distributing without K12's written consent is prohibited.

Instructions

Day 1

Who's Who

Today you will spend some time online reviewing important individuals whose work and ideas changed society between 1300 and 1800. As you review online flash cards and unit reviews, think about the people who significantly changed European thought. Then on the Innovators of the Modern World sheet, list the individuals (who lived between 1300 and 1800) whose ideas and works you believe had the greatest influence on the modern world. As you review and complete the sheet, try to identify a significant impact each individual had on the world. Completing the sheet is the first step in your research. Next, choose one individual from the Innovators of the Modern World sheet to research and write an essay about.

Day 2

Organizing Thoughts

Begin to research the individual that you chose as the subject for your essay. You should use your textbook and online resources to help you gather information about the person. Be sure to take notes as you research your subject. Then write a thesis statement and create an outline to help organize your information.

Research

Begin your research by going to Grolier's online encyclopedia and reading article(s) on the individual you selected. Write down the important information on the Taking Notes sheet. Also reread any information you can find in the textbook about this person.

To find other online sources, try a search engine such as Yahooligans, or use several of the search engines found at these websites. The links to these websites can be found in Resources.

- TekMom: Search Tools for Students
- Ivy's Search Engine Resources for Kids

After you have completed your research, use the Expository Essay Plan to help you organize your information. You'll begin writing the essay on **Day 3**.

Day 3

Writing the Essay

1. Place your outline and Taking Notes sheet where you can see them easily as you compose your essay. If you need additional information to support your ideas, find it now. Remember, your outline and essay should match each other exactly.
2. Use your thesis statement from your Taking Notes sheet to introduce your essay. The introduction should get the reader's attention and set the scene, so you may want to add some historical information or an explanation before or after the thesis statement. Be sure your introduction tells the reader what you will be writing about. Don't write more than four or five sentences.
3. Follow your outline as you write the body of your essay. Use the topic sentences you wrote in your outline. Explain or support your topic sentences with information from the corresponding section of your outline. Write a concluding sentence that connects back to the thesis statement. Follow the same procedure to write each of the supporting paragraphs.
4. Write a concluding paragraph that summarizes the main ideas of your essay and restates your thesis statement in some way. Write no more than four or five sentences.

© 2016 K12 Inc. All rights reserved.
Copying or distributing without K12's written consent is prohibited.

ASSESS

Lesson Assessment: Writing from Research *(Offline)*

You will complete an offline assessment covering some of the main points of this lesson. Your assessment will be scored by the teacher.

© 2016 K12 Inc. All rights reserved.
Copying or distributing without K12's written consent is prohibited.

Name ______________________ Date ______________________ 

Taking Notes

As you research, remember that you are looking for specific information about the person's accomplishments. The information needs to indicate how the individual influenced society.

You may have to leave some sections of the chart blank because the information is not available, and you may have more information in some sections than in others.

General Information

Born: ______________________

Died: ______________________

Where he lived: ______________________

Where he was educated: ______________________

Other general information: ______________________

____

____

____

Specific Accomplishment(s) and/or Contribution(s) ______________________

____

____

____

© 2016 K12 Inc. All rights reserved.
Copying or distributing without K12's written consent is prohibited.

Taking Notes

Impact of Accomplishments (How did this person's accomplishments influence or change the way people in Europe and/or the world thought or lived?)

____

____

____

____

Writing the Thesis

Now it is time to answer the Guiding Question. Using your chart, think about two or three main points you want to make, and what details will support each of the points. Why do you think this person is so important? What did the person do? What was the impact of his contributions?

- Write your answer in one sentence.
- Use third person—don't use the words "I," "we," or "you."

Thesis: ____________________ was an innovator who had enormous impact on

society because ______________________________________

____

© 2016 K12 Inc. All rights reserved.
Copying or distributing without K12's written consent is prohibited.

Name ______________________ Date ______________________

Innovators of the Modern World, 1300 to 1800

Person	Time Period	Field(s)	Accomplishments/Contributions	Impact

It is time to choose the person that you want to write about. Which of these individuals do you think most significantly influenced European thought? Whose ideas or work resulted in the greatest changes in society?

The person I will write about is: ______________________

© 2016 K12 Inc. All rights reserved.
Copying or distributing without K12's written consent is prohibited.

Name Date 

Expository Essay Plan

An expository essay instructs, provides information, or explains. In this essay, you are presenting information and explaining why you think the ideas and work of the individual you chose had an impact on European thought. But before you begin writing the essay, you need to organize the information you've gathered by creating an outline.

Directions:

1. Your Taking Notes sheet should have helped you identify and organize the information you found while doing your research. Now it is time to create an outline to organize the information in the way you will present it in your essay. You may decide not to use all the information you gathered, but be sure you do not leave out anything that you believe is important to support your thesis.

2. Your essay should include an introductory paragraph, supporting paragraphs, and a concluding paragraph. Each paragraph should cover one main topic and should correspond to a Roman numeral (I., II., III.) on the outline. The main topics should cover:

    - The person's accomplishment and contributions
    - The impact of his accomplishments or contributions on European thought

3. Write a topic sentence for each paragraph of your essay. Be sure it tells the reader what the section will be about and how the information relates to your thesis statement. Your topic sentence for the introductory paragraph might say something like "Johannes Gutenberg's invention changed the way people communicated." A topic sentence for the second paragraph—the first main topic—might be something like "Gutenberg's printing press changed the way books were produced and the way knowledge was communicated."

4. Decide which pieces of information you will use to support your topic sentences. (These ideas or groups of facts are called *subtopics*.) Subtopics follow capital letters and periods (A., B., C.) on your outline. Add this information beneath your topic sentence.

5. You can further divide subtopics into specific facts. In an outline, specific facts follow Arabic numerals and periods (1., 2., 3., 4.).

6. End your outline and essay with a concluding paragraph.

© 2016 K12 Inc. All rights reserved.
Copying or distributing without K12's written consent is prohibited.

Student Guide
Lesson 2. Optional: Your Choice

You may use today's lesson time to do one or more of the following:

- Complete work in progress.
- Complete the Beyond the Lesson activity in any lesson in this unit.
- Review the Time Line in the Resources section.
- Go on to the next lesson.

Please mark this lesson complete to proceed to the next lesson in the course.

PREPARE

Approximate lesson time is 60 minutes.

© 2016 K12 Inc. All rights reserved.
Copying or distributing without K12's written consent is prohibited.

Student Guide

Unit 9: Semester Review and Assessment
Lesson 1: Semester Review: Units 1, 2, 3, and 4

It's time to look back and pull together the material studied this semester. Reviewing in preparation for a semester assessment provides an excellent opportunity to make inferences and see connections that you may not have noticed earlier. Review isn't just a way to do well—it's a way to learn something new, as well.

You've finished! Now it's time to pull together what you have learned this semester. You've learned a lot, so we'll review it unit by unit. Let's start by taking a look at the following units.

- Beginning
- A Renaissance Begins in Europe
- The Spread of New Ideas
- New Powers in Asia

Lesson Objectives

- Demonstrate mastery of important knowledge and skills taught in the Beginning unit.
- Demonstrate mastery of important knowledge and skills taught in A Renaissance Begins in Europe unit.
- Demonstrate mastery of important knowledge and skills taught in The Spread of New Ideas unit.
- Demonstrate mastery of important knowledge and skills taught in the New Powers in Asia unit.

PREPARE

Approximate lesson time is 60 minutes.

Materials

For the Student

History Journal

LEARN

Activity 1: Early Modern World *(Online)*

Activity 2: History Journal *(Offline)*

Instructions

Review what you learned this semester by going through your History Journal. You should look at:

- Completed activity sheets, including Reading Guides
- Printouts of online activities
- Map activities
- Keywords and definitions
- Offline assessments

Remember to focus your offline review on these units.

© 2016 K12 Inc. All rights reserved.
Copying or distributing without K12's written consent is prohibited.

- Beginning
- A Renaissance Begins in Europe
- The Spread of New Ideas
- New Powers in Asia

© 2016 K12 Inc. All rights reserved.
Copying or distributing without K12's written consent is prohibited.

Student Guide
Lesson 2: Semester Review: Units 5, 6, and 7

Continue to pull together the material studied this semester by reviewing it unit by unit. Focus on the following units today:

- Europe Seeks Asia and Meets the Americas
- Exploration Changes the World
- Changing Empires, Changing Ideas

Lesson Objectives

- Demonstrate mastery of important knowledge and skills taught in the Changing Empires, Changing Ideas unit.
- Demonstrate mastery of important knowledge and skills taught in the Europe Seeks Asia and Meets the Americas unit.
- Demonstrate mastery of important knowledge and skills taught in the Exploration Changes the World unit.

PREPARE

Approximate lesson time is 60 minutes.

LEARN

Activity 1: Expanding the Known World *(Online)*

Activity 2: Offline *(Offline)*

Instructions

Review what you learned this semester by going through your History Journal. You should look at:

- Completed activity sheets, including Reading Guides
- Printouts of online activities
- Map activities
- Keywords and definitions
- Offline assessments

© 2016 K12 Inc. All rights reserved.
Copying or distributing without K12's written consent is prohibited.

Student Guide
Lesson 3. Optional: Your Choice

You may use today's lesson time to do one or more of the following:

- Complete work in progress.
- Complete the Beyond the Lesson activity in any lesson in this unit.
- Review the Time Line in the Resources section.
- Go on to the next lesson.

Please mark this lesson complete to proceed to the next lesson in the course.

PREPARE

Approximate lesson time is 60 minutes.

© 2016 K12 Inc. All rights reserved.
Copying or distributing without K12's written consent is prohibited.

Student Guide
Lesson 4: Semester Assessment

Today you will take the Semester Assessment.

Lesson Objectives

- Define *humanism* as a movement that stressed the wisdom of the classics and the dignity of humans and human potential.
- Define the Scientific Revolution.
- Describe artistic and political achievements in China under the Ming dynasty.
- Describe English explorations in the sixteenth century and the explorers who led them.
- Describe Renaissance cities as catalysts for change at the close of the Middle Ages.
- Describe the causes and results of England's conflict with Spain.
- Describe the Columbian Exchange.
- Describe the Japanese feudal system and the role of the samurai and the code of bushido.
- Describe the reasons for European interest in traveling by sea to Asia in the fifteenth century.
- Explain how Renaissance art differed from medieval art.
- Identify Copernicus.
- Identify Dias as the Portuguese explorer who first rounded the southern tip of Africa.
- Identify Elizabeth I and her accomplishments.
- Identify Johannes Gutenberg as the fifteenth-century inventor of the modern printing press.
- Identify John Locke.
- Identify Louis XIV.
- Identify Machiavelli as the Italian author of *The Prince*.
- Identify major artists of the Northern Renaissance (including Van Eyck, Dürer, and Holbein) and their accomplishments.
- Identify Martin Luther.
- Identify significant individuals and events in the English Civil War.
- Identify the major Florentine artists including Donatello, Brunelleschi, Masaccio, Botticelli, da Vinci, and their achievements.
- Identify the Tokugawa shogunate and its reasons for closing Japan to foreign influence.
- Identify Voltaire, Montesquieu, Diderot, and Condorcet.
- Locate on a map the route Magellan took, the major land areas and bodies of water on the route, and the distance the expedition traveled.
- Locate Russia on a map and identify its boundaries, major land features, and cities.
- Recognize how Renaissance ideas spread beyond Italy.
- Recognize key goals, events, problems, and people in the settlement of the English colonies in North America.
- Recognize Newton's achievements in science and mathematics and his impact on the field of scientific study.
- Recognize that the Islamic world experienced hardships at the hands of Mongol conquerors during the time of the European Middle Ages.

© 2016 K12 Inc. All rights reserved.
Copying or distributing without K12's written consent is prohibited.

- Recognize that the people in the African kingdoms identified themselves with members of their own tribe, not with the inhabitants of the entire continent.
- Recognize the work of Descartes and Bacon in developing reliable ways to acquire knowledge.
- Review basic geography skills.
- Summarize Galileo's achievements and the obstacles he faced.
- Summarize the major achievements and characteristics of Aztec civilization.
- Summarize the major achievements and characteristics of Inca civilization.
- Summarize the major achievements and characteristics of Maya civilization.
- Trace on a map the route of Columbus's first voyage, and identify San Salvador as his landing point.
- Define *kremlin* and explain Ivan's purpose in restoring the Kremlin in Moscow.
- Define the Reformation.
- Define the Renaissance as a period of artistic and literary achievement in Europe from the late fourteenth to the early seventeenth centuries, inspired by new interest in the classics.
- Describe the belief in purgatory and indulgences and how indulgences came to be given in exchange for money.
- Describe the effects of colonization on the peoples of the colonized territories.
- Describe the Mongol conquest of Russia.
- Explain the origins of the terms "Protestant" and "Catholic".
- Explain why the native population declined so rapidly and describe how the Spanish government responded to the decline.
- Give examples of goods that Europeans wanted from the Americas.
- Identify Akbar as the ruler of the Mughal Empire who practiced religious and cultural tolerance in India.
- Identify Dante as the fourteenth-century Italian poet who wrote *The Divine Comedy*.
- Identify Erasmus.
- Identify Isabella d'Este as a "Renaissance woman" who ruled a city-state and made it a center of learning and art.
- Identify Ivan III as Ivan the Great and describe his accomplishments.
- Identify Ivan IV as Ivan the Terrible, and describe how he earned his nickname.
- Identify John Calvin.
- Identify Osman as the Muslim, Turkish nomad who founded the Ottoman Empire in the thirteenth century.
- Identify Pedro Cabral.
- Identify Petrarch as the fourteenth-century Italian scholar known as the father of humanism.
- Identify Prince Henry the Navigator as the Portuguese patron of sea expeditions.
- Identify Teresa of Avila.
- Identify the Reformation.
- Identify Thomas More.
- Identify Vladimir as the tenth-century Grand Prince of Kiev who ordered Russians to convert to Orthodox Christianity.
- Review the late Middle Ages in Europe and Asia.

© 2016 K12 Inc. All rights reserved.
Copying or distributing without K12's written consent is prohibited.

PREPARE

Approximate lesson time is 60 minutes.

ASSESS

Semester Assessment: First Semester: MS World History II, Part 1

(*Online*)

Complete the computer-scored portion of the Semester Assessment. When you have finished, complete the teacher-scored portion of the assessment and submit it to your teacher.

Semester Assessment: First Semester: MS World History II, Part 2

(*Offline*)

Complete the teacher-scored portion of the Semester Assessment and submit it to your teacher.

© 2016 K12 Inc. All rights reserved.
Copying or distributing without K12's written consent is prohibited.

Student Guide

Unit 10: Age of Democratic Revolutions
Lesson 1: The World Turned Upside Down: The American Revolution

Revolutions cause dramatic change. England's revolution marked the beginning of a long period of change. Educated men and women began discussing John Locke's ideas about the purpose of government. People in France, the British colonies in North America, and the Spanish colonies in South America grew more and more unhappy with their situations. Talk of revolution even spread to Russia. People became convinced that it was time for change. Did they dare revolt? How bloody would a revolution be? Could they create better governments?

Lesson Objectives

- Summarize the attitude of most colonists toward Britain in 1763 and the reasons for their attitude.
- Explain why Parliament imposed taxes after 1763 and why the colonists reacted as they did.
- Describe the events that led to war between Britain and the colonies.
- Identify Montesquieu, Locke, and Jefferson and their political ideas.
- Summarize the arguments Thomas Paine put forth in *Common Sense,* and their influence on colonial opinion regarding independence.
- Summarize the major ideas of the Declaration of Independence.
- Identify George Washington and his contributions to the revolution.
- Describe the disadvantages the American army faced and the importance of French aid in winning the war.
- Summarize the reasons for a Constitutional Convention in 1787 and its accomplishments.
- Identify the U.S. Constitution as the world's oldest functioning written constitution.
- Review historical events.

PREPARE

Approximate lesson time is 60 minutes.

Materials

For the Student

- Making Sense of Common Sense
- Reading Guide
- The Human Odyssey, Volume 2 edited by Klee, Cribb, and Holdren
- History Journal

© 2016 K12 Inc. All rights reserved.
Copying or distributing without K12's written consent is prohibited.

Keywords and Pronunciation

Enlightenment : era in the eighteenth century when thinkers valued logic, reason, and scientific method

tyranny : abuse of power; according to John Locke, the actions of a ruler who "makes not the law, but his will, the rule"

LEARN

Activity 1: Declaring and Winning Independence *(Offline)*

Instructions

Day 1

Read

Read the Part 3 Introduction and Chapter 1, from the beginning to "Declaring Independence," pages 349–361, and complete Day 1 of the Reading Guide. When you have finished, use the Lesson Answer Key to check your work, and then place the Reading Guide in your History Journal.

Making Sense of Common Sense

Most American colonists in 1763 were proud of their English heritage. By the summer of 1776, after Thomas Paine published Common Sense , their sentiments had changed dramatically.

Plain-speaking Paine had a lot to say about relations between the colonists and Britain. Much of what he had to say he recorded in his pamphlet Common Sense . Study what he said by completing Putting Words in Thomas Paine's Mouth sheet.

Day 2

Read

Read Chapter 1, from "Declaring Independence" to the end of the chapter, pages 361–367, and complete Day 2 of the Reading Guide. When you have finished, use the Lesson Answer Key to check your work, and then place the Reading Guide in your History Journal.

Declaring Independence and Acting Independently

After you have finished your reading assignment, go online to complete the Declaring Independence activity. When you have finished the activity, stay online and complete the Separation of Powers activity.

Day 3

Asking the Tough Questions!

Pretend you are a newspaper reporter on a special assignment. Your job is to interview one of the characters from Chapter 1 of Part 3. Choose a character, then write a paragraph explaining to your editor why interviewing that particular person will give your newspaper's readers a real insight into the events of the American Revolution.

Then, draw up a list of questions for your interviewee—and provide the answers you think the interviewee might give. Use a question-and-answer format. On one line, write your initials followed by a colon and the question. On the next line, write the interviewee's initials followed by a colon and the answer.

For example:

RC: Mr. Jefferson, how did the Enlightenment shape your ideas about government?

TJ: A very good question, I must say. When I first read John Locke and Montesquieu...

© 2016 K12 Inc. All rights reserved.
Copying or distributing without K12's written consent is prohibited.

This sample question is indeed a good one. Enlightenment ideas were extremely important during the American Revolution. Try to get your interviewee to talk about those ideas. Other questions might include:

- How did you feel after the British victory at Fort Ticonderoga?
- How important was it to have the French on our side?
- How difficult was it to get colonial soldiers to train and fight with discipline?
- How great an achievement was the Constitutional Convention?

ASSESS

Lesson Assessment: The World Turned Upside Down: The American Revolution (*Online*)

You will complete an online assessment covering the main objectives of this lesson. Your assessment will be scored by the computer.

LEARN

Activity 2. Optional: The World Turned Upside Down: The American Revolution *(Online)*

© 2016 K12 Inc. All rights reserved.
Copying or distributing without K12's written consent is prohibited.

Name ______________________________ Date ______________________________ 

Putting Words in Thomas Paine's Mouth

Use pages 359–360 of the textbook to fill in the blanks below.

1. Paine insisted that institutions of government should be reasonable. Was it reasonable for a king to rule colonies far away? Paine answered with a resounding ____________________.

2. When Paine said "'Tis time to part," he meant that the colonies should become ____________________ of Britain.

3. According to Paine, "Of more worth is one honest man to society" than ____________________.

4. Paine described a king as ____ ____.

5. To Paine, "there is something very absurd, in supposing a continent to be perpetually governed by an ____________________."

Use the excerpt from *Common Sense* on pages 360-361 to answer the following in your own words:

6. Paine argued that "the parent of America" is not England but Europe. What evidence did he present for his argument? ____
____
____

7. Paine argued that the king was not a proper power to govern the American people. Why?
____
____
____

© 2016 K12 Inc. All rights reserved.
Copying or distributing without K12's written consent is prohibited.

Collision Course

Many colonists agreed with Paine's "common sense." The colonies and "the mother country" began to drift apart.

The chart below shows the British point of view. Fill in the colonists' point of view on each issue.

British Point of View	Colonists' Point of View
Colonists should pay taxes to support the army.	
London should rule the colonies.	
A king should be head of the country.	
The colonies should stay tied to "the mother country."	

What was the result of these differing points of view? ______________________________

____

____

© 2016 K12 Inc. All rights reserved.
Copying or distributing without K12's written consent is prohibited.

Name Date 

Reading Guide

Day 1

Read

Reading Guide

1. The English philosopher who wrote, in his *Two Treatises of Government,* that all people have natural rights, was ______________________________.

2. Name two rights that John Locke discussed.

3. Why were Britain's colonists so proud to be part of the British Empire in 1763? Give at least two reasons.

4. Why did many colonists refer to Britain as "the mother country"?

5. True or False? Britain had always kept careful control of the colonies, giving the appointed governors the power to tax and enact laws for the colonists.

6. The colonists despised the new taxes imposed in 1765 by the ____________ Act. Why was it so named?

7. What did the colonists mean when they cried, "No taxation without representation"?

8. Name the French Enlightenment author of *The Spirit of the Laws* who defined tyranny as "the exercise of power beyond right."

© 2016 K12 Inc. All rights reserved.
Copying or distributing without K12's written consent is prohibited.

Name Date 

9. What was the Boston Massacre, and why did it upset people in the colonies so much?

10. Why in 1773 did a group of colonists disguise themselves as Indians, make their way to Boston Harbor, and board three British cargo ships?

11. What was "the shot heard 'round the world"?

12. What was *Common Sense* in the American Revolution?

Day 2

Read

13. In the Declaration of Independence, Thomas Jefferson argued for certain "unalienable rights" that were endowed by the Creator. What were those rights?

14. The leader of the Continental Army was ______________________________. Name two of his achievements.

15. What disadvantages did the Continental Army face?

16. Why did the Americans need French help?

17. Colonists who remained loyal to Britain were known as______________or______________.

© 2016 K12 Inc. All rights reserved.
Copying or distributing without K12's written consent is prohibited.

Name Date

18. The last major battle of the American Revolution was fought at_______________in Virginia.

19. The government for the new United States was described in a document called the ____________________________________. What weaknesses did this government have?

20. Why did Americans call a Constitutional Convention in 1787?

21. What is unique about the U.S Constitution?

Explore and Discuss

You have described the event known as "the shot heard 'round the world." Now that you have finished the chapter, think again about that phrase. It comes from a poem written by Ralph Waldo Emerson in 1837. Why do you think Emerson used that phrase?

© 2016 K12 Inc. All rights reserved.
Copying or distributing without K12's written consent is prohibited.

Student Guide
Lesson 2: The French Revolution

Lesson Objectives

- Summarize Enlightenment ideas that promoted revolution in France.
- Describe the reigns of absolute monarchs in France.
- Describe the social structure of France and its influence on French life.
- Summarize the circumstances and events that led to the French Revolution.
- Compare the Declaration of the Rights of Man with the Declaration of Independence.
- Explain the revolutionaries' criticisms of the Church.
- Describe the events of the Reign of Terror.
- Recognize reforms made by the National Convention.
- Explain how Napoleon came to power.
- Identify major positions of the political spectrum.

PREPARE

Approximate lesson time is 60 minutes.

Materials

For the Student

- Declaration of the Rights of Man
- Lesson Answer Key
- Reading Guide
- The French Revolution: What Happened and When

The Human Odyssey, Volume 2 edited by Klee, Cribb, and Holdren

History Journal

Keywords and Pronunciation

Bastille (bah-STEEL)
dauphin (doh-FAN)
guillotine (GIH-luh-teen)
Liberté, égalité, fraternité (lee-behr-TAY, ay-ga-lee-TAY, fra-tehr-nee-TAY)
Maximilien Robespierre (mahk-see-meel-yan ROHBZ-pyehr)
Napoleon Bonaparte (nuh-POHL-yuhn BOH-nuh-pahrt)
Vive l' assemblée (veev lah-sahm-blay)
Vive la république (veev lah ray-poob-leek)

© 2016 K12 Inc. All rights reserved.
Copying or distributing without K12's written consent is prohibited.

LEARN

Activity 1: The French Revolution *(Offline)*

This lesson is designed to be completed in 3 class sessions.

Day 1

Read

Read Chapter 2, from the beginning to “Storming the Bastille and Starting a Revolution,” pages 368–374, and complete Day 1 of the Reading Guide. When you have finished, use the Lesson Answer Key to check your work, and then place the Reading Guide in your History Journal.

That's Class!

French people in the eighteenth century belonged to one of three classes, known as estates. The First Estate was made up of members of the clergy, such as bishops and priests of the Catholic Church. The Second Estate was made up of nobles. And the Third Estate was made up of everyone else in French society—98 percent of the population.

These class distinctions were very rigid. “Commoners” could not become members of the nobility, no matter how wealthy they became. Hundreds of years earlier, when the Estates-General was formed, nobles and high ranking clergy were almost the only people who could obtain any real wealth. But over time, things had changed and many members of the Third Estate, or commoners, owned businesses that made them rich. The rigid class structure really angered many French people.

What's more, France at this time was almost bankrupt, and the people with power (members of the First and Second Estates and the king himself) needed the cooperation of the people with money (many members of the Third Estate). The stage was set for conflict and, ultimately, violent revolution.

See how rigid the French social system was by completing the “French Estates” online activity.

Day 2

Read

Read Chapter 2, from “Storming the Bastille and Starting a Revolution” to “Terror and Equality,” pages 374–380, and complete Day 2 of the Reading Guide. When you have finished, use the Lesson Answer Key to check your work, and then place the Reading Guide in your History Journal.

Declaring the Rights of Man and the Citizen

Complete the “Declaration of the Rights of Man” activity. When you have finished, compare your answers with those in the Lesson Answer Key.

Day 3

Read

Read Chapter 2, from “Terror and Equality” to the end, pages 380–383, and complete Day 3 of the Reading Guide. When you have finished, use the Lesson Answer Key to check your work, and then place the Reading Guide in your History Journal.

What Happened and When?

Complete the French Revolution: What Happened and When? activity. When you have finished, compare your dates and order of events with those in the Lesson Answer Key.

A Spectrum of Political Opinion

Another way to make sense of the various events and movements of the French Revolution is to see them as part of a political spectrum.

© 2016 K12 Inc. All rights reserved.
Copying or distributing without K12's written consent is prohibited.

The dictionary defines spectrum as "a continuous range." A political spectrum, therefore, is a continuous range of political opinion. Typically, political spectrums range from left to right—from the extreme left to moderate left to the center, and from the center to moderate right to the extreme right. Politically speaking, someone on "the left wing" of the political spectrum favors change, and someone on "the right wing" of the political spectrum opposes change.

To learn more about the political spectrum in revolutionary France, complete the Political Spectrum activity online. (One more word on definitions: status quo means the way things are at the moment, before there is any change.)

ASSESS

Lesson Assessment: The French Revolution (*Online*)

You will complete an online assessment covering the main objectives of this lesson. Your assessment will be scored by the computer.

LEARN

Activity 2. Optional: The French Revolution *(Online)*

© 2016 K12 Inc. All rights reserved.
Copying or distributing without K12's written consent is prohibited.

The French Revolution

Day 1

Read

Reading Guide

1. Name two of the Enlightenment ideas that promoted revolution in France.
   people have natural rights; government should represent the people; rights should be written in a constitution

2. What kind of power did France's absolute monarchs possess?
   they had almost unlimited powers; they were all-powerful

3. Name the three estates into which French society was divided. Who were the members of each of the three estates?
   the First Estate (clergy); the Second Estate (nobles); the Third Estate ("commoners")

4. Look closely at the cartoon on page 371. Describe in your own words what it is trying to say.
   The "commoners" are carrying the nobles and the clergy; the Third Estate supports the other two estates; commoners are the only ones in society who do any real work; nobles and clergy are lazy

5. True or false? It was easy for a "commoner" to change his estate by acquiring wealth.
   false

6. Why did Louis XVI call a meeting of the Estates-General in 1789? How long had it been since such a meeting had been called?
   He needed money. The Estates-General had not met for 175 years.

7. One of the advantages of the First and Second Estates is that their members did not have to pay taxes.

8. Unfair taxes angered members of the Third Estate. But what would have happened if the Third Estate had tried to get the First and Second Estates to pay taxes? How would the estates have voted in the Estates-General?
   The First and Second Estates would have voted against the Third Estate.

9. If the Third Estate would be constantly outvoted, two to one, by the other two estates, how could commoners ever hope to gain a fairer share of power?
   by ending the Estates General and its division of people into estates; by having people vote instead of having estates vote

10. Deputies of the Third Estate took the Tennis Court Oath, swearing not to disband until they had drafted a new constitution.

11. What was the new name the deputies gave themselves?
    the National Assembly

© 2016 K12 Inc. All rights reserved.
Copying or distributing without K12's written consent is prohibited.

Day 2

Read

Reading Guide

12. After the formation of the National Assembly, the Paris mob decided to get in on the action by storming the Bastille.

13. What was the mob hoping to find in this building? What did they find?
    arms and ammunition, prisoners; just seven prisoners

14. True or false? The new National Assembly wanted to immediately get rid of the monarchy completely.
    false

15. American revolutionaries drew up a Declaration of Independence. What kind of declaration did the French write?
    the Declaration of the Rights of Man

16. Why did the revolutionaries dislike the Church? Give at least two reasons.
    It was too wealthy; it was too powerful; religion ran contrary to reason.

Declaration of the Rights of Man

1. Declaration of Independence
2. Supreme Being
3. Enlightenment
4. John Locke; *philosophes*
5. liberty, property, security, resistance to oppression
6. powers
7. Answers may vary but could include: Frenchmen fighting on the side of the Americans had seen that royal power could be broken; they learned about the ideas that inspired the American Revolution; Lafayette returned to France with ideas about liberty
8. Answers may vary but could include references to constitutional monarchy, the Glorious Revolution in England, the writings of Locke about the exercise of power beyond right, the divine right of kings, particular behavior of particular kings

© 2016 K12 Inc. All rights reserved.
Copying or distributing without K12's written consent is prohibited.

Day 3

Read

Reading Guide

17. What was the Reign of Terror?
    It was the period during the revolution when thousands of citizens were executed because they had been labeled (often wrongly) as enemies of the revolution.

18. Among the reforms of the National Convention were free primary education for all boys and girls, equal inheritance for both sons and daughters, and the abolition of slavery in the French colonies.

19. To whom did the Directors turn for help against their enemies? Why did they think that he could help them?
    Napoleon; he had an army and they thought they could control him

20. Napoleon took control of France by seizing power from the Directory. Soon he wielded as much power as a dictator.

21. If moderates had maintained control of the revolution, how do you think it would have turned out? If reactionaries had seized control, what would they have done?
    If the moderates had maintained control, it would have turned into a constitutional monarchy. If the reactionaries had seized control, there would have been a return to the days of absolute monarchs.

Thinking Cap Question:

Was there anything poor Louis XVI could have done to stop the revolution, to maintain the monarchy, or even to save his own head? Or, by 1789 was there nothing the king could have done?

Answer could include that he could have: lived more frugally, avoided calling the Estates-General, sided with the Third Estate, embraced the constitution, not tried to flee France
Or there was nothing he could have done, because of the demands for change by the Third Estate, the poverty of the people, the reactionary positions of the First and Second Estates.

What Happened and When?

Spring 1789: The Estates-General meets.
June 20, 1789: Members of the National Assembly take the Tennis Court Oath.
July 14, 1789: Paris mob storms the Bastille.
August 1789: The National Assembly issues the Declaration of the Rights of Man.
October 1789: Parisians move the royal family from Versailles to the capital.
August 1792: Paris mob imprisons the royal family.
September 1792: Convention declares France a republic.
January 21, 1793: King Louis XVI is executed.
Spring 1793: Robespierre begins to rule France like a tyrant during the Reign of Terror.
October 16, 1793: Marie Antoinette is executed.
July 28, 1794: Robespierre's execution brings the Directory to power.
1799: Napoleon Bonaparte seizes power from the Directory.

© 2016 K12 Inc. All rights reserved.
Copying or distributing without K12's written consent is prohibited.

Name Date 

Reading Guide

Day 1

Read

Reading Guide

1. Name two of the Enlightenment ideas that promoted revolution in France.

2. What kind of power did France's absolute monarchs possess?

3. Name the three estates into which French society was divided. Who were the members of each of the three estates?

4. Look closely at the cartoon on page 371. Describe in your own words what it is trying to say.

5. True or false? It was easy for a "commoner" to change his estate by acquiring wealth.

6. Why did Louis XVI call a meeting of the Estates-General in 1789? How long had it been since such a meeting had been called?

7. One of the advantages of the First and Second Estates is that their members did not have to pay ________________.

© 2016 K12 Inc. All rights reserved.
Copying or distributing without K12's written consent is prohibited.

Name Date 

8. Unfair taxes angered members of the Third Estate. But what would have happened if the Third Estate had tried to get the First and Second Estates to pay taxes? How would the estates have voted in the Estates-General?

9. If the Third Estate would be constantly outvoted, two to one, by the other two estates, how could commoners ever hope to gain a fairer share of power?

10. Deputies of the Third Estate took the ______________________ Oath, swearing not to disband until they had drafted a new constitution.

11. What was the new name the deputies gave themselves?

Day 2

Read

12. After the formation of the National Assembly, the Paris mob decided to get in on the action by storming the ____________________ .

13. What was the mob hoping to find in this building? What did they find?

14. True or false? The new National Assembly wanted to immediately get rid of the monarchy completely.

15. American revolutionaries drew up a Declaration of Independence. What kind of declaration did the French write?

© 2016 K12 Inc. All rights reserved.
Copying or distributing without K12's written consent is prohibited.

Name ______________________________ Date ______________________________ 

16. Why did the revolutionaries dislike the Church? Give at least two reasons.

Day 3

Read

17. What was the Reign of Terror?

18. Among the reforms of the National Convention were free ______________ for all boys and girls, equal ______________ for both sons and daughters, and the abolition of ______________ in the French colonies.

19. To whom did the Directors turn for help against their enemies? Why did they think that he could help them?

20. Napoleon took control of France by seizing ______________ from the Directory. Soon he wielded as much power as a ______________ .

21. If moderates had maintained control of the revolution, how do you think it would have turned out? If reactionaries had seized control, what would they have done?

Thinking Cap Question:

Was there anything Louis XVI could have done to stop the revolution, to maintain the monarchy, or even to save his own head? Or, by 1789 was there nothing the king could have done?

© 2016 K12 Inc. All rights reserved.
Copying or distributing without K12's written consent is prohibited.

The French Revolution: What Happened and When?

The French Revolution was a whirlwind of events: declarations and executions, armed mobs and armed invasions, new governments and new personalities. To help make sense of these key events—and the order in which they happened—rearrange the events below in chronological order. Use your textbook to assign dates to each event, and place them in order on the chronological chart.

King Louis XVI is executed.

Parisians move the royal family from Versailles to the capital.

Robespierre's execution brings the Directory to power.

The Estates-General meets.

Paris mob storms the Bastille.

Paris mob imprisons the royal family.

Robespierre begins to rule France like a tyrant during the Reign of Terror.

Marie Antoinette is executed.

Napoleon Bonaparte seizes power from the Directory.

The convention declares France a republic.

The National Assembly issues the Declaration of the Rights of Man.

Members of the National Assembly take the Tennis Court Oath.

© 2016 K12 Inc. All rights reserved.
Copying or distributing without K12's written consent is prohibited.

The French Revolution: What Happened and When?

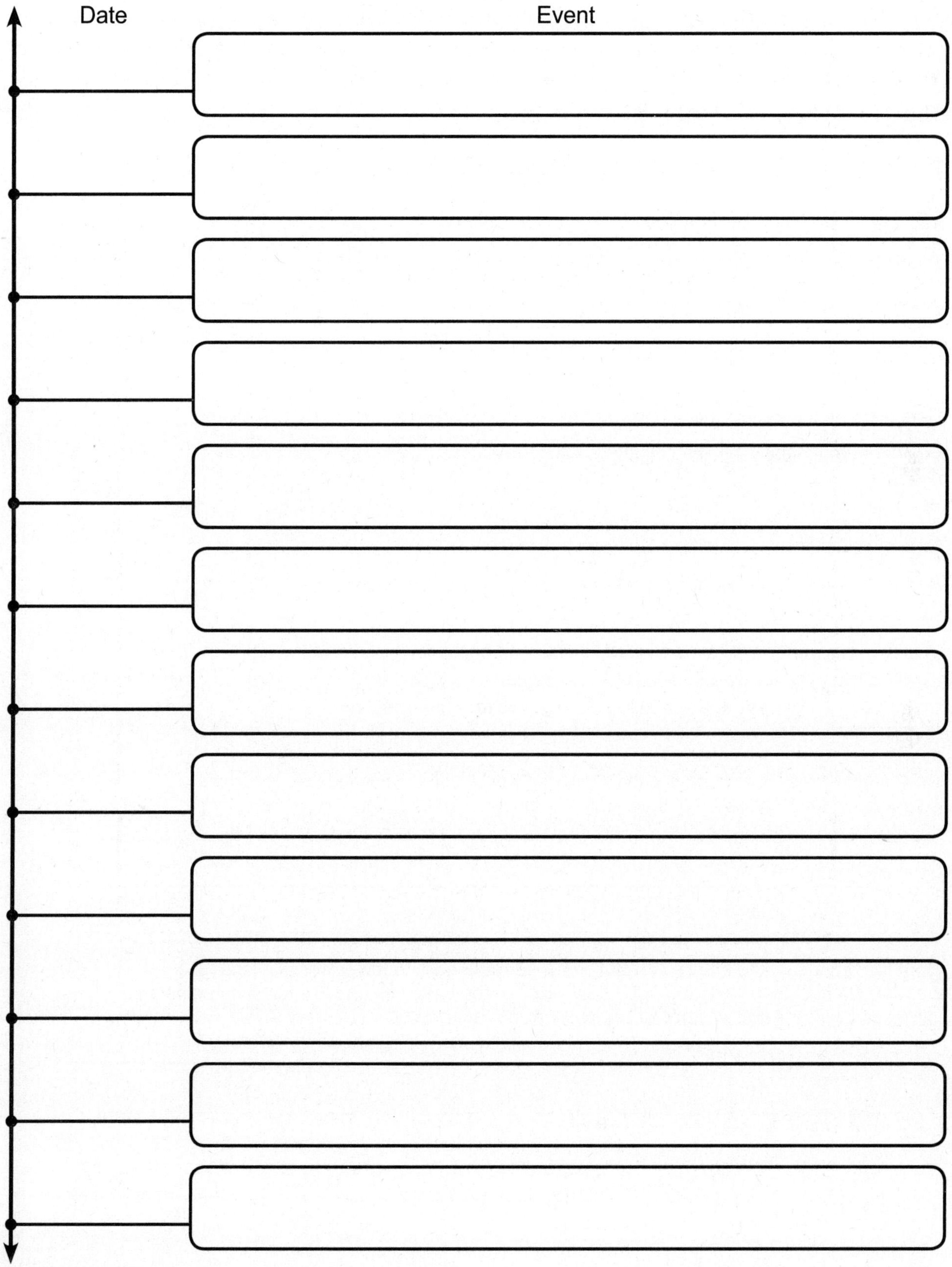

Date	Event

© 2016 K12 Inc. All rights reserved.
Copying or distributing without K12's written consent is prohibited.

Declaration of the Rights of Man

In August 1789, a month after the fall of the Bastille, the National Assembly issued a Declaration of the Rights of Man. Answer the following questions about this important document, which became one of the defining documents of the French Revolution.

1. Thirteen years before the French, revolutionaries in America had penned a similar document, known as the ______________________.

2. The American document spoke of a Creator who endowed rights; the Declaration of the Rights of Man similarly made reference to a ______________________.

3. Like the American document, the French Declaration expressed many ideas from the age of ______________________.

4. Both drew on the idea of "natural law" from the English philosopher ______________________ and the French thinkers known as the ______________________.

5. The American document spoke of rights such as "life, liberty, and the pursuit of happiness." Name three rights recognized in the French document: ______________, ______________ and ______________.

6. Thirteen years after writing the Declaration of Independence, the U.S. ratified its Constitution. The U.S. Constitution and the French Declaration both saw the need for a separation of ______________.

7. How might French involvement in the American Revolution have influenced the ideas contained in the Declaration of the Rights of Man?

____

____

____

8. Both the American and French Revolutions were challenges to the power of a king. Is it possible for people to enjoy the rights expressed in the American and French documents and *still* have a king? If not, why not? If so, how?

____

____

____

© 2016 K12 Inc. All rights reserved.
Copying or distributing without K12's written consent is prohibited.

Student Guide
Lesson 3: Napoleon: From Revolution to Empire

Lesson Objectives

- Recognize the effects of Napoleon's rule on Europe.
- Summarize the major steps in Napoleon's rise to power.
- Describe Napoleon's reforms and their significance to the people of France.
- Explain how Napoleon was able to finance wars and win territory.
- Describe the Continental System and the consequences of imposing the system.
- Explain the reasons for Napoleon's invasion of Russia and his failure to defeat Russia.
- Summarize the events that led to Napoleon's final defeat at Waterloo.
- Identify on a map major physical and political features of Europe.

PREPARE

Approximate lesson time is 60 minutes.

Materials

For the Student

- Europe's Changing Face
- Napoleon: Hero or Tyrant?
- Opinions
- Reading Guide
- Say What?

The Human Odyssey, Volume 2 edited by Klee, Cribb, and Holdren

History Journal

LEARN

Activity 1: Napoleon: From Revolution to Empire *(Offline)*

Instructions

This lesson is designed to be completed in 4 class sessions.

Day 1

Read

Read Chapter 3, from the beginning to "Catastrophe in Russia," pages 384–394, and complete Day 1 of the Reading Guide. When you have finished, use the Lesson Answer Key to check your work, and then place the Reading Guide in your History Journal.

That's Your Opinion!

Napoleon was a man of action. He did some things that helped France and the revolution and some things that harmed France. His actions stirred intense opinions among French men and women. Some people had positive reactions to what Napoleon did, some had negative reactions—and some people (at different points in time) had both!

© 2016 K12 Inc. All rights reserved.
Copying or distributing without K12's written consent is prohibited.

Pretend you are a member of the Third Estate living during Napoleon's era and state your opinions about Napoleon's actions on the Opinions sheet.

Day 2

Read

Read Chapter 3, from "Catastrophe in Russia" to the end, pages 394–399, and complete Day 2 of the Reading Guide. When you have finished, use the Lesson Answer Key to check your work, and then place the Reading Guide in your History Journal.

Putting Napoleon on the Map

Napoleon transformed the map of Europe. And when the allied powers eventually defeated him, they redrew that map at the Congress of Vienna. To see how, complete the Europe's Changing Face sheet.

Day 3

"Say What?"

Examine famous quotations by or about Napoleon on the "Say What?" sheet. Compare your answers to the "Say What?—Answer Key."

Political Cartoons—Seriously Funny

Political and military leaders such as Napoleon cared what people thought about them. They went to great lengths to "cultivate their image" before the people—to make sure they looked good. Go online and visit the website Looking Backward, Looking Forward: Public Opinion and Art. Scroll down to examine the Napoleon portrait there. Doesn't he appear regal, dignified, confident, and poised?

But cartoonists often do the opposite. By exaggerating certain characteristics and by "poking fun," they try to ridicule important leaders, to make them appear less grand, less scary. Political cartoons, as they are known, can get a simple message across very effectively. Go to the website Liberty, Equality, Fraternity: Exploring the French Revolution and examine the Napoleon cartoons there.

For more information on political cartoons, visit the website Graphic Witness: Political Cartoon or go to Grolier's Online Encyclopedia and search "political cartoons." Then go to the Library of Congress site and complete the "It's No Laughing Matter" activity. You'll learn about symbolism, exaggeration, labeling, analogy, and irony—all things to help you develop your own political cartoons tomorrow.

Day 4

Have Fun with Napoleon: Making Political Cartoons

You've read a lot about Napoleon—what he said, what others said about him, what he achieved. But sometimes a picture speaks a thousand words. Now you're going to take what you've learned from the chapter and the earlier activities—and design your own political cartoons about the great/not-so-great French emperor. Complete the "Napoleon: Hero or Tyrant" activity.

ASSESS

Lesson Assessment: Napoleon: From Revolution to Empire (*Online*)

You will complete an online assessment covering the main objectives of this lesson. Your assessment will be scored by the computer.

© 2016 K12 Inc. All rights reserved.
Copying or distributing without K12's written consent is prohibited.

Name Date 

Say What?

Napoleon left us many memorable quotations. And much has been said about him. Explain each of the quotations below—is it something Napoleon said? Or something said about him? What does it mean? Why might Napoleon or someone else have said it? Does the quotation favor Napoleon? The first has been done for you.
At the end, complete the "Napoleon in a Nutshell" section.

"I am the Revolution."

Who: Napoleon

Meaning: Napoleon said this about his own role; it justified his all-powerful position.

Favorable? Most people today would say it is not favorable.

"My forces are three times greater than yours."

"You have won battles without cannon, crossed rivers without bridges, made forced marches without shoes…"

"If you wish to be a success in the world, promise everything, deliver nothing."

"the little corporal"

"Enemy and Disturber of the Tranquility of the World"

"Vive l'Empereur!"

"soldier of the Revolution"

© 2016 K12 Inc. All rights reserved.
Copying or distributing without K12's written consent is prohibited.

Say What?

Napoleon in a Nutshell

Choose your favorite quotation about Napoleon and explain why it best sums up the nature of the man.

Quotation: ____

____

What it tells us about Napoleon: ____

____

____

© 2016 K12 Inc. All rights reserved.
Copying or distributing without K12's written consent is prohibited.

Name ______________________________ Date ______________________________ 

Reading Guide

Day 1

Read

1. Napoleon was born on the Mediterranean island of ____________________ and later lived in the French capital, ____________ .

2. Napoleon the soldier gained political power by first gaining military power. He rose through the ranks of the __________ at the beginning of the Revolution. He helped put down a __________________________ uprising in Paris. And he took command of a new French army in________________.

3. How did Napoleon rise from first consul to emperor?

4. Name three reforms Napoleon made that improved the lives of the people of France.

5. How did Napoleon raise soldiers for his army?

6. What was the name of the North American territory that Napoleon sold to the United States to help pay for his wars?

7. To attack the island of Britain, Napoleon had to cross the ______________________.

8. To defeat Britain, Napoleon devised the _________________ System, which banned Europeans from buying and selling with the (trade-dependent) island nation.

9. Name one country from southwestern Europe that refused to participate in the Continental System.

10. Portugal and Spain make up the _________________ Peninsula.

© 2016 K12 Inc. All rights reserved.
Copying or distributing without K12's written consent is prohibited.

Name Date 

Day 2

Read

11. Which other (huge) country also tried to break away from the Continental System?

12. When the Royal Navy defeated the French fleet, Napoleon marched his army all the way across Europe to invade ________________ .

13. To build up his enormous army for the invasion of Russia, Napoleon raised soldiers from ________________ as well as from France.

14. True or false? Napoleon invaded Russia because the Russians would not let Napoleon put his brother on the Russian throne.

15. Napoleon made it all the way to the Russian capital. What is the name of that city?

16. What strategy did the Russians use to defeat Napoleon?

17. Napoleon escaped from the island of______________, raised an ________ in Paris, and tried to defeat the ____________ before the Prussians arrived on the field of battle.

18. Napoleon gave the conquered peoples of Europe a unified legal system known as the ___________________ . However, many Europeans resented being ruled by Napoleon, whom they regarded as a ___________________ .

19. After defeating Napoleon, the allies redrew the border of Europe at a congress, or meeting, of their leaders. In which European city was the congress held?

© 2016 K12 Inc. All rights reserved.
Copying or distributing without K12's written consent is prohibited.

Name Date 

Explore and Discuss

History is full of "what ifs." What if Napoleon had been defeated in Italy? What if the Continental System had worked? What if the French had won the battle of Trafalgar? What if the Prussians had been delayed at Waterloo?

Consider these questions:

1. What if Napoleon had never been born? (In what ways would history have been different? Do you think someone else would have done what Napoleon did? Why?)
2. The French Revolution began as a struggle for the rights of the people against a single ruler with all the power. It ended by giving all power to another single ruler. Why do you think that happened?

© 2016 K12 Inc. All rights reserved.
Copying or distributing without K12's written consent is prohibited.

Name ______________________ Date ______________________ 

Europe's Changing Face

1. Consulting the maps on pages 392 and 393 and the atlas at the back of the textbook, label the following on your map:

France	Kingdom of Italy	Britain
Austrian Empire	Spain	Prussia
Portugal	Sweden	Germany
Russian Empire	Holland	

Label the following cities:

Paris	Moscow	Waterloo	Vienna

Label the following physical features:

Alps	English Channel	Northern European Plain

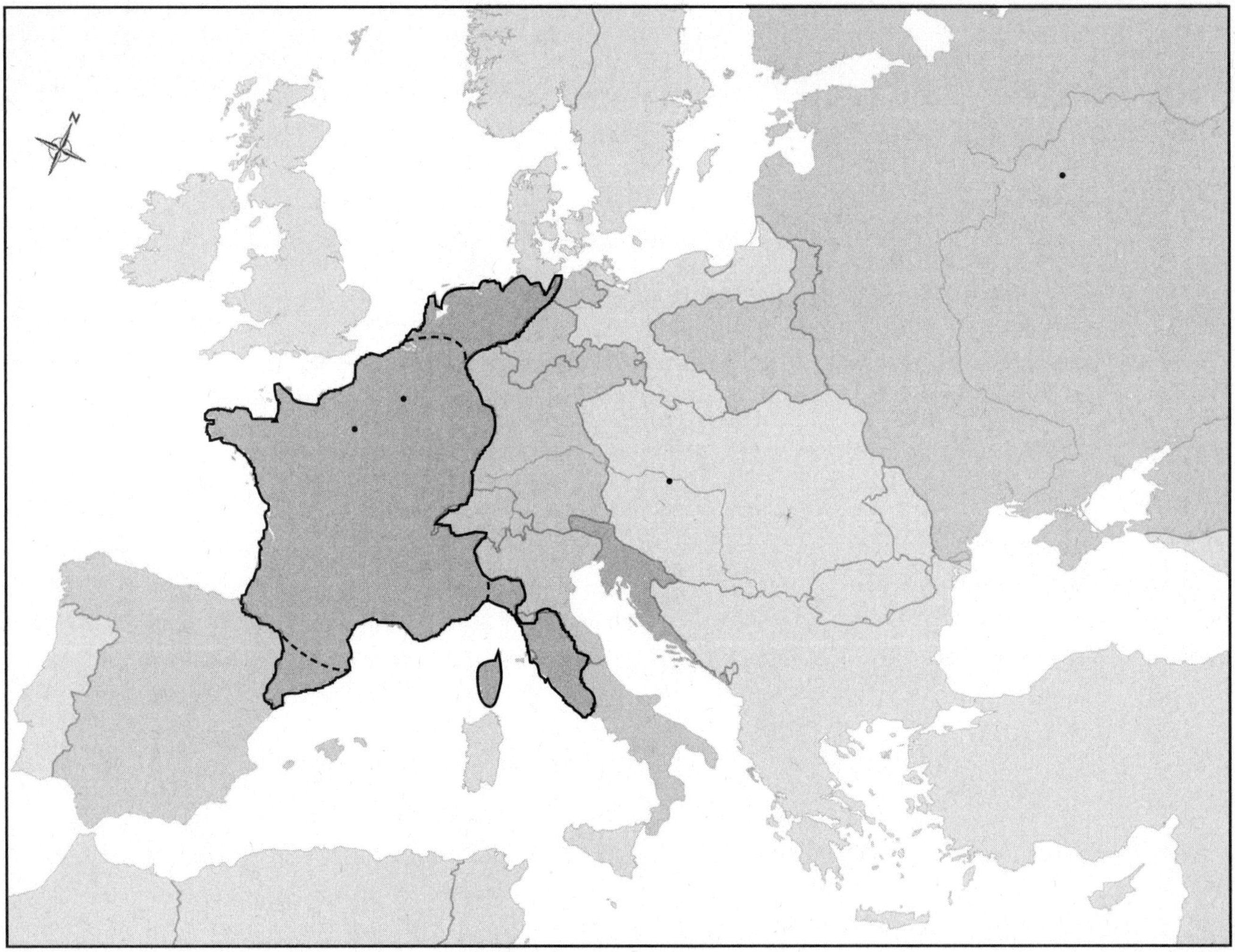

© 2016 K12 Inc. All rights reserved.
Copying or distributing without K12's written consent is prohibited.

Name ______________________________ Date ______________________________ 

Europe's Changing Face

2. Napoleon's first foreign victory was in ________________. Look at the map in the Atlas at the back of your textbook. What physical feature, or barrier, stands between France and this country? ________________ If you need a clue, take another look at the first picture in this chapter.

3. But geography couldn't slow Napoleon for long. He went on to win great victories on battlefields all over Europe. Now we're going to see just how successful Napoleon was. Use a pencil or marker to indicate the extent of the French Empire in 1812, then color the empire light blue or light purple if you have it, like the map on pages 392–393. (Consider to be within the empire the "allies of France" indicated in the map legend.)

4. Quite an empire, huh? But he didn't get all of Europe. Circle Britain in red on the map. What makes it different from the other countries of Europe? What separates Britain from France? Britain is an ______________, separated from France and its all-conquering Napoleon by the ____________________________. Unable to attack Britain because of its powerful navy, Napoleon instead tried to use his Continental System to subdue the island nation.

5. But there's another little country right at the southwestern edge of Europe that Napoleon didn't get either. You see it? It's on the western side of the ________________ Peninsula. What is its name? ________________

   Circle this country in red on the map. Draw a line in red between this circle and the circle around Britain. This symbolizes the trade that went on between these two nations, much to the annoyance of Napoleon.

6. Yes, Napoleon was really annoyed. For his Continental System to work, he had to control all of the continent. And when the Spanish began to break away from French control, Napoleon decided to send an army down into the Iberian Peninsula. Draw an arrow in red from France down into the Iberian Peninsula, to indicate the invading French army.

7. Now we (just like Napoleon) are going to look east—all the way across Europe to the borders of the Russian Empire. That's a long way, isn't it? Use a ruler and the scale bar on page 393 of the chapter to calculate the distance from Paris to the Russian border: ________________ miles. That's where Napoleon marched his armies next. Draw an arrow in red from France through Prussia and across the Russian frontier. Much of this territory is part of the Northern European Plain—flat land, good for Napoleon's quick-moving armies.

8. Russia was Napoleon's next target. It was mainly flat, too. But geography and climate—specifically, the Russian winter—proved too much for Napoleon this time. His army was almost wiped out on the seemingly endless march across the frozen Russian steppes. Calculate the distance from the Russian border to Moscow: ______________ miles.

9. After the catastrophe in Russia, Napoleon lived to fight another day. But his defeat at Waterloo marked the end. The victorious allied powers met in Vienna in 1815 to redraw the map of Europe and put France back in its place. To see how far they shrunk Napoleon's once-great realm, use a black marker and trace around the faint, dashed line on the map. This was France in 1815.

© 2016 K12 Inc. All rights reserved.
Copying or distributing without K12's written consent is prohibited.

That's *Your* Opinion!

Pretend you are a Parisian—a member of the old Third Estate. You live in the capital during the time of the revolution and Napoleon's rise to power. You believe in liberty, equality, and fraternity. You didn't like the king, but in your opinion he shouldn't have been executed. Exercise your opinion as the following events unfold in revolutionary France....

1. Army captain Napoleon fights well in battles against the Revolution's enemies in the provinces. How do you feel about the activities of the young officer?

2. What's your opinion on Napoleon's promotion to the rank of brigadier general at the young age of 24?

3. How do you feel about Napoleon's success at helping put down a royalist uprising in Paris?

4. How do most French people feel about the victories of "the little corporal" in Italy?

5. Do you approve of his overthrow of the Directory?

6. Napoleon becomes first consul. Then he makes himself consul for life! Does that worry you?

© 2016 K12 Inc. All rights reserved.
Copying or distributing without K12's written consent is prohibited.

7. And how about Napoleon, the "soldier of the Revolution," becoming...*emperor?* Can you believe it? Will he carry out the goals of the Revolution—liberty, equality, and fraternity? Or will he use all his power for his own benefit and forget the rest of us?

8. Whether consul, emperor, or just plain conqueror, Napoleon leads France into 16 years of almost continuous warfare. What, *mon ami*, is your opinion of that?

9. And Napoleon topples the Spanish king and puts his brother Joseph on the throne! Tell me, does that influence your feelings about him?

10. Sum it up for me: Have your opinions on Napoleon changed over the years? Why or why not?

© 2016 K12 Inc. All rights reserved.
Copying or distributing without K12's written consent is prohibited.

Name Date 

Napoleon: Hero or Tyrant?

As you've learned, there were some positive aspects of Napoleon's rule and some negative aspects. You could say, they are two sides of the same coin. Show those two sides by drawing two political cartoons. One cartoon should show Napoleon as hero, the other Napoleon as tyrant. Remember to use the tools of the political cartoonist: symbolism, exaggeration, labeling, analogy, and irony.

Napoleon as hero

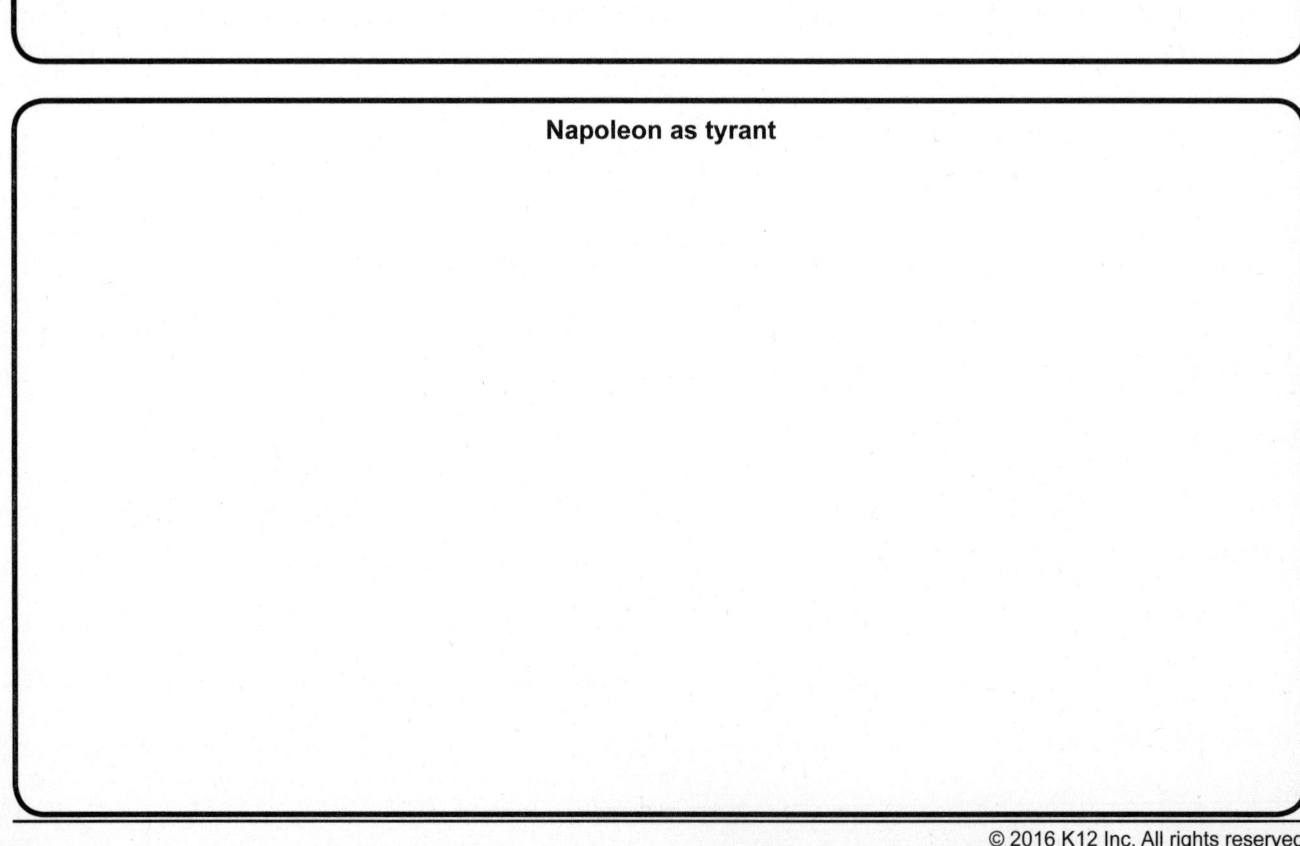

Napoleon as tyrant

© 2016 K12 Inc. All rights reserved.
Copying or distributing without K12's written consent is prohibited.

Student Guide
Lesson 4. Optional: Your Choice

PREPARE

Approximate lesson time is 60 minutes.

© 2016 K12 Inc. All rights reserved.
Copying or distributing without K12's written consent is prohibited.

Student Guide
Lesson 5: Latin American Independence Movements

Lesson Objectives

- Describe the social and political structure of Latin American colonies in 1800.
- Identify significant leaders of nineteenth century Latin American independence movements and their accomplishments and failings.
- Explain why attempts to establish republics in Latin America were less successful than in the United States.
- Identify major physical, political, and cultural features of Latin America.

PREPARE

Approximate lesson time is 60 minutes.

Materials

For the Student

- Ask the Revolutionary
- Mapping Out Latin America
- Off the Charts!
- Reading Guide

The Human Odyssey, Volume 2 edited by Klee, Cribb, and Holdren

History Journal

Keywords and Pronunciation

caudillos (kaw-DEEL-yohs) : military strongmen who seized power in South American nations after their liberation from Spain

Dolores (doh-LOH-res)

Francisco de Miranda (fran-SEES-koh day mee-RAHN-dah)

Ignacio Allende (uh-YEN-day)

José de San Martín (hoh-SAY day san mahr-TEEN)

Miguel Hidalgo y Costilla (mee-GEHL ee-DAHL-goh ee kahs-TEE-yah)

Querétaro (kay-RAY-tah-roh)

Rio de Janeiro (REE-oh day zhuh-NER-oh)

Simón Bolívar (see-MOHN buh-LEE-vahr)

LEARN

Activity 1: Latin American Independence Movements *(Offline)*

© 2016 K12 Inc. All rights reserved.
Copying or distributing without K12's written consent is prohibited.

Instructions

Day 1

Read

Read Chapter 4, from the beginning to "San Martín, Hero of the South," pages 400– 406, and complete Day 1 of the Reading Guide. When you have finished, use the Lesson Answer Key to check your work, and then place the Reading Guide in your History Journal.

Mapping Out Latin America

See what you know about the geography of this part of the world by completing each of the numbered steps on the Mapping Out Latin America sheet. You may wish to refer to the maps in the chapter and in the Atlas at the back of your textbook to complete the activity.

Day 2

Read

Read Chapter 3, from "San Martín, Hero of the South" to the end, pages 406–415, and complete Day 2 of the Reading Guide. When you have finished, use the Lesson Answer Key to check your work, and then place the Reading Guide in your History Journal.

Charting Latin America's Leaders

Show what you know about the leaders of Latin America's independence movements by filling in the boxes in the Off the Charts! sheet. (Some of the boxes have already been filled in, just to give you a head start.) Compare your answers to the suggested answers in the Lesson Answer Key.

Day 3

The Revolutionary Americas

The British colonies that became the United States and the Spanish and Portuguese colonies that became the nations of Latin America had some things in common. But their struggles for independence and their experiences after independence were quite different. See what you know about these differences by completing the Revolutionary Americas activity online.

Ask the Revolutionary

Pretend you have a chance to interview each of Latin America's revolutionary leaders about his struggle to win independence by filling out the Ask the Revolutionary sheet. When you have finished, compare your answers to those suggested in the Ask the Revolutionary Answer Key.

ASSESS

Lesson Assessment: Latin American Independence Movements (*Online*)

You will complete an online assessment covering the main objectives of this lesson. Your assessment will be scored by the computer.

© 2016 K12 Inc. All rights reserved.
Copying or distributing without K12's written consent is prohibited.

Name Date

Off the Charts!

Complete the chart by filling in the information about each leader.

	Miranda	Bolívar	San Martín	Hidalgo
Creole or peninsulare?			creole	
Born in		Venezuela		
Family background				the son of a middle class creole who ran a hacienda, or ranch
Before becoming a revolutionary				provincial creole priest
Sources of ideas, inspiration		traveled to Spain; read Enlightenment thinkers such as Locke, Voltaire, Montesquieu		

© 2016 K12 Inc. All rights reserved.
Copying or distributing without K12's written consent is prohibited.

Off the Charts!

	Miranda	Bolívar	San Martín	Hidalgo
Goals in own words			"the prompt conclusion of the war [and] the organization of the different republics"	
Territory tried to liberate			Argentina, Chile, Peru	
Difficulties		troops loyal to Spain fought back, recovered liberated territory		
Major accomplishment			served as Protector of Peru after it won its independence	

© 2016 K12 Inc. All rights reserved.
Copying or distributing without K12's written consent is prohibited.

Name Date 

Mapping Out Latin America

1. On the map, draw a line in red pencil around Latin America.
2. With a green pencil, draw a line around South America.
3. Which major Latin American country lies north of South America? Label it on the map.
4. Latin America is bordered by four bodies of water. Label them.
5. A range of mountains runs the length of South America, along the western coast. Indicate the mountain range with a series of mountain symbols (^^^^^^) and label the range.
6. Trace the course of two of South America's important rivers—the Amazon River and the Orinoco River. Label the rivers.
7. Add the following country labels:

Venezuela	Colombia	Brazil	Argentina
Chile	Peru	Ecuador	

8. Add the following city labels:

Caracas	Rio de Janeiro	Buenos Aires	Lima

© 2016 K12 Inc. All rights reserved.
Copying or distributing without K12's written consent is prohibited.

Name ______________________________ Date ______________________________ 

Reading Guide

Day 1

Read

1. Settlers in the colonies of Latin America belonged to different classes. *Peninsulares* were ____ .

2. Creoles formed another class of people in the Latin American colonies. *Creoles* were __________________________.

3. What is a *mestizo*? (If you do not remember, see page 254.)

4. Latin America stretches all the way from __________________________ in the north to the tip of ____________________ in the south.

5. Latin America is so named because the majority of the people there speak ____________ or ________________, both of which developed from Latin.

6. One of the early leaders of the Latin American independence movements was Francisco de ________________. He learned much about the political freedom when he visited ______________________ .

7. Miranda was chosen by ____________________ to lead an uprising against Spanish rule in ________________ .

8. Bolívar eagerly read Enlightenment writers such as ______________________ and ____________________ .

9. True or false? Miranda's uprising against the Spanish was successful.

10. Miranda spent his last years in __________________________________ .

© 2016 K12 Inc. All rights reserved.
Copying or distributing without K12's written consent is prohibited.

Name ______________________________ Date ______________________________ 

11. Eventually, Bolívar led a revolutionary army that freed Venezuela, whose people hailed him with the Spanish title ____________________, which in English means ____________________.

Day 2

Read

12. In which South American country was José de San Martín regarded as the greatest hero?

13. San Martín led a rebel army across the ____________________ mountains, from Argentina to ____________________.

14. Who was the Chilean with the Irish family name who became the first leader of his liberated nation?

15. Of all their colonies in South America, the Spanish prized ____________________ above the rest. After San Martín helped liberate it, he ruled it as ____________________.

16. True or false? Bolívar believed that the people of Peru were ready to rule themselves and did not need strong leadership.

17. True or false? Bolívar hoped to form a large nation covering much of South America.

18. Latin Americans often faced political chaos after winning their liberation. This allowed ______________________________________ to rise to power.

19. The people of the new Latin American nations did not have a history of electing their own representatives, passing laws, or charting their own future. That's why attempts to establish ____________________ in Latin America were less successful than in the ____________________ ____________________.

20. What was the largest colony in South America and what language did the colonists there speak?

21. When Brazil declared its independence, it was a ____________________, unlike the Spanish-speaking colonies, which became republics.

© 2016 K12 Inc. All rights reserved.
Copying or distributing without K12's written consent is prohibited.

Name Date 

22. This colonist led a rebellion against Spanish rule. The Spanish captured and executed him. But he is remembered as the father of Mexican independence. Who was he?

23. The father of Mexican independence was not a military leader or a political figure. Instead, he was a ________________ .

24. Mexico dates its independence to the day on which Father Hidalgo ________________ and gave the cry that sparked a revolution.

25. Three large bodies of water border Latin America. To the west is the ________________ Ocean, to the East is the ________________ Ocean, and to the northeast is the ________________ Sea.

26. True or false? The Alps run down the east coast of South America.

Explore and Discuss

Now that you've learned about revolutions and liberation movements in both North and South America, consider these questions:

What characteristics did colonies and liberation movements in the United States and Latin America share?

In what ways were the colonies and liberation movements in these two parts of the Americas different?

© 2016 K12 Inc. All rights reserved.
Copying or distributing without K12's written consent is prohibited.

Name Date 

Ask the Revolutionary

Pretend you are interviewing each of Latin America's revolutionary leaders about his struggle to win independence. Fill in the answers you think each leader would have given to the following questions.

Francisco de Miranda, why did your attempt to liberate Venezuela fail so badly even though you had Bolívar's support?

Simón Bolívar, what was your greatest achievement?

And what was your bitterest disappointment?

© 2016 K12 Inc. All rights reserved.
Copying or distributing without K12's written consent is prohibited.

Ask the Revolutionary

José de San Martín, you fought bravely for Spain in Europe. Why did you feel so strongly about freeing South America from Spanish rule?

What was the toughest challenge you faced?

Miguel Hidalgo y Costilla, you are remembered as the father of Mexican independence. That's a great achievement, but looking back, is there anything you would have done differently?

© 2016 K12 Inc. All rights reserved.
Copying or distributing without K12's written consent is prohibited.

Student Guide
Lesson 6: The Russia of the Romanovs

Lesson Objectives

- Describe how Russia differed from western Europe in the sixteenth and seventeenth centuries and explain why.
- Describe the social structure of Russian society.
- Identify Peter the Great.
- Locate on a map the city of St. Petersburg and the boundaries of Russia.
- Recognize the significance of warm water ports for Russia.
- Identify Catherine the Great.
- Describe the lives of Russia's serfs.
- Identify Alexander I.
- Describe the Decembrist Uprising.

PREPARE

Approximate lesson time is 60 minutes.

Materials

For the Student

- Class-Conscious Russia
- Reading Guide
- Water, Water Everywhere
- What's So Great?

The Human Odyssey, Volume 2 edited by Klee, Cribb, and Holdren

History Journal

Keywords and Pronunciation

Caucasus (KAW-kuh-suhs)

Cossacks : wild-looking Russian cavalrymen

Crimea (kriy-MEE-uh) : large peninsula on the Black Sea

Hermitage : Catherine the Great's residence, which became a center of culture and a great art museum

---

LEARN

Activity 1: The Russia of the Romanovs *(Offline)*

© 2016 K12 Inc. All rights reserved.
Copying or distributing without K12's written consent is prohibited.

Instructions

Day 1

Read

Read Chapter 5, from the beginning to "Serfdom Endures and Expands," pages 416–423, and complete Day 1 of the Reading Guide. When finished, use the Lesson Answer Key to check your work, and then place the Reading Guide in your History Journal.

Water, Water Everywhere...

See what you know about the geography of Russia, particularly its coastlines and ports. Complete the Water, Water Everywhere... sheet. When you have finished, compare your answers to those in the Lesson Answer Key.

Class-Conscious Russia

Like many countries in the seventeenth and eighteenth centuries, Russia was divided into a number of social classes. Russia, though, may have been a little more divided by class than most. See how by completing the Class-Conscious Russia sheet. When you have finished, compare your answers to those in the Lesson Answer Key.

Day 2

Read

Read Chapter 5, from "Serfdom Endures and Expands" to the end, pages 423–429, and complete Day 2 of the Reading Guide. When you have finished, use the Lesson Answer Key to check your work, and then place the Reading Guide in your History Journal.

Mapping the Growth of an Empire

Yesterday in the Water, Water Everywhere... activity, you learned that Russia was the biggest country in the world in 1689, when Peter the Great came to power. In the years that followed, the biggest country in the world grew even bigger as various rulers expanded Russia's borders. Find out more about that expansion as you complete the online Mapping the Growth of the Empire activity.

What's So Great About the Romanovs?

To learn more about the greatest achievements of Peter, Catherine, and Alexander, pretend you're a journalist conducting an interview with each of the tsars toward the end of their lives. Show what you've learned about each of the rulers by answering for them on the What's So Great About the Romanovs? sheet. You'll also want to get them to talk about their one great failure—their inability to improve the lives of Russia's serfs. When you have finished, compare your answers to those suggested in the Lesson Answer Key.

Day 3

Two Time Lines

There were dramatic changes in Russia between the time of Peter the Great and the death of Alexander I. But life was changing in the rest of Europe and the Americas, too. Compare the changes in Russia and elsewhere in the world by completing the Two Time Lines activity online.

Field Trip: Visiting St. Petersburg and Its Hermitage Museum

St. Petersburg is one of the great treasures of Russia. And the Hermitage—Catherine the Great's private residence within the Winter Palace of the Romanovs—is one of the great treasures of St. Petersburg. Today the Hermitage is a world-famous art museum in the heart of the historic city. Visit both by going to the State Hermitage Museum website.

Click the English language option. Read the two-paragraph overview of the Hermitage, then click the "Virtual Visit" icon in the upper right corner.

© 2016 K12 Inc. All rights reserved.
Copying or distributing without K12's written consent is prohibited.

Now you're ready to begin your tour of St. Petersburg and the Hermitage. Begin by taking a look at the surrounding city—Peter the Great's magnificent Window on the West. In the menu on the left, click "Outside Views" then "Views of the Historical Centre of St. Petersburg." The map will show you the location of the Hermitage, on the banks of the Neva, just where the river splits into two branches.
Check out the panoramic views. As you do so, note the modern things that would not have been there in Catherine's day: traffic lights and cars, motorized watercraft, radio or TV masts, telephone wires, the red, white, and blue flag of today's Russian state.

Next, click "Hermitage" in the upper left corner, then "Views From the Roofs" on the right. You can see the spectacular sights of St. Petersburg from the top of the Hermitage—by day, by night, under blue skies, and in mid-winter.

Note the sights that would have been there when Catherine was empress: the church spires and the grand cathedrals, sculptures, bridges, the wonderful greens, golds, yellows, and blues of the buildings, and of course, the Neva River itself.

When you've finished, write a field trip report of about a page or so on your visit to St. Petersburg and the Hermitage.

ASSESS

Lesson Assessment: The Russia of the Romanovs (*Online*)

You will complete an online assessment covering the main objectives of this lesson. Your assessment will be scored by the computer.

© 2016 K12 Inc. All rights reserved.
Copying or distributing without K12's written consent is prohibited.

Name Date 

Reading Guide

Day 1

Read

1. Name two movements that had changed the Western world by the seventeenth century but had barely touched Russia.

2. What practice or institution most differentiated Russia from the West?

3. Serfs were peasants who were bound by law to the __________ on which they worked.

4. Which tsar assumed the throne in 1689? What was his family name?

5. Peter was a great reformer. In 1696 he set off on an 18-month tour of ____________________, the first Russian ruler to venture abroad during times of ______________ .

6. Name two of Peter's reforms.

7. Perhaps Peter's greatest achievement was the construction of a port on the Baltic Sea called ____________ ______________________. His greatest failing was to leave unreformed the institution of ___________ .

8. In 1762 a German-born princess named Empress _____________________ came to the throne. She promoted _____________________ ideas and fostered the arts.

9. Catherine also modernized Russia. Name two of her reforms.

10. In the end, however, Catherine did little to improve the lot of the vast majority of her subjects—the ____________________ .

© 2016 K12 Inc. All rights reserved.
Copying or distributing without K12's written consent is prohibited.

Name _______________ Date _______________ 

Day 2

Reading Guide

11. Russia's serfs lived in single-room cabins made of ____________________. They did not own the ______________ upon which they toiled and possessed few ________________ under the law.

12. Name one of the ways in which a serf could "escape" the hardships of his life.

13. In 1801, Catherine the Great's grandson ascended the throne as ____________________. She had always referred to her beloved grandson as ____________________ .

14. How did the new tsar delight Russian liberals when he assumed power?

15. War with which country halted Alexander's plans to reform Russia?

16. In the year________, the Russians defeated the French emperor, ____________________, and forced his army to retreat from the city of ________________ .

17. After Alexander died, revolutionaries launched a failed attempt to overthrow the Russian government. Their rebellion was known as the ________________________ .

© 2016 K12 Inc. All rights reserved.
Copying or distributing without K12's written consent is prohibited.

Name Date 

Explore and Discuss

Catherine the Great's reign was characterized by good intentions that were rarely fulfilled. On page 425 of your textbook you can see some of her good intentions in the seven passages from Catherine's Instruction, which she wrote to guide officials as they drafted a new law code.

Read each passage carefully. Then go back and pick out a keyword (or several keywords) that indicate what Catherine thought was important. Select keywords that reflect her enlightened ideas and what she valued. (The first one has been filled out for you.)

1. natural liberty, supreme good
2.
3.
4.
5.
6.
7.

Like Peter the Great before her and Tsar Alexander after her, Catherine came to power as a leader who at first looked capable of delivering real change but ultimately failed to transform Russia in the way that it most needed—by abolishing serfdom.

Why, despite the efforts of these accomplished leaders, did serfdom prove so difficult to eliminate?

© 2016 K12 Inc. All rights reserved.
Copying or distributing without K12's written consent is prohibited.

Name Date 

Water, Water Everywhere

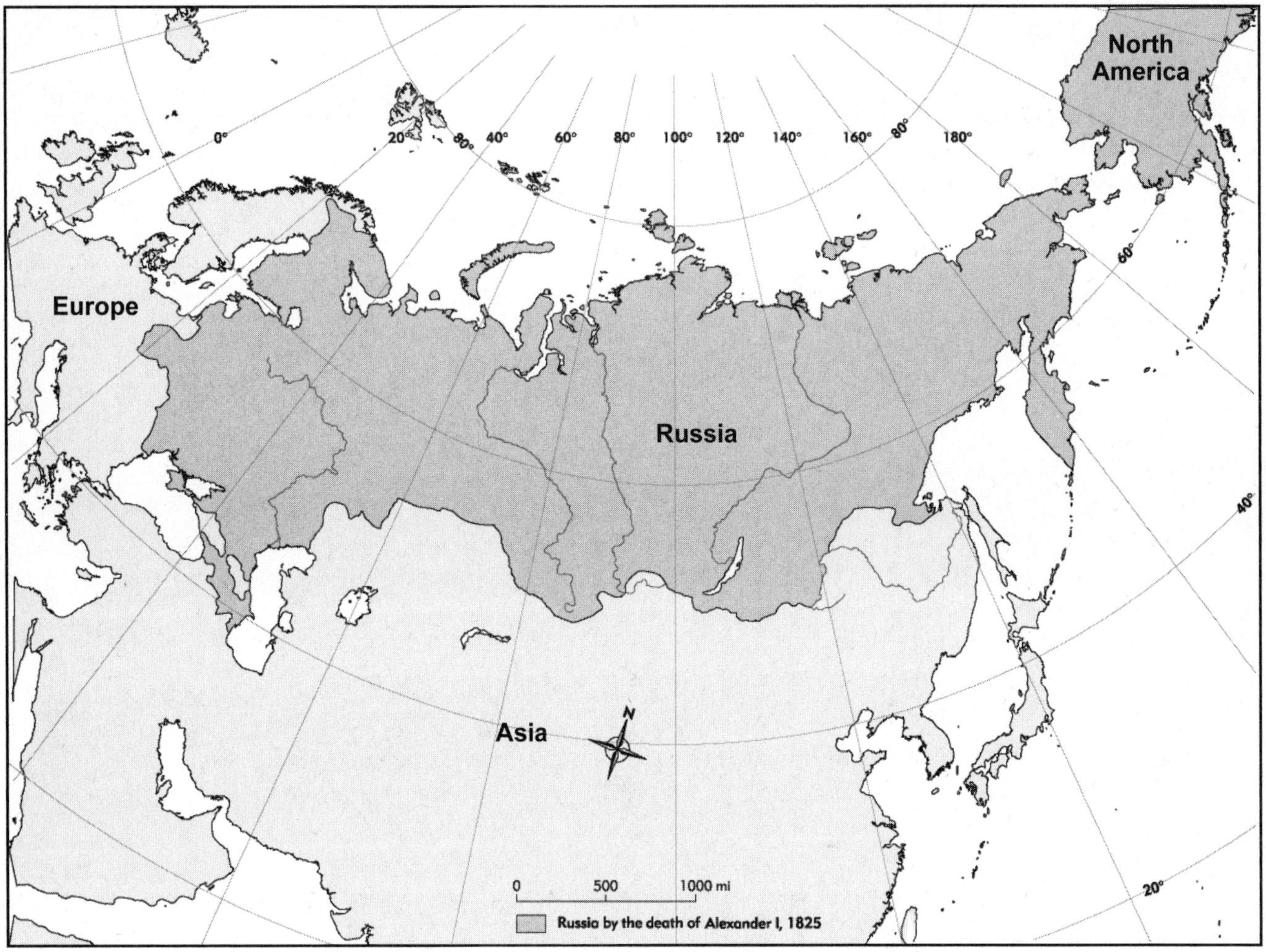

North America
Europe
Russia
Asia
0 500 1000 mi
Russia by the death of Alexander I, 1825

1. Take a good look at this map of Russia. What will immediately strike you is the size of the country; Russia was the biggest country in the world (as it still is today). It was also the country with the longest coastline in the world. Take a blue pencil and trace the various coastlines of mainland Russia. Using a ruler and the scale bar on the map, estimate the length of Russia's coastline. How long is it?

2. At about what latitude is the longest portion of Russia's coastline? Name 3 other places in the world at that latitude.

3. Label the following bodies of water. (Consult the map on page 418 of the chapter, if you need to).

Arctic Ocean	Bering Sea	Caspian Sea
Black Sea	Baltic Sea	White Sea

© 2016 K12 Inc. All rights reserved.
Copying or distributing without K12's written consent is prohibited.

Water, Water Everywhere

4. Wow! There are a lot of seas, aren't there? Now draw a dot on the map to indicate the location of the city of Archangel and then label it. It was Russia's only major port during the early part of Peter the Great's reign. Because this port is so far north, on the shores of the White Sea, it was frozen solid for six months of every year.

5. How do you think Russia's geography contributed to her lagging behind western Europe for so long?

6. Peter was determined to gain more ports for Russia. Why did he need more ports? In general, what benefits would more ports confer on Russia? Answer the questions by writing a brief paragraph.

7. Peter sent his army to fight the Turks and capture the port of Azov, which gave Russia access to the Black Sea. Draw a dot on the map to indicate the location of Azov and then label it. With a red pencil, draw an arrow from Azov through the Black Sea out into the Mediterranean Sea. It will show the route Russian ships began to take to reach the West.

8. Peter's armies also seized part of the Baltic coastline from the Swedes. There Peter built a new port city and capital for Russia—St. Petersburg. Draw a dot on the map to indicate the location of St. Petersburg and then label it. With a red pencil, draw an arrow from St. Petersburg through the Baltic Sea and out toward the rest of western Europe.

© 2016 K12 Inc. All rights reserved.
Copying or distributing without K12's written consent is prohibited.

Name Date 

Class-Conscious Russia

Each of the statements below describes the life of a typical Russian. Identify the class or position of the person.

1. "My family ruled Russia for more than 300 years. I guess you could say that, just like my father and his father before him, I'm all-powerful. I have a special title. What is it?"

2. "My family is bound to the land on which we work. We have as few rights as slaves. On official records, we are even listed as the property of those who own the fields we till. What are we known as?"

3. "We are powerful and grand figures in Russia. We own much of the country's land. We grow our whiskers long, which is in keeping with Russian tradition. Sometimes we're called nobles, but we also have another, Russian name. What is it?"

4. "I am the head of the Orthodox Church of Russia. The head of that Church has a unique name. What is it?"

5. "I am a poor man from the Russian countryside. I have a small plot of land with which I try to feed my family. What class do I belong to?"

6. "I am a believer in the new ideas from Europe that are intended to liberate people from ignorance and backwardness. What am I known as?"

© 2016 K12 Inc. All rights reserved.
Copying or distributing without K12's written consent is prohibited.

Name Date 

What's So Great About the Romanovs?

Pretend you are interviewing three of the Russian leaders: Peter the Great, Catherine the Great, and Alexander I. Fill in the answers you think each leader would have given to the following questions.

Peter the Great:
Tsar Peter, how did your country differ from the rest of Europe and the Americas when you became tsar?

Why did you feel you had to travel to western Europe in 1697?

You have never been one to be bashful about your greatest achievements. What were they?

And, if I may be so bold, Your Majesty, how about your greatest failure?

© 2016 K12 Inc. All rights reserved.
Copying or distributing without K12's written consent is prohibited.

What's So Great About the Romanovs?

Catherine the Great:
Empress, history remembers you as Catherine the Great, one of Russia's most outstanding rulers. In what ways did you modernize Russia?

Your Majesty, you were a monarch who valued education highly. Why did you think education was so important for Russians?

You like to be thought of as a new kind of Russian monarch, one inspired by the new ideas of the European Enlightenment. Why was it so difficult to make Enlightenment ideas work in Russia?

Why were you unable to end serfdom?

© 2016 K12 Inc. All rights reserved.
Copying or distributing without K12's written consent is prohibited.

What's So Great About the Romanovs?

Alexander I:
Your Majesty, you were the grandson of Catherine the Great. What can you tell me about your childhood and your early education?

Monsieur Alexander, unlike some earlier rulers, you were never known as "the Great." But what do you consider your greatest achievement?

In later years, you changed your opinion about some of the new thinking that came out of France. Why did you change your mind?

Your Majesty, why were you unable to improve the lives of the majority of your subjects, the serfs?

© 2016 K12 Inc. All rights reserved.
Copying or distributing without K12's written consent is prohibited.

Student Guide
Lesson 7: Unit Review

Lesson Objectives

- Demonstrate mastery of important knowledge and skills in this unit.

PREPARE

Approximate lesson time is 60 minutes.

LEARN
Activity 1: Age of Democratic Revolutions *(Online)*
Instructions
History Journal Review

Now, review the unit by going through your History Journal. You should:

- Look at activity sheets and Reading Guides you completed in this unit.
- Review unit keywords.
- Read through any writing assignments you completed during the unit.
- Review any offline assessments you took during the unit.

Skim through the chapters in The Human Odyssey: Our Modern World that you read in this unit.
Don't rush through. Take your time. Your History Journal is a great resource for a unit review.
Online Unit Review

Go online to review the following:

- Flash Cards: Age of Democratic Revolutions
- Declaring Independence
- Separation of Powers
- French Estates
- Political Spectrum
- Napoleon's Life
- The Revolutionary Americas
- Mapping the Growth of an Empire
- Unit 10 Review

© 2016 K12 Inc. All rights reserved.
Copying or distributing without K12's written consent is prohibited.

Student Guide
Lesson 8: Unit Assessment

Lesson Objectives

- Recognize major causes, events, and results of the American Revolution.
- Identify major causes, events, and results of independence movements in Latin America.
- Recognize major causes and events of the French Revolution.
- Summarize major ideas and the significance of key documents of the American Revolution and Republic.
- Identify key figures in the Latin American independence movements and their accomplishments.
- Identify Peter the Great, Catherine the Great, and Alexander I and their goals, accomplishments, and failures.
- Identify Napoleon and his primary accomplishments and failures.
- Explain major differences between Russia and western Europe in the seventeenth and eighteenth centuries.
- Summarize the attitude of most colonists toward Britain in 1763 and the reasons for their attitude.
- Summarize the circumstances and events that led to the French Revolution.
- Describe Napoleon's reforms and their significance to the people of France.
- Identify on a map major physical and political features of Europe.
- Describe the social and political structure of Latin American colonies in 1800.
- Identify major physical, political, and cultural features of Latin America.
- Trace significant positions on the political spectrum.
- Identify important physical and political features on maps of Europe and Latin America.
- Identify significant individuals and their contributions to the American Revolution and early republic.

PREPARE

Approximate lesson time is 60 minutes.

Materials

For the Student

Question Review Table

ASSESS

Unit Assessment: Age of Democratic Revolutions, Part 1 (*Online*)

Complete the computer-scored portion of the Unit Assessment. When you have finished, complete the teacher-scored portion of the assessment and submit it to your teacher.

© 2016 K12 Inc. All rights reserved.
Copying or distributing without K12's written consent is prohibited.

Unit Assessment: Age of Democratic Revolutions, Part 2 (*Offline*)

Complete the teacher-scored portion of the Unit Assessment and submit it to your teacher.

LEARN

Activity 1. Optional: Optional Unit Assessment Review Table *(Online)*

© 2016 K12 Inc. All rights reserved.
Copying or distributing without K12's written consent is prohibited.

Assessment Date

Unit 10: Age of Democratic Revolutions

Before you retake the Unit Assessment, use the table to figure out which activities you should review.

Question Review Table

Circle the numbers of the questions that you missed on the Unit Assessment. Review the activities that correspond with these questions.

Age of Democratic Revolutions, Part 1

Question	Lesson	Review Activity
1	1: The World Turned Upside Down: The American Revolution 5: Latin American Independence Movements	Declaring and Winning Independence Latin American Independence Movements
2, 7	2: The French Revolution	The French Revolution
3,4	5: Latin American Independence Movements	Latin American Independence Movements
5,6	1: The World Turned Upside Down: The American Revolution	Declaring and Winning Independence
8,9,10,11	3: Napoleon: From Revolution to Empire	Napoleon: From Revolution to Empire
12	3: Napoleon: From Revolution to Empire 5: Latin American Independence Movements 6: The Russia of the Romanovs	Napoleon: From Revolution to Empire Latin American Independence Movements The Russia of the Romanovs
13,14	6: The Russia of the Romanovs	The Russia of the Romanovs

© 2016 K12 Inc. All rights reserved.
Copying or distributing without K12's written consent is prohibited.

Age of Democratic Revolutions, Part 1

Question	Lesson	Review Activity
1, 2, 3, 6,7,8	6: The Russia of the Romanovs	The Russia of the Romanovs
4	2: The French Revolution	The French Revolution
5	1: The World Turned Upside Down: The American Revolution 2: The French Revolution	Declaring and Winning Independence The French Revolution

© 2016 K12 Inc. All rights reserved.
Copying or distributing without K12's written consent is prohibited.

Student Guide
Unit 11: Revolutions in Arts, Industries, and Work
Lesson 1: Romantic Art in an Age of Revolution

Lesson Objectives

- Recognize that the early nineteenth century revolution in the arts known as Romanticism rejected the ideas of the Enlightenment.
- Describe Romanticism.
- Identify Jean-Jacques Rousseau.
- Identify major writers, artists, and composers of the Romantic period and the kinds of works they are known for.

PREPARE

Approximate lesson time is 60 minutes.

Materials

For the Student

- Reading Guide
- Romanticism's Other Target
- What Makes a Painting "Romantic"?

The Human Odyssey, Volume 2 edited by Klee, Cribb, and Holdren

History Journal

Keywords and Pronunciation

Strum und Drang (shturm oont DRAHNG)
Émile (ay-MEEL)
Eugene Delacroix (del-uh-KWAH)
Franz Joseph Haydn (frahnz YOH-sef HIY-dn)
Horatii (huh-RAY-shee-iy)
Jacques-Louis David (zhahk LOO-ee dah-veed)
Jean-Jacques Rousseau (zhahn-zhahk roo-SOH)
Johann Wolfgang von Goethe (YOH-hahn VOULF-gahng vahn GUR-tuh)
Ludwig van Beethoven (LOOD-vihg vahn BAY-toh-vuhn)
Wolfgang Amadeus Mozart (WOULF-gang ahm-uh-DAY-uhs MOHT-sahrt)

LEARN
Activity 1: Romantic Art in an Age of Revolution *(Offline)*

© 2016 K12 Inc. All rights reserved.
Copying or distributing without K12's written consent is prohibited.

Instructions

This lesson is designed to be completed in **2** class sessions.

Day 1

Read

Read Chapter 6, from the beginning to "John Constable: Painter of Gentle Landscapes," pages 430–438, and complete Day 1 of the Reading Guide. When you have finished, you should use the Lesson Answer Key to check your work, and then place the Reading Guide in your History Journal.

Enlightenment versus Romanticism

Romanticism differed from the earlier thinking of the Enlightenment in many ways. See just how these two movements were different by completing the Enlightenment versus Romanticism online activity.

Let's Get Romantic

Romanticism affected all areas of artistic endeavor. Today, we'll take a quick look at writers whose words show what it meant to be part of the Romantic movement. Complete the Romantic Words online activity to see the boldness, passion, and "wildness" of these Romantic writers.

Romanticism's Other Target: The Industrial Revolution

You've seen how Romanticism reacted against the ideas of the Enlightenment. It also rebelled against another historical development that was transforming the face of the Western world—the Industrial Revolution.

By completing the Satanic Mills sheet, you will see how one English poet, William Blake, viewed the changes taking place in his country.

Day 2

Read

Read Chapter 6, from "John Constable: Painter of Gentle Landscapes" to the end of the chapter, pages 438–443, and complete Day 2 of the Reading Guide. When you have finished, you should use the Lesson Answer Key to check your work, and then place the Reading Guide in your History Journal.

What Makes a Painting "Romantic"?

We've seen how Romantic writers expressed themselves. Now we're going to consider how the Romantic movement affected painters. Complete the Romantic Painting sheet.

ASSESS

Lesson Assessment: Romantic Art in an Age of Revolution (*Online*)

You will complete an online assessment covering the main objectives of this lesson. Your assessment will be scored by the computer.

LEARN

Activity 2. Optional: Romantic Art in an Age of Revolution *(Online)*

© 2016 K12 Inc. All rights reserved.
Copying or distributing without K12's written consent is prohibited.

Name Date 

Romantic Art

Chapter Six describes Eugene Delacroix as the Byron of painters. Look at the painting of that great English poet, Lord Byron, during the Greek War of Independence, on page 437 of the textbook. Doesn't Byron look every inch a symbol of the "free man"—an individual not bound to the routine of an increasingly mechanized, impersonal world? He appears as a champion of a great cause, a man who shapes his own destiny.

These are the Romantic qualities that helped inspire Delacroix. Let's consider in more detail his painting *Liberty Leading the People,* which you can find on page 440 of your textbook.

Answer the following questions about the painting:

1. What historical event does *Liberty Leading the People* depict?

2. What viewpoint or attitude toward the event do you think Delacroix tried to convey?

3. Who is holding aloft the French flag and what is she doing?

4. What kinds and classes of people are depicted? Why?

5. Why do you think Delacroix painted himself—the well-dressed man with the top hat—into the scene?

6. What emotions does the painting evoke?

© 2016 K12 Inc. All rights reserved.
Copying or distributing without K12's written consent is prohibited.

Name ____________________ Date ____________________ 

Reading Guide

Day 1

Read

Reading Guide

1. Romanticism was a reaction against the order, harmony, and reason of the ____________ period. It represented a revolution in the ____________ .

2. Instead of emphasizing order, harmony, and reason, Romanticism sought truth in ____________.

3. Name the French philosophe who paved the way for the Romantic movement and name two of his beliefs.

4. Complete his famous quote: "Man is born free, and ____________________ ."

5. What was the name and nationality of the author of *The Sorrows of Young Werther?* He was a member of the *Sturm und Drang* movement of authors. What does Sturm und Drang mean?

6. Name the poet who found inspiration in the natural beauty of the English Lake District.

7. Byron traveled to __________ to help its people fight against the Ottomans. He once declared, "I was born for ____________ ."

Day 2

Read

Reading Guide

8. ____________ was a landscape artist who loved to paint the scenery where he grew up, around the River Stour in ____________ .

9. ______________ was a French painter who loved to paint scenes from the exotic places he visited. He also painted *Liberty Leading the People* during the 1830 rebellion.

© 2016 K12 Inc. All rights reserved.
Copying or distributing without K12's written consent is prohibited.

Name Date

10. ____________________ was a German Romantic artist who painted wild landscapes, such as rocky seacoasts and dark forests.

11. Name the composer who began in the Classical style, became increasingly influenced by Romanticism, and whose music was inspired by the natural world.

Explore and Discuss

As you've seen, Romanticism was very much a reaction against the emphasis on reason that was so important to the Enlightenment. It was also a reaction against the Industrial Revolution with its factories and pollution and overcrowded living conditions that, as you'll see in a later lesson, was starting to spread across Europe.

Why might Romanticism have been at odds with such developments?

© 2016 K12 Inc. All rights reserved.
Copying or distributing without K12's written consent is prohibited.

Name Date 

Satanic Mills

Read the poem "Jerusalem" by William Blake, and then answer the questions that follow.

Jerusalem

And did those feet in ancient time
Walk upon England's mountain green?
And was the holy Lamb of God
On England's pleasant pastures seen?

And did the Countenance Divine
Shine forth upon our clouded hills?
And was Jerusalem builded here
Among these dark Satanic mills?

Bring me my bow of burning gold!
Bring me my arrows of desire!
Bring me my spear! O clouds, unfold!
Bring me my chariot fire.

I will not cease from mental fight,
Nor shall my sword sleep in my hand
'Til we have built Jerusalem
In England's green and pleasant land.

1. In the first stanza, how does Blake describe England in that "ancient time" before industrialization?

2. In the second stanza, into what does the Industrial Revolution turn England?

3. What image does Blake evoke in the third stanza?

4. In the fourth stanza, what course of action does he propose?

© 2016 K12 Inc. All rights reserved.
Copying or distributing without K12's written consent is prohibited.

Student Guide
Lesson 2: Britain Begins the Industrial Revolution

Lesson Objectives

- Define Industrial Revolution.
- Identify the factors that allowed the Industrial Revolution to begin first in England.
- Identify Adam Smith and what he is known for.
- Summarize the major ideas of *The Wealth of Nations.*
- Describe the advances made in the textile industry in England in the eighteenth century.
- Describe the beginnings of the coal and iron industries.
- Identify the achievements of individuals who made major contributions to the Industrial Revolution in England.
- Explain the significance of the steam engine to industry.
- Recognize that the changes in manufacturing brought hardships to many people.

PREPARE

Approximate lesson time is 60 minutes.

Materials

For the Student

- In Grandma's Day
- Reading Guide
- The Wealth of Nations
- Why Britain?

The Human Odyssey, Volume 2 edited by Klee, Cribb, and Holdren

History Journal

LEARN

Activity 1: Britain Begins the Industrial Revolution *(Offline)*

Instructions

This lesson is designed to be completed in 3 class sessions.

Day 1

Read

Read Chapter 7, from the beginning to "From Handmade to Machine-made," pages 444–449, and complete Day 1 of the Reading Guide. When you have finished, use the Lesson Answer Key to check your work, and then place the Reading Guide in your History Journal.

A Wealth of Meaning in The Wealth of Nations

Carry out some primary source analysis by completing the Wealth of Nations sheet. When you have finished, use the answer key to check your work.

© 2016 K12 Inc. All rights reserved.
Copying or distributing without K12's written consent is prohibited.

You've Got to Hand It to Mr. Smith!

See how Adam Smith's capitalist economy can work for the good of all by completing the Invisible Hand activity online.

Day 2

Read

Read Chapter 7, from "From Handmade to Machine-made" to the end of the chapter, pages 451–457, and complete Day 2 of the Reading Guide. When you have finished, use the Lesson Answer Key to check your work, and then place the Reading Guide in your History Journal.

Why Britain?

Why did the Industrial Revolution begin in Great Britain? Because of Adam Smith? No, not just because of Adam Smith, although he was an important contributor. In the eighteenth century, all the necessary factors came together in Britain. See what they were by completing the Why Britain? sheet. When you have finished, use the answer key to check your work.

Building a Better Mousetrap

Inventors are always trying to come up with improved ways of doing things and constructing machines that operate more efficiently. It's a bit like building a better mousetrap!

See how British inventors during the Industrial Revolution took machines and methods that already existed, and then improved them, by completing the Better Mousetrap activity online.

Day 3

"Ah, the Changes I've Seen…"

Pretend you lived during the Industrial Revolution in Great Britain—and that when your grandmother was a child, many of the changes brought about by the Industrial Revolution had not yet taken place.

Like many kids, you just can't imagine how things were before so many important inventions changed life so completely. And like many grandparents, Grandma has seen a lot of the changes take place.

You've got a lot of questions for her. Complete the In Grandma's Day sheet by filling out the answers Grandma might have provided.

Activity 2. Optional: Britain Begins the Industrial Revolution *(Online)*

ASSESS

Lesson Assessment: Britain Begins the Industrial Revolution (*Online*)

You will complete an online assessment covering the main objectives of this lesson. Your assessment will be scored by the computer.

© 2016 K12 Inc. All rights reserved.
Copying or distributing without K12's written consent is prohibited.

Why Britain?

Here are the factors that led to the Industrial Revolution in Britain. In the spaces provided, complete the explanation of the importance of each of the factors.

Abundant water power to

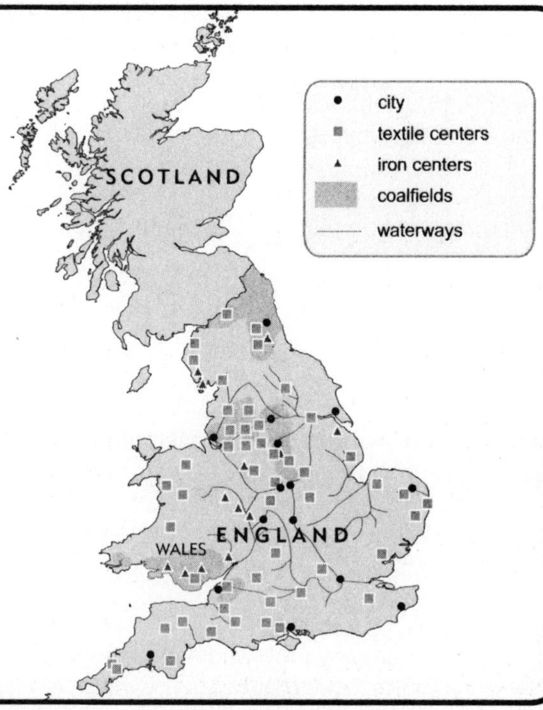

Banks willing to lend money, or capital, in support of

Textile industry inventions such as

Plentiful supplies of iron ore for the manufacture of

Plentiful supplies of coal for

Growing city populations for

Good harbors and ships for

Inventors and thinkers such as

Smith supporters in government who

© 2016 K12 Inc. All rights reserved.
Copying or distributing without K12's written consent is prohibited.

Name Date 

The Wealth of Nations

You've probably read books such as the plays of Shakespeare or the King James version of the Bible that are written in an older kind of English that sounds strange to the modern ear. Well, Adam Smith didn't exactly live in the days of King James, but he did live more than two hundred years ago. And back then, the English that people spoke wasn't what we would call "modern."

Not surprisingly, therefore, Smith's *Wealth of Nations* uses language that may at first appear hard to understand. But with a little work, it's not too difficult to figure out what he was saying and to translate it into today's English.

Take, for example, Smith's opening statement on page 450 of the textbook:

"The greatest improvements in the productive powers of labor…seem to have been the effects of the division of labor."

Today we might say something like this:

The best way to get improved results from workers is to have each of them perform a different task in the manufacturing process.

Now "translate" into everyday speech the following excerpts from *The Wealth of Nations,* which are also taken from page 450 of the textbook:

1. "[Shoemakers] find it for their interest to employ their whole industry in a way in which they have some advantage over their neighbors, and to purchase…whatever else they have occasion for."

   Translation:

2. "Man has almost constant occasion for the help of his brethren, and it is in vain for him to expect it from their benevolence only."

   Translation:

3. "He will be more likely to prevail if he can interest their self-love in his favor, and show them that it is for their own advantage to do for him what he requires of them."

   Translation:

4. "…any man [who] employs capital in the support of industry…neither intends to promote the public interest…He intends only his own gain; and he is in this…led by an invisible hand to promote an end which was no part of his intention."

© 2016 K12 Inc. All rights reserved.
Copying or distributing without K12's written consent is prohibited.

Name Date 

Translation:

5. “By pursuing his own interest, he frequently promotes that of the society more effectually than when he really intends to promote it.”

Translation:

© 2016 K12 Inc. All rights reserved.
Copying or distributing without K12’s written consent is prohibited.

Name ______________________________ Date ______________________________ 

Reading Guide

Day 1

Read

Reading Guide

1. If *industry* is how things are made, and a *revolution* is an extreme change, then what is an industrial revolution?

2. The Industrial Revolution replaced human and animal power with ______________ power.

3. During the Industrial Revolution, people moved from the____________ to ____________ .
   In addition, _____________ replaced______________ as the centers of production.

4. In which country did the Industrial Revolution begin?

5. Adam Smith was born in______________, he wrote a book called __________________,
   and today is considered to be the father of___________________ .

6. Smith believed that the actions of government often hurt the proper functioning of the economy. Name one such government action.

7. In *The Wealth of Nations,* Smith wrote that markets produced the things that society needed because of the operation of the "_______________ hand." This idea forms the basis of a ________________ economy.

8. According to Smith, the economy worked best when consumers and producers acted in their own self-_________________.

9. Smith also believed that groups of businessmen, known as monopolies, could also hurt the economy. What did he think monopolies would do?

© 2016 K12 Inc. All rights reserved.
Copying or distributing without K12's written consent is prohibited.

Name ______________________________ Date ______________________________ 

Day 2

Read

Reading Guide

10. In which industry did the Industrial Revolution begin?

11. ____________________ invented the flying shuttle, and ____________________ invented the spinning jenny.

12. Richard Arkwright's ____________________ could make stronger thread than the spinning jenny, and it could make 80 strands at once.

13. Edmund Cartwright invented a mechanical loom powered by a ____________________ or a ____________________ .

14. What important source of power lay beneath England's central and northern hills—a resource important to the development of the iron industry?

15. Underground springs often flooded coal mines and had to be pumped out with a crude steam engine known as the Miner's Friend. Name the University of Glasgow student asked to repair one of these broken-down engines in 1763.

16. This Scottish student went on to invent his own, improved ____________-driven steam engine that could power all kinds of machines and gave a huge boost to the Industrial Revolution.

17. An English immigrant to the United States named ____________________ brought with him extensive knowledge of textile machinery. He built America's first successful ____________________ .

18. Because of steam power, ships no longer had to depend on ________________, and mills no longer had to use ________________ for power. Steam-powered machines could work at rates faster than ________________ ever could.

19. Despite its advantages, the Industrial Revolution also brought many hardships. Name two.

© 2016 K12 Inc. All rights reserved.
Copying or distributing without K12's written consent is prohibited.

Name Date 

Short Answer Questions

What was so revolutionary about the Industrial Revolution? In other words, what was the great change that came about because of the Industrial Revolution?

Which countries did the Industrial Revolution first affect?

Even though the Industrial Revolution began in the eighteenth century, not all countries today have undergone an industrial revolution. Why not?

© 2016 K12 Inc. All rights reserved.
Copying or distributing without K12's written consent is prohibited.

Name Date 

In Grandma's Day

1. Grandma, when you were young, you worked at home and spun wool into yarn. But that was before the Industrial Revolution. What kind of spinning wheel did you use?

2. Didn't work back then seem very slow and leisurely?

3. In those days before there were textile mills, you worked in your own home—a cottage in a small village. How did you like that way of working?

4. Some people hated the new machines. When they began to appear, were you worried they would threaten your job?

5. And then you had to leave the countryside and move to the city for a new job in the growing textile industry. Did you go willingly? Was your new house nice or did you have to live in horrible slums?

6. What was the biggest difference made by machines like the flying shuttle and the spinning jenny?

7. How did your life change when you began to work with the new machines? Was it better or worse than before? Did you feel you were rushing all the time?

8. Do you think the cloth made by machines was better—or was it just produced faster?

9. Looking back, are you nostalgic for "the old days"? What do you miss most?

10. What is the best thing the Industrial Revolution has brought us?

© 2016 K12 Inc. All rights reserved.
Copying or distributing without K12's written consent is prohibited.

Student Guide
Lesson 3. Optional: Your Choice

PREPARE

Approximate lesson time is 60 minutes.

© 2016 K12 Inc. All rights reserved.
Copying or distributing without K12's written consent is prohibited.

Student Guide
Lesson 4: A Revolution in Transportation and Communication

Lesson Objectives

- Describe the need for better roads in the 1700s and 1800s and the attempts to improve roads.
- Explain how better transportation led to more trade and lower prices for goods.
- Describe the rise of canal building in the late 1700s and early 1800s.
- Identify Fulton and his contribution to steam-powered boats.
- Identify Stephenson and his contribution to railroad travel.
- Trace the development of railroads in the first half of the nineteenth century.
- Recognize the changes that the revolution in transportation and manufacturing brought.
- Identify Morse and his contribution to rapid communication.

PREPARE

Approximate lesson time is 60 minutes.

Materials

For the Student

A Day in the Life

Reading Guide

The Human Odyssey, Volume 2 edited by Klee, Cribb, and Holdren

History Journal

LEARN

Activity 1: A Revolution in Transportation and Communication *(Offline)*

Instructions

This lesson is designed to be completed in 3 class sessions.

Day 1

Read

Read Chapter 8, from the beginning to the end of page 467, and complete Day 1 of the Reading Guide. When you have finished, use the Lesson Answer Key to check your work, and then place the Reading Guide in your History Journal.

When It's Easier by Water

The Erie Canal has been called the Eighth Wonder of the World. Over the centuries, lots of things have been dubbed the Eighth Wonder of the World—yet the canal is a spectacular engineering feat.

Go online and find out just how spectacular it is by taking a virtual tour at the Erie Canal. There, you'll be able to see historical and contemporary images of the canal, its locks, aqueducts, and bridges, as well as read about its history.

© 2016 K12 Inc. All rights reserved.
Copying or distributing without K12's written consent is prohibited.

Then use what you've learned on the website and its various subsites to answer the following questions in your History Journal. Compare your answers with those in the Lesson Answer Key.

1. Which two bodies of water does the Erie Canal link?
2. Why was the canal called "Clinton's big ditch"?
3. Why did canals have towpaths?
4. What is the purpose of locks?
5. Compare some of the historical and contemporary photographs and images of the Erie Canal. What is the canal most often used for today?

The "Rail Way" to Develop Industry

A first train ride is always an exciting event. Fanny Kemble, a popular British actress of the early nineteenth century, certainly thought so.

George Stephenson invited Kemble to the opening of the Liverpool and Manchester Railway. Go online and read Kemble's account of her first train ride to Manchester (be sure to scroll down the page).

The two cities linked by the railroad, Liverpool and Manchester, became major industrial centers in a rapidly industrializing Britain. The "starved-looking weaver" in Kemble's account seemed to realize what the arrival of the railroad meant. It meant "the triumph of machinery"—or in other words, of industrialization.

Review how the establishment of railroads spurred industrial development by answering these questions in your History Journal.

1. British railroads began to link towns that grew into major industrial centers. Why did towns with railroad stations develop more quickly than those without them? Why did rail transportation spur industrialization?
2. The building of a railroad was itself a major undertaking, creating jobs for thousands of workers and requiring shipments of various kinds of raw materials and finished products. Name some of the jobs that would be created in a city—and the kinds of products and materials that would be required—when the city's leaders decided to build and operate a railroad line.
3. Today, railroads and locomotives evoke strong emotions in many people, such as nostalgia, sentimentality, and romanticism. This is especially true about steam engines. But nowadays, even though railroads are still important for hauling freight, they carry fewer passengers than in the past. If you have never traveled by train, would you like to? Explain the reasons for your answer. If you have traveled by train, describe the experience.

Day 2

Read

Read Chapter 8, from "On the Move" to the end of the chapter, pages 468–473, and complete Day 2 of the Reading Guide. When you have finished, use the Lesson Answer Key to check your work, and then place the Reading Guide in your History Journal.

Talking in Code

Morse developed a code that used dots (.) and dashes (-) to represent letters of the alphabet. Every letter in the alphabet was represented by a combination of dots or dashes. For example, in Morse Code the letter a is represented by a dot and a dash (.-), and the letter o by three dashes (---).

© 2016 K12 Inc. All rights reserved.
Copying or distributing without K12's written consent is prohibited.

A telegraph operator could use this code to send a message immediately to another telegraph operator, miles away. First he would take his message and convert it into Morse Code. Then he would tap out on a telegraph line the dots and dashes of the coded message, using pauses in his tapping to indicate the beginning of a new word.

The "receiving" operator would do the reverse. First he would record the series of dots and dashes—the message in Morse Code. Then he would translate the coded message of dots and dashes into regular letters and words.

Go online and check out Morse's alphabet at the GCI Morse Code Translator website.

The first coded message that Morse sent across the telegraph was this one:

What Hath God Wrought

This is how those four words look in Morse Code (with forward slashes to indicate a pause that separated the words):

.-- .... .- - / .... .- - .... / --. --- -.. / .-- .-. --- ..- --. .... -

WHAT HATH GOD WROUGHT

Below is another coded message using Morse's system of dots and dashes. Decipher the message using the online guide at the GCI Morse Code Translator website. Then follow the instructions given in the message.

– — ...- . / — -. / - — / - .... . / -. . -..- - / .- -.-. - .. ...- .. - -.–

A Day in the Life…

Think about all the usual things you do on a day-to-day basis—what you eat, what you wear, where you go, and other things like that.

For example, you might have orange juice from Florida and cereal from the Midwest for breakfast. You might ride to the mall in a car manufactured in Japan that runs on fuel brought from oilfields in the Middle East. You might walk around the mall in sneakers made in Thailand as you shop for a shirt exported from China or a sweater from Ireland. For lunch, who knows? Mexican tacos? An Italian submarine sandwich? French fries? When you get home, you want to check in with some friends to make plans for the weekend. Do you pick up the phone? Type out an e-mail? Or send an instant message or a text message?

You'll continue with this activity tomorrow. For the moment, just think about the things you do on a typical day.

Day 3

A Day in the Life (continued)…

Complete the activity you began last time by filling out the A Day in the Life sheet.

© 2016 K12 Inc. All rights reserved.
Copying or distributing without K12's written consent is prohibited.

ASSESS

Lesson Assessment: A Revolution in Transportation and Communication (*Online*)

You will complete an online assessment covering the main objectives of this lesson. Your assessment will be scored by the computer.

© 2016 K12 Inc. All rights reserved.
Copying or distributing without K12's written consent is prohibited.

Name Date 

A Day in the Life

In the spaces in the left column, list ten things that you regularly do on any given day. When you have finished, list in the right column how you would have done those things had you lived in the late 1700s.

Imagine having to *walk* to a friend's house to set up plans for a day together! Makes you wonder what you do with all that "extra" time in your day, doesn't it?

Daily Life Today	Daily Life in the Late 1700s

© 2016 K12 Inc. All rights reserved.
Copying or distributing without K12's written consent is prohibited.

Name ______________________________ Date ______________________________ 

Reading Guide

Day 1

Read

Reading Guide

1. Describe the condition of roads in the late 1700s.

2. What effect might the condition of roads have on trade? Why?

3. ____________________ were roads with gates and guards and could only be used after payment of a toll.

4. Name one advantage of the slightly raised roads built by John McAdam on a foundation of crushed rock.

5. In the early 1800s, improved roads in Britain led to increased trade and lower____________.

6. The realization that it has always been easier to move heavy cargo over_____________ than over land led to a surge in the building of______________in the late 1700s and early 1800s.

7. Describe the development of canals in Britain.

8. Canal building also became popular in the United States. Name a famous American canal.

9. _________________ gets popular credit for "inventing the steamboat." He was not only a gifted inventor, but he was also a good_______________who managed to establish a regular steamboat service.

© 2016 K12 Inc. All rights reserved.
Copying or distributing without K12's written consent is prohibited.

Name ______________________________ Date ______________________________

10. In addition to sailing on rivers and lakes, some steamboats even made it across the ______________ Ocean.

11. Name the inventor of the *Rocket*—the man acknowledged as the "Father of the Railroad."

12. As with canal construction, railroad construction also took off in ______________________, where some began talking of building a railroad all the way to the Pacific Ocean.

Day 2

Read

Reading Guide

13. How did the transportation revolution also lead to a manufacturing revolution?

14. ______________________ invented the electric telegraph, as well as a special code to use on the telegraph, called ______________________.

15. How did the electric telegraph spread across the United States?

Explore and Discuss

What means of transportation or communication breakthroughs might the future still hold? How would they affect you, the society in general, and our economy?

© 2016 K12 Inc. All rights reserved.
Copying or distributing without K12's written consent is prohibited.

Student Guide
Lesson 5: Hard Times

Lesson Objectives

- Describe conditions for factory workers in the early nineteenth century.
- Recognize that the workforce included children as young as six and women who were paid less than men.
- Describe living conditions for poor workers in industrial cities.
- Explain the link between lack of sanitation and disease and death rates.
- Identify Charles Dickens and the impact of his writing.
- Identify Queen Victoria.
- Give examples of attempted reforms in industrial cities.
- Identify Karl Marx and what he is known for.
- Summarize the major ideas in Marx's writing.
- Identify Charles Darwin and what he is known for.
- Summarize the major ideas in Darwin's writing.
- Recognize that Thomas Malthus's ideas about population growth influenced politics and literature.

PREPARE

Approximate lesson time is 60 minutes.

Materials

For the Student

- Child Labor
- Oily Business
- Reading Guide

The Human Odyssey, Volume 2 edited by Klee, Cribb, and Holdren

History Journal

Keywords and Pronunciation

Das Kapital (dahs kahp-ee-TAHL)

bourgeoisie (bourzh-wah-ZEE) : the middle class

communism : economic system envisioned by Karl Marx in which the government plans the economy and owns most of the land, factories, and other property, and all citizens share in the common wealth

Galápagos (guh-LAH-puh-guhs)

proletariat : factory laborers and others who work for wages

© 2016 K12 Inc. All rights reserved.
Copying or distributing without K12's written consent is prohibited.

LEARN

Activity 1: Hard Times *(Offline)*

Instructions

This lesson is designed to be completed in 3 class sessions.

Day 1

Read

Read Chapter 9, from the beginning to "Karl Marx Criticizes Capitalism," pages 475–483, and complete Day 1 of the Reading Guide. When you have finished, use the Lesson Answer Key to check your work, and then place the Reading Guide in your History Journal.

How Hard Was It?

There are many elements in the study of history. It is the study of famous people. It is the chronology of key events. And it's an examination of the "forces" that make things happen. History is also the study of ordinary people doing "ordinary" things. Ordinary people are a major part of history, too.

You will go online to look at primary sources that shed light on the ordinary people of the mid and late 1800s. As you look at these primary sources, complete the Child Labor activity.

How Hard Are Things Today?

Now that you've looked at primary sources that shed light on the ordinary people of the mid and late 1800s, take a look at how things have changed today. Find out more about current child labor laws in the United States.

Go online and visit the Child Labor Education Project: U.S. Federal Child Labor Law website, and then answer the following questions in your History Journal:

1. What is the minimum age for (nonagricultural) employment?
2. How many hours a week may someone of this age work when school is in session and when it is not?
3. What is the federal minimum wage?
4. What do you think is the worst teen job and why?

What Should Have Been Done?

There is a saying—hindsight is 20/20. This means that when we look at the past, we have perfect vision. Of course, that isn't always the case. We don't know what would have happened in history if people had done things differently, or what influenced them at the time. But thinking about what should have been done in the past can help us understand things more fully.

Using your perfect, 20/20 vision, write in your History Journal an account of what might have been done about:

- child labor
- women's wages
- safety in the workplace
- working conditions in general.

If you do not have enough time to complete this activity on Day 1, begin your Day 2 lesson by completing this activity.

© 2016 K12 Inc. All rights reserved.
Copying or distributing without K12's written consent is prohibited.

Read Chapter 9, from “Karl Marx Criticizes Capitalism” to “Darwin Sees Competition in Nature,” pages 483–486, and complete Day 2 of the Reading Guide. When you have finished, use the Lesson Answer Key to check your work, and then place the Reading Guide in your History Journal.

Communism on the Move

From its origins with Marx, Engels, and a handful of followers, communism spread to dominate some parts of the world. Go online and see how the ideas of Marx gained popularity by completing the Communism on the Move activity.

Day 3

Read

Read Chapter 9, from “Darwin Sees Competition in Nature” to the end, pages 486–489, and complete Day 3 of the Reading Guide. When you have finished, use the Lesson Answer Key to check your work, and then place the Reading Guide in your History Journal.

Theoretically Speaking...

Darwin’s writings, and the work of the many scientists who have followed him, are still controversial today. Members of your family may have different views on “Darwinism.” Discuss what you’ve learned with an adult.

Mankind’s Ongoing Struggle

Darwin and Malthus talked about the struggle for limited resources—and the impact that this struggle may have had. We still live in a world of limited resources. For most people in the United States and other wealthy countries, life is not a struggle for food. In many parts of the world, however, it is. Even in the richest nations, some resources are limited. Oil is a good example of a limited resource.

Find out the impact a limited supply of oil has had—and may have in the future—by completing the Oily Business activity.

ASSESS

Lesson Assessment: Hard Times (*Online*)

You will complete an online assessment covering the main objectives of this lesson. Your assessment will be scored by the computer.

© 2016 K12 Inc. All rights reserved.
Copying or distributing without K12’s written consent is prohibited.

Name Date 

Oily Business

Oilfields around the world produce petroleum that is turned into the gasoline we use in automobiles. But there is a limited supply of oil on Earth—and an ever-increasing demand. What effects will this have?

1. What will happen to gasoline prices if demand increases and supplies remain the same or drop?

2. What effect will the cost of gasoline have on the demand for various types of vehicles? What automobiles are likely to sell well? Why?

3. What effect will sales of certain types of cars and trucks have on employment in cities like Detroit where the manufacturing of most large vehicles takes place?

4. How might automobile manufacturing in Detroit change?

5. How might gasoline prices affect sales of motor scooters?

6. On a bigger scale, how might the struggle for limited oil resources affect relations between countries?

© 2016 K12 Inc. All rights reserved.
Copying or distributing without K12's written consent is prohibited.

Name Date 

Child Labor

Primary sources like the one you are about to read give historians remarkable insight into the past. In the 1830s, reformers in the British Parliament began to interview young people about their working conditions in factories. Read the following firsthand account of questions posed to a young woman named Elizabeth Bentley and the answers she provided. When you have finished, answer the questions that follow.

> At what age did you begin to work at a factory?
> *When I was six years old.*
>
> What were your hours of labour in the mill?
> *From five in the morning till nine at night when they were busy.*
>
> What time was allowed for your meals?
> *Forty minutes at noon.*
>
> Did your labour keep you constantly on your feet?
> *Yes, there are so many frames and they run so quickly.*
>
> Suppose you flagged a little, or were too late, what would they do?
> *Strap us.*
>
> Severely?
> *Yes.*
>
> Could you eat your food well in that factory?
> *No indeed, I had not much to eat, and the little I had I could not eat, my appetite was so poor, and it being covered with dust.*

1. How many abuses can you count in Elizabeth Bentley's testimony? List them all. (You can probably find one for every question asked.)

2. Why might her parents have allowed Elizabeth to perform such work?

3. Why did factory owners hire children like Elizabeth instead of getting adults to do the job?

4. If factory owners and families both wanted child labor to continue, should Parliament still have pressed ahead to reform the system? Why or why not?

© 2016 K12 Inc. All rights reserved.
Copying or distributing without K12's written consent is prohibited.

Children also performed many jobs in America's urban centers, which industrialized later than those in Britain. Go online and visit the History Place website.

Scroll through the pictures and read some of the accounts. Pick one of the child occupations shown and write a diary entry for a typical day in the life…

Dear Diary,

© 2016 K12 Inc. All rights reserved.
Copying or distributing without K12's written consent is prohibited.

Name ______________________ Date ______________________ 

Reading Guide

Day 1

Read

Reading Guide

1. Describe working conditions for factory workers in the early nineteenth century.

2. In addition to men, __________ and ____________ also worked in factories and mills.

3. What was the major difference between the way men and women were paid?

4. Working conditions were bad. But for industrial workers, living conditions could be just as bad. Give two examples of such conditions.

5. ________________________ wrote *A Christmas Carol, Oliver Twist, Bleak House,* and *Little Dorrit.* He described an industrial city called Coketown in his 1854 novel, ________________ .

6. In addition to entertaining his readers, what impact did his work have on society?

7. ________________________ ruled England between 1837 and 1901. Name some of the values she emphasized during her reign.

8. Various reformers sought to improve conditions for the industrial poor during the mid-nineteenth century. How did they try to make workplaces safer places to work?

9. What efforts were made to improve the lot of overworked workers?

© 2016 K12 Inc. All rights reserved.
Copying or distributing without K12's written consent is prohibited.

Name Date 

10. What development made the streets of London safer?

11. Which sanitation improvement helped reduce disease in the British capital?

Day 2

Read

Reading Guide

12. ____________________ was a socialist writer who called for the overthrow of capitalism. His major works were *The Communist Manifesto* and ____________________.

13. He believed that the working class and the middle class struggled against each other for a greater share of ____________. After a revolution staged by the working class, personal ____________ would no longer exist.

14. What name did he and others use for the working class? What did he call the middle class?

Day 3

Read

Reading Guide

15. ________________________ was an English scientist who proposed a theory known as "natural selection."

16. The idea that living things have changed over time appeared in the book, ________________ in 1859.

17. Thomas Malthus believed that population growth would exceed food supply. How did his beliefs influence society?

© 2016 K12 Inc. All rights reserved.
Copying or distributing without K12's written consent is prohibited.

Name Date 

Explore and Discuss

Most of us now lead more comfortable lives than the men, women, and children who worked in factories and mills during the nineteenth century. But is it possible that in a hundred years' time, people will look back on the present era and describe it as "hard times"? What could they think was hard about life today?

Did the Industrial Revolution bring positive changes in countries like Great Britain? Give reasons for your answers.

© 2016 K12 Inc. All rights reserved.
Copying or distributing without K12's written consent is prohibited.

Student Guide
Lesson 6: Slavery in the Modern World

Lesson Objectives

- Recognize that Enlightenment ideas about human rights conflicted with the reality of life for most people in the world at the time.
- Describe the slave trade in Africa as it existed by 1700.
- Describe the transatlantic slave trade and its consequences.
- Explain the relationship between slavery and the growth of racism.
- Trace on a map the major routes the slave trade took.
- Recognize that slavery still exists in parts of the world today.
- Compare and contrast the European and Muslim slave trade of Africans with earlier slave systems.
- Identify major leaders of the abolition movement, what they are known for, and the results of their work.
- Summarize the experiences of Equiano.
- Give examples of the kinds of work slaves did in the Americas and the economic factors that encouraged it.
- Describe slavery in the Muslim world.

PREPARE

Approximate lesson time is 60 minutes.

Materials

For the Student

Reading Guide

The Human Odyssey, Volume 2 edited by Klee, Cribb, and Holdren

History Journal

Keywords and Pronunciation

boycott (BOY-kaht) : to join together in refusing to buy, sell, or use something or to have any dealings with someone

Olaudah Equiano (oh-LOW-duh ek-wee-AHN-oh)

racism : the belief that some races of people are morally, culturally, or physically superior to others

Saint-Domingue (sehn-daw-MEHNG)

Toussaint L'Ouverture (too-SEHN loo-vair-tyour)

© 2016 K12 Inc. All rights reserved.
Copying or distributing without K12's written consent is prohibited.

LEARN

Activity 1: Slavery in a Changing World *(Offline)*

Instructions

This lesson is designed to be completed in 3 class sessions.

Day 1

Read

Read Chapter 10, from the beginning to "Slavery and Racism," pages 490–501, and complete Day 1 of the Reading Guide. When you have finished, use the Lesson Answer Key to check your work, and then place the Reading Guide in your History Journal.

Up Close and Personal: Reading a Primary Source

Read again the account by Olaudah Equiano, "Aboard a Slave Ship," on pages 496–497. When you've finished, answer the following questions in your History Journal, and then compare your answers to those in the Lesson Answer Key

1. Why did slavers treat slaves so inhumanely, like squeezing so many of them together in the holds of their ships?
2. How did the slavers try to justify their actions?
3. What explains the slavers' unnecessarily harsh treatment of slaves, like throwing overboard the fish they did not intend to eat rather than giving it to the starving Africans?
4. How might enslaved Africans view not just their slavers but all white people?

Day 2

Read

Read Chapter 10, from "Slavery and Racism" to the end, pages 501–507, and complete Day 2 of the Reading Guide. When you have finished, use the Lesson Answer Key to check your work, and then place the Reading Guide in your History Journal.

Mapping out the Slave Trade

The maps on pages 494 and 507 of chapter 10 show the routes of the slave trade from Africa to the Americas and to the Middle East. They indicate the great distances slaves traveled from their homelands. But they fail to communicate the numbers of people who took those routes. Find out about the relative importance of those routes now by completing the African Slave Routes activity. When you've finished the African Slave Routes activity, answer these questions in your History Journal and check your answers with those in the Lesson Answer Key.

1. Why were so many slaves needed in Brazil and the Caribbean?
2. With relatively few slaves being sent to North America, how did it end up with one-third of the New World's slaves by the mid-nineteenth century?
3. Why did most slaves in the United States end up in the southern states?

Day 3

Slavery Time Line

The transatlantic slave trade endured for centuries. It was not a single event, but a succession of events that saw the trade begin, grow, change, and eventually disappear. Trace the developments of the slave trade to the New World by completing the Slave Trade Time Line activity.

© 2016 K12 Inc. All rights reserved.
Copying or distributing without K12's written consent is prohibited.

Abolition Time Line

The Slavery Time Line shows the events surrounding the slave trade, concluding with the abolition of the practice. But a time line oversimplifies events. The 1833 entry, for example, marks the end of Britain's involvement in the trade. However, a whole series of events led to that milestone. On the time line, click on the date 1833 to find out just how complicated a process outlawing slavery was.

ASSESS

Lesson Assessment: Slavery in the Modern World (*Online*)

You will complete an online assessment covering the main objectives of this lesson. Your assessment will be scored by the computer.

© 2016 K12 Inc. All rights reserved.
Copying or distributing without K12's written consent is prohibited.

Name ______________________________ Date ______________________________ 

Reading Guide

Day 1

Read

Reading Guide

1. Did Enlightenment ideas about human rights apply to most people around the world in the eighteenth century?

2. For centuries, Africans enslaved other Africans. Name the two later slave trades that transported millions of Africans to distant lands to work.

3. Slaves marched to the Indian Ocean on Africa's east coast were shipped to______________.

4. Slaves marched to the west coast of Africa were shipped across the____________________ Ocean to the_____________________ .

5. What killed more than one-third of the slaves before they even reached the coast?

6. Most slaves who were shipped to the Americas worked on_________________ plantations.

7. What machine made cotton farming profitable and increased the demand for slaves? Name some of the other kinds of work that slaves performed in the Americas.

8. Name the African slave who wrote an account of his experiences in Africa and the Americas and who eventually bought his freedom from his owner, a British naval officer.

Day 2

Read

Reading Guide

9. Why did racism help strengthen the acceptance of slavery?

© 2016 K12 Inc. All rights reserved.
Copying or distributing without K12's written consent is prohibited.

Name ____________________ Date ____________________

10. ____________________ was a young Anglican clergyman who began the abolitionist movement in Britain. He enlisted to the cause a British member of parliament and famous orator named ____________________.

11. ____________________ was an American abolitionist who also helped organize the world's first conference on women's rights. "We hold these truths to be self-evident: that all ____________________ are created equal."

12. When did slavery finally come to an end in the Muslim world?

© 2016 K12 Inc. All rights reserved.
Copying or distributing without K12's written consent is prohibited.

Student Guide
Lesson 7: Unit Review

PREPARE

Approximate lesson time is 60 minutes.

LEARN
Activity 1: Revolutions In Arts, Industries, and Work *(Online)*

© 2016 K12 Inc. All rights reserved.
Copying or distributing without K12's written consent is prohibited.

Student Guide
Lesson 8: Unit Assessment

You've finished the unit. Now it's time to take the Unit Assessment.

Lesson Objectives

- Identify Adam Smith and what he is known for.
- Describe the transatlantic slave trade and its consequences.
- Define the Industrial Revolution.
- Explain why the Industrial Revolution began in England in the eighteenth century.
- Describe the Romantic movement in the arts of the early nineteenth century.
- Describe conditions for factory workers in the early nineteenth century.
- Identify major events and individuals of the Industrial Revolution.
- Identify major contributors to the Romantic movement and what they are known for.
- Identify major inventors and inventions of the transportation and communications revolution and the results of their accomplishments.
- Identify Dickens, Marx, and Darwin, and what they are known for.
- Describe living and working conditions for early industrial workers.
- Identify major leaders of the abolitionist movement and what they are known for.

PREPARE

Approximate lesson time is 60 minutes.

Materials

For the Student

Question Review Table

ASSESS

Unit Assessment: Revolutions in Arts, Industries, and Work, Part 1 (*Online*)

Complete the computer-scored portion of the Unit Assessment. When you have finished, complete the teacher-scored portion of the assessment and submit it to your teacher.

Unit Assessment: Revolutions in Arts, Industries, and Work, Part 2 (*Offline*)

Complete the teacher-scored portion of the Unit Assessment and submit it to your teacher.

LEARN

Activity 1: Optional Unit Assessment Review Table *(Online)*

© 2016 K12 Inc. All rights reserved.
Copying or distributing without K12's written consent is prohibited.

Assessment Date

Unit 11: Revolutions in Arts, Industries, and Work

Before you retake the Unit Assessment, use the table to figure out which activities you should review.

Question Review Table

Circle the numbers of the questions that you missed on the Unit Assessment. Review the activities that correspond with these questions.

Revolutions in Arts, Industries, and Work, Part 1

Question	Lesson	Review Activity
1,2,3	2: Britain Begins the Industrial Revolution	Britain Begins the Industrial Revolution
4	1: Romantic Art in an Age of Revolution	Romantic Art in an Age of Revolution
5	6: Slavery in the Modern World	Slavery in a Changing World

Revolutions in Arts, Industries, and Work, Part 2

Question	Lesson	Review Activity
3,4,6,7,	2: Britain Begins the Industrial Revolution	Britain Begins the Industrial Revolution
1	1: Romantic Art in an Age of Revolution	Romantic Art in an Age of Revolution
2	6: Slavery in the Modern World	Slavery in a Changing World
8,9,10,11	Throughout Unit	

© 2016 K12 Inc. All rights reserved.
Copying or distributing without K12's written consent is prohibited.

Student Guide

Unit 12: Picturing Your Thoughts
Lesson 1: Picturing Your Thoughts

Lesson Objectives

- Review knowledge gained in the Age of Democratic Revolutions and the Revolutions in Arts, Industries, and Work units.
- Conduct research on examples of progress and hardship in the period from 1700 to 1900.
- Write a thesis statement based on research.
- Support a thesis statement visually.

PREPARE

Approximate lesson time is 60 minutes.

Materials

For the Student

The Human Odyssey, Volume 2 edited by Klee, Cribb, and Holdren

Keywords and Pronunciation

collage : an artwork made by gluing pieces of paper, fabric, photographs, and other objects to a flat surface
inquisitor : one who examines or investigates
juxtaposition : the placing together of two or more contrasting things for the sake of effect
thesis : the focus or main idea of an essay. A thesis states what the essay will prove.

LEARN

Activity 1: Picturing Your Thoughts *(Offline)*

Instructions

Day 1

Read, Browse, Peruse

You have written essays before. Often, an essay proves something by presenting factual evidence to support a thesis. Sound familiar? You are about to review Part 3 of the textbook, choose a topic, do some research, and prepare to write a thesis. But instead of supporting your thesis in writing, you are going to make a collage—a carefully arranged collection of images, graphs, charts, short quotations, drawings, maps, and so on. The collage will support your thesis, perhaps as well as a thousand words would. Let's get started by answering some questions you might have.

- What's a thesis statement?
- Your thesis statement comprises the sentence or two that tells the reader (and you) what your essay is going to prove.
- What will the thesis be about?
- Your thesis will be about progress and hardship during the period from 1700 to 1900.
- What does a thesis look like?

© 2016 K12 Inc. All rights reserved.
Copying or distributing without K12's written consent is prohibited.

Let's use an example from a time period you've studied earlier in the course. Here's a thesis statement related to progress and hardship during the Age of Exploration in the 1500s:

Spanish settlement in the Americas during the 1500s brought wealth and new products to many Europeans, but Native Americans suffered death and the loss of wealth and land.

Are there facts and evidence to support this statement? Sure. You could find a lot of information in your text and in other sources. Now, could you support the statement with images instead of paragraphs? Could you use pictures, drawings, statistics, quotations, and maps instead of words?

So, how will you get started?

Review the contents of Units 10 and 11, which correspond to Part 3 of the textbook. As you do so, think about particular examples of progress and hardship during the period from 1700 to 1900.

This may seem like a lot of ground to cover (in the textbook, Part 3 runs from pages 348–515). However, that's where the words browse and peruse come in. Look at the illustrations and their captions, pay attention to the chapter subheadings, and scan the text. But you should only read text about subjects that relate to the topic of progress and hardship. Pay particular attention to the review lessons at the end of Units 10 and 11.

Make a list of topics that fit the theme of progress and hardship. Was there both progress and hardship as a result of the American or French Revolution? Was there both progress and hardship during the Industrial Revolution? What other topics fit the theme?

Once you've identified several examples, you're ready to move on to the next stage.

Doing the Research

Using online and printed sources, begin to research two or three of the topics you have identified that exemplify progress and hardship during the period from 1700 to 1900. As you do so, think about which example you would like to develop further.

The kinds of facts you should try to find include:

- quotes from relevant parties
- visuals such as paintings, portraits, or maps
- facts, figures, and statistics

During your research, narrow your focus to the example that you think works best.

Day 2

Write a Thesis

Now it's time to write your thesis—the focus or main idea of an essay. Remember, a thesis states what the essay will prove.

© 2016 K12 Inc. All rights reserved.
Copying or distributing without K12's written consent is prohibited.

Write a short statement about the topic you selected on Day 1 (try to get it down to a single sentence). The statement should answer the question: in what way was there both progress and hardship in this area?

Make sure your thesis is a strong one that addresses both the progress and the hardship.

Re-Research

Now continue with your research, this time to gather information (visual and statistical as well as written) in support of your thesis.

Look at the same types of information you did during yesterday's research. In other words, collect supportive visual and statistical information as well as written information. Collect quotes from people at the time that back up your thesis. Find relevant excerpts from laws, declarations, or other official documents. Make notes of statistics that seem to add weight to your views. Create graphs, charts, or other ways to represent information. Think about visuals that will provide a little context or color. Either draw them yourself or print images from the Internet.

For example, if you were working on the sample thesis ("Spanish settlement in the Americas during the 1500s brought wealth and new products to many Europeans, but Native Americans suffered death and the loss of wealth and land") you might gather the following:

- Quotations from explorers, kings, merchants, and so on.
- Drawings of the gold and silver the explorers found in the Americas.
- Magazine pictures of products that went to Europe such as potatoes, tomatoes, squash, and so on.
- Advertisements in Europe about going to the Americas.
- Statistics about wealth in Europe.
- Statistics on the decline of Native Americans because of European diseases.
- Maps of land claims before and after colonization.
- Pictures of the Spanish taking gold and silver.
- Government documents from the time.
- Letter from Bartolome de Las Casas about the abuse of Indians.

You could handwrite the quotes or find them on the Internet and print them out. Illustrations, maps, paintings, diagrams, and so on can be drawn and colored by you, photocopied from the textbook or other sources, or printed from the Internet. Create charts and graphs to quickly and effectively represent facts, figures, and statistics.

Once you have completed this activity, you'll have all the raw materials you will use to complete this lesson tomorrow.

Day 3

Picture This!

A picture, they say, is worth a thousand words. Now's your chance to prove it.

Rather than writing an essay about the issue in your thesis, you'll use the images, quotes, graphs, and other things that you gathered yesterday. Glue them on a large sheet of paper to form a collage that supports your thesis statement.

Think carefully about the layout of the collage. Consider the following:

© 2016 K12 Inc. All rights reserved.
Copying or distributing without K12's written consent is prohibited.

- Should the collage be divided in two, perhaps to show things "before" and "after" or to compare the progress with the hardship?
- Is the thesis statement featured prominently?
- Should the content of the collage move chronologically from left to right or from top to bottom?
- Should you use arrows to show a progression of events?
- Do you want to use labels?
- What is the best way to juxtapose different elements? (For example, to support the exploration thesis, include a painting showing the wealth of the conquistadors next to one illustrating the enslavement of the Native Americans.)

Day 4

Presentation

You should finish up your collage and then present it to a member of your family and explain its meaning. Be ready to answer questions and to provide clarifications.

ASSESS

Lesson Assessment: Picturing Your Thoughts *(Offline)*

You will complete an offline assessment covering some of the main points of this lesson. Your assessment will be scored by the teacher.

© 2016 K12 Inc. All rights reserved.
Copying or distributing without K12's written consent is prohibited.

Student Guide

Unit 13: Nations Unite and Expand
Lesson 1: Growing Nationalism in Italy and Germany

- Define *nationalism* and *imperialism.*
- Recognize major causes, events, and individuals in the unification of German and Italy.
- Recognize major causes, events, individuals, and results of the American Civil War.
- Describe the second Industrial Revolution.
- Identify major contributors to the second Industrial Revolution and what they are known for.
- Explain the reasons for the new imperialism of the late nineteenth century.
- Locate on a map major colonial claims in Africa and Asia.
- Describe the effects of colonization on the peoples of the colonized territories.

Lesson Objectives

- Identify the causes of Italian and German unification.
- Identify major events and individuals in the unification of Italy.
- Identify Bismarck and his role in German unification.
- Describe the means Bismarck used to make Germany a unified and powerful nation.
- Define *nationalism.*
- Recognize Napoleon's role in the nationalist movements of the nineteenth century in Europe.
- Recognize the origin of Vatican City as the smallest nation in the world.
- Explain *volksgeist* and its influence on the German peoples.
- Identify the Holy Roman Empire and its situation in the 1800s.
- Locate major German states on a map.

PREPARE

Approximate lesson time is 60 minutes.

Materials

For the Student

- Reading Guide
- Unified Germany
- Unified Italy

The Human Odyssey, Volume 2 edited by Klee, Cribb, and Holdren

History Journal

© 2016 K12 Inc. All rights reserved.
Copying or distributing without K12's written consent is prohibited.

Keywords and Pronunciation

Reichstag (RIYKS-tahk)
volksgeist (FOLKS-giyst)
Alsace (al-SAS)
Baden (BAH-dn)
chancellor : the title for the head of government in some countries
Count di Cavour (kuh-VUR)
Giuseppe Garibaldi (joo-ZEP-pay gah-ree-BAHL-dee)
Giuseppe Mazzini (joo-ZEP-pay maht-SEE-nee)
Lorraine (luh-RAYN)
nationalism : a strong feeling of attachment to one´s own country
prime minister : the leader of a parliamentary government

LEARN

Activity 1: Growing Nationalism in Italy and Germany *(Offline)*

This lesson is designed to be completed in 3 class sessions.

Day 1

Read

Read Chapter 1 from the beginning to "Growing Nationalism in German Lands," pages 522–531, and complete Day 1 of the Reading Guide. When you have finished, use the Lesson Answer Key to check your work, and then place the Reading Guide in your History Journal.

Italy in 1848 and 1870

Study the map of Italy prior to its unification on page 528 and then complete the map on the Unified Italy sheet to represent Italy after its unification. You may use the map on page 529 to help you. Your finished map should have the lands colored like on the map on page 529.

Day 2

Read

Read Chapter 1, from "Growing Nationalism in German Lands" to the end, pages 531–537, and complete Day 2 of the Reading Guide.

Germany in 1848 and 1871

Study the map of Germany prior to its unification on page 532 and then complete the map on the Unified Germany sheet to represent Germany after its unification. Use the map on page 536 to help you complete this activity. Your finished map should have the same colored lands as the map on page 536.

Day 3

Compare and Contrast

Today you will compare and contrast the means used to unify Italy to those used to unify Germany by completing the Compare and Contrast online activity. You may use the maps and textbook to help complete this activity.

Major Roles

Some people played major roles in the unification of Germany and Italy. Complete the Major Roles activity. In this activity you will create flash cards describing the roles that some of these major players had in the unification of Germany and Italy.

© 2016 K12 Inc. All rights reserved.
Copying or distributing without K12's written consent is prohibited.

ASSESS

Lesson Assessment: Growing Nationalism in Italy and Germany (*Online*)

You will complete an online assessment covering the main objectives of this lesson. Your assessment will be scored by the computer.

© 2016 K12 Inc. All rights reserved.
Copying or distributing without K12's written consent is prohibited.

Name ______________________________ Date ______________________________ 

Unified Italy

Follow the directions below to create a map of unified Italy. For assistance, you may refer to the map on page 529 of your textbook.

1. The Kingdom of Sardinia—also known as Piedmont—was the only major state on the Italian peninsula not ruled by a foreign power. On the map, color Piedmont green. Also color the box in the legend green.

2. The French and Piedmontese clashed with the Austrians in 1859. When the fighting ended, the Austrians had lost their hold on all the northern Italian states except Venice. Color the Lombardy area red. In the legend, draw a box and color it red. Then write "Territory added in 1859" to the right of the box.

© 2016 K12 Inc. All rights reserved.
Copying or distributing without K12's written consent is prohibited.

Unified Italy

3. In 1860, the newly liberated states in northern Italy—Tuscany, Modena, Parma, and the Papal States—decided to join the Kingdom of Sardinia. Color these states blue and add a blue box with the label "Territory added in 1860" to the legend.

4. In 1860, the people in the Kingdom of the Two Sicilies were rebelling against their rulers, who were members of the Spanish royal family. Garibaldi and his men landed in Sicily and defeated the kingdom's forces. Garibaldi then marched on Naples, the capital of the Kingdom of the Two Sicilies. The king fled without a fight and Garibaldi now controlled all of southern Italy. Color the Kingdom of the Two Sicilies (Sicily and the lands surrounding Naples) blue because this territory was also added in 1860.

5. In 1866, Venice broke away from Austria and joined Italy. Color the Venice area yellow and add a yellow box with the label "Territory added in 1866" to the legend.

6. In 1870, Victor Emmanuel II marched into Rome and declared it his capital. Color the Rome area orange and add an orange box with the label "Territory added in 1870" to the legend.

© 2016 K12 Inc. All rights reserved.
Copying or distributing without K12's written consent is prohibited.

Name Date

Unified Germany

Follow the directions below to create a map of Unified Germany. For assistance, you may refer to the map on page 536.

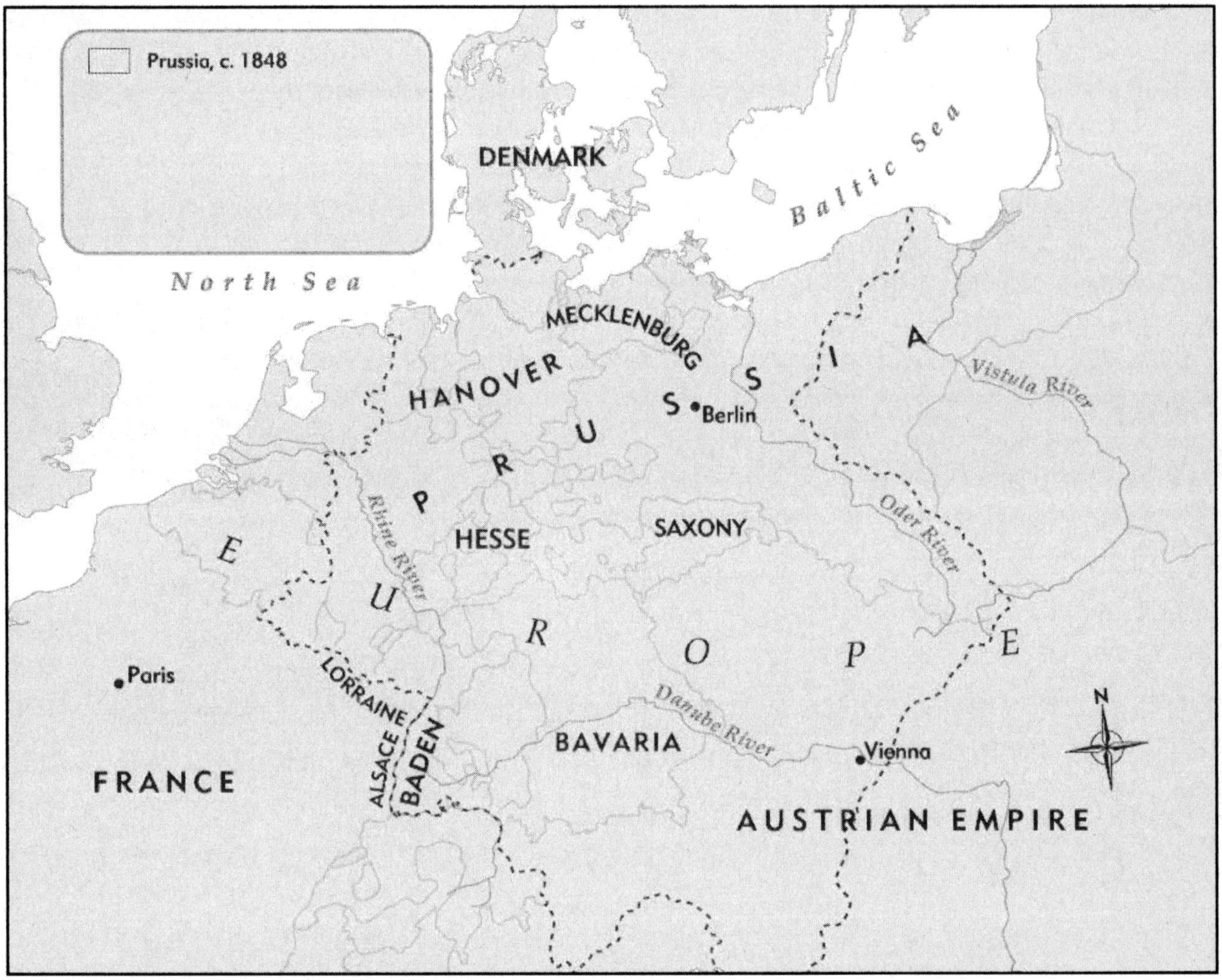

1. In 1815, after the defeat of Napoleon, the German kingdoms and states once again became independent. They formed the German Confederation. A confederation is a group of kingdoms or states that are allied. On the map of Germany, outline the German Confederation boundary line in brown.

2. The German-speaking people lived in 39 states ruled by various kings, princes, and dukes. The most powerful state was Austria and the next most powerful was Prussia. Other Germans lived in kingdoms such as Bavaria and Hanover, or duchies such as Baden or Hesse. Color the lands of Prussia and the box for "Prussia, c. 1848" in the legend yellow.

© 2016 K12 Inc. All rights reserved.
Copying or distributing without K12's written consent is prohibited.

Unified Germany

3. In 1862, the King of Prussia appointed Bismarck as his chancellor. Under Bismarck, Prussia began producing more iron and building more railroads. By 1866, Prussia was engaged in war with Austria and defeated Austria in what was known as the Seven Week War. Twenty-two states joined Prussia and a new organization, the North German Confederation, was formed in 1867. Color the boundary line for the North German Confederation orange. Add an orange line with the label "North German Confederation" to the legend.

4. Color the lands surrounding Hesse, Hanover, Saxony, and Mecklenburg green. Add a green box with the label "Territory added in 1867" to the legend.

5. On July 19, 1870, France declared war on Prussia. This war took even less than seven weeks. On September 2, the main French army surrendered and handed over Napoleon III himself. Four months later, the Parisians surrendered their capital. Bismarck declared the birth of the German Empire, which included every German state except Austria. He also demanded that France turn over Alsace and Lorraine. Color Alsace, Lorraine, Baden, and the lands around Bavaria red. Add a red box with the label "Territory added in 1871" to the legend.

© 2016 K12 Inc. All rights reserved.
Copying or distributing without K12's written consent is prohibited.

Name Date 

Reading Guide

Day 1

Read

1. When did Italy and Germany emerge as independent nations?

2. How did Napoleon play a role in the nineteenth century movements to unify Germany and Italy?

3. The strong sense of attachment or belonging to one's own country is called ____________.

4. Describe some of the methods young Italian students used to express their support for a unified Italy.

5. Who was Giuseppe Mazzini?

6. The Young Italy movement organized uprisings against foreign rule of Italy. Were these uprisings successful? What did the organization persuade many Italians to believe?

7. Who was Giuseppe Garibaldi? What did he do to earn the title "Hero of Two Worlds"?

8. Garibaldi's troops came to be known as____________________ because their uniforms were red robes that butchers had thrown away.

© 2016 K12 Inc. All rights reserved.
Copying or distributing without K12's written consent is prohibited.

Name _______________ Date _______________ 

9. Describe the major events that led to the unification of Italy.

10. In 1929, the Roman Catholic Church recognized Italy as a nation with its capital at Rome, and Italy recognized _______________ as an independent state. Vatican City, a 109-acre territory in the city of Rome, is the world's _______________.

Day 2

Read

11. What was unity like among the German-speaking people in the Holy Roman Empire before and after Napoleon?

12. Some Germans began to build on an idea proposed by German philosophers. These thinkers wrote that each nation has its own _______________, which means the soul of the people.

13. Who was Otto von Bismarck?

14. What was Bismarck's role in German unification? Describe the strategies he used to make Germany a unified and powerful nation.

© 2016 K12 Inc. All rights reserved.
Copying or distributing without K12's written consent is prohibited.

Student Guide
Lesson 2: The United States Fights and Unites

Lesson Objectives

- Describe the economic differences between the North and the South.
- Trace on a map the expansion of the United States from 1800 to 1860.
- Recognize that most countries had abolished slavery by the early 1800s.
- Identify Jefferson Davis and Abraham Lincoln and what they are known for.
- Summarize the major events of the Civil War.
- Explain why the Civil War is considered the first modern war.
- Summarize the results of the American Civil War.
- Describe the building of the transcontinental railroad and its significance.

PREPARE

Approximate lesson time is 60 minutes.

Materials

For the Student

Reading Guide

Keywords and Pronunciation

daguerreotype (duh-GEH-roh-tiyp)
Louis Daguerre (lwee dah-gair)

LEARN

Activity 1: Changing Nation *(Offline)*

Instructions

This lesson is designed to be completed in 3 class sessions.

Day 1

Read

Read Chapter 2 from the beginning to "The First Modern War", pages 538–549, and complete Day 1 of the Reading Guide. When you have finished, use the Lesson Answer Key to check your work, and then place the Reading Guide in your History Journal.

Changing Nation

During the first hundred years, the United States kept growing until its territory extended all the way from the Atlantic Ocean to the Pacific Ocean. But keeping such a large country unified was not easy. In the 1850s, the industrial North and the agricultural South threatened to tear the nation apart over the issue of slavery. Go online to the Changing Nation map activity to see how the United States expanded and how it nearly split apart.

© 2016 K12 Inc. All rights reserved.
Copying or distributing without K12's written consent is prohibited.

Day 2

Read

Read Chapter 2, from "The First Modern War" to the end of the chapter, pages 549–557 and complete Day 2 of the Reading Guide.

The Vital Link

To find out more about the amazing ingenuity the railroad workers used to build the railroad that finally linked the nation, go online to visit the PBS: Transcontinental Railroad website. Why do you think the railroad tracks were being laid faster in some regions and more slowly in others?

As you explore the PBS history animation about the transcontinental railroad, think about the challenges and obstacles the Central Pacific (CP) and the Union Pacific (UP) railroad companies had to face and how they overcame them. If you were to create a video game or a board game about the race to link the nation, which challenges would you include in your game? Discuss your choices with an adult.

Be sure to consider the geography of the region, the weather, and how the builders would get their supplies.

Day 3

Taking a Stand

The United States was dramatically transformed by the Civil War. Four long years of fighting had killed hundreds of thousands and destroyed homes, crops, factories, and railroads. Despite the terrible devastation, the United States was an enormous country with vast resources and ingenious citizens. During the war many citizens had been forced to abandon their traditional way of life and to learn new skills and roles. The war had settled once and for all that the United States should be one, unified country. But, what kind of nation should it be?

Pretend to be a newspaper editor looking at the state of the nation at the end of the Civil War. Write an editorial suggesting some steps Americans should take to heal and rebuild the nation.

An editorial is a brief article written to influence public opinion about an issue or event. A good editorial includes constructive criticism and offers solutions. Like other essays, an editorial should have a brief introduction, a body, and a powerful conclusion. The main idea should be well supported with facts or evidence.

Remember to pick your topic or angle wisely and research it. Then, carefully craft your thesis statement, or main idea. Write an outline that includes your supporting evidence and your conclusion. Then, write your editorial. Be sure to proofread it carefully before you send it to the press!

ASSESS

Lesson Assessment: The United States Fights and Unites (*Online*)

You will complete an online assessment covering the main objectives of this lesson. Your assessment will be scored by the computer.

© 2016 K12 Inc. All rights reserved.
Copying or distributing without K12's written consent is prohibited.

Name Date 

Reading Guide

Day 1

Read

Reading Guide

1. In 1803 the United States bought a large chunk of territory from Napoleon; it became known as the Louisiana Purchase. Where was the territory and how did if affect the size of the young nation?

2. How did the United States acquire the territory that extends from Texas to California?

3. The United States grew by leaps and bounds, quickly acquiring territory from Great Britain, France, Spain, and Mexico. Unifying the enormous young nation was a tremendous challenge. What issue threatened to destroy the unity?

4. How had Britain and the Latin American nations dealt with the issue of slavery?

5. Compare life in the North and the South by filling in the chart.

	North	South
Type of farming		
Population		
Cities		
Work force		
Attitude toward slavery		

© 2016 K12 Inc. All rights reserved.
Copying or distributing without K12's written consent is prohibited.

Name Date 

6. Many Southerners believed that the federal government could not force its laws onto the states. This idea is called ______________________ .

7. Label each of the following statements L if it describes Lincoln, D if it describes Davis, and B if it describes both.

   Born in Kentucky _______

   Grew up as a Southern gentleman _______

   Taught himself to read and write _______

   Served four terms in the state legislature _______

   Served in the United States Senate _______

   Called slavery a "moral, social, and political evil"_______

   His greatest loyalty was to his state _______

   His greatest loyalty was to his country _______

   Became president of his country _______

8. How did the southern states react when Lincoln was elected president in 1860?

9. The Civil War began on April 12, 1861 when Confederate soldiers fired on Fort Sumter in Charleston, South Carolina. Why did the North and the South believe the war would be short?

10. The Confederates won their first major victory at the Battle of ____________________ .

11. Why was the Confederate army so successful during the first two years of the Civil War?

12. Why was Great Britain inclined to help the South even though Britain had abolished slavery?

13. For Lincoln and the North, the war began as a fight to preserve the __________, but later became a war to end slavery with a document called the __________________________ .

© 2016 K12 Inc. All rights reserved.
Copying or distributing without K12's written consent is prohibited.

Name Date 

14. Why did Lee decide to invade the North?

15. The battle that turned the tide of war in favor of the North was ________________ .

16. Who delivered the Gettysburg Address? Why? What vision did it present?

17. In what ways was Ulysses S. Grant a very effective military leader?

Day 2

Read

Reading Guide

18. How did factories contribute to the Civil War?

19. How did new weapons affect the war?

20. What impact did the American Civil War have on the history of Germany?

21. How did news from the battlefields reach the public?

© 2016 K12 Inc. All rights reserved.
Copying or distributing without K12's written consent is prohibited.

Name Date 

22. Shortly after the Civil War two new amendments were added to the Constitution. What were they about?

23. In 1865, Americans made slavery illegal. What was the status of slavery in other countries?

24. How did the Civil War change the role of women?

25. How did the Civil War affect life in the South?

26. On May 10, 1869, in Promontory Point, Utah, a rowdy crowd joyously celebrated "the completion of the greatest enterprise ever yet undertaken." How did the construction of the transcontinental railroad change the nation?

27. Who built the transcontinental railroad?

28. What major obstacles did they face when they were building the railroad?

© 2016 K12 Inc. All rights reserved.
Copying or distributing without K12's written consent is prohibited.

Name Date 

Thinking Cap Questions

29. Why do many scholars consider the Civil War the first modern war?

30. How did the Civil War transform the nation?

31. After gold was discovered in California in 1849, politicians were eager to build a transcontinental railroad and began to argue about the route. Why did people want the railroad to pass through their region of the country?

© 2016 K12 Inc. All rights reserved.
Copying or distributing without K12's written consent is prohibited.

Student Guide
Lesson 3: Age of Innovation

Lesson Objectives

- Explain how steel led to a second industrial revolution.
- Identify Alexander Graham Bell and his accomplishments.
- Identify Thomas Edison and his accomplishments.
- Identify Guglielmo Marconi and his accomplishments.
- Describe advances in fuels in the late 1800s.
- Identify Andrew Carnegie and his accomplishments.
- Describe the evolution of the bicycle into the automobile.

PREPARE

Approximate lesson time is 60 minutes.

Materials

For the Student

Innovators and Innovation

The Human Odyssey, Volume 2 edited by Klee, Cribb, and Holdren

History Journal

Keywords and Pronunciation

Andrew Carnegie (KAHR-nuh-gee)
Gottlieb Daimler (GAHT-leeb DIYM-lur)
Guglielmo Marconi (gool-YEL-moh mahr-KOH-nee)
Gustave Eiffel (GOUS-tahv IY-fuhl)
Heinrich Hertz (HIYN-rik hurts)
Patent : an official document from the government stating that an inventor owns his or her invention and has the right to make, use, or sell it

---

LEARN

Activity 1: Innovators and Innovations *(Offline)*

Instructions

Day 1

Read

Read Chapter 3, from the beginning to "Getting There: From Velocipede to Bicycle" pages 558–565, and complete as much as possible of the Innovators and Innovations chart.

© 2016 K12 Inc. All rights reserved.
Copying or distributing without K12's written consent is prohibited.

The Wizard of Menlo Park

When you have finished reading the textbook, and filling out as much of the chart as possible, go online to read a very short piece of historical fiction. Historical fiction is usually based on very careful research into the lives and times of historical characters. The writer tries to make an historical event come to life. In order to do that, he may supplement his research with details from his imagination. In The Wizard of Menlo Park: Thomas Edison, you will accompany a young journalist to an interview with Thomas Edison.

When you have finished reading the story, write a paragraph in your History Journal or in the Online Notebook about Thomas Edison. In your opinion, what made him such a successful inventor? Make sure you cite specific facts and examples to support your opinion.

Flash Card Maker: Innovators

Go online to create Flash Cards of Henry Bessemer, Andrew Carnegie, Alexander Graham Bell, Thomas Edison, and Samuel Morse.

Day 2

Read

Read Chapter 3, from "Getting There: From Velocipede to Bicycle" to the end of Chapter 3, pages 565–571, and finish the Innovators and Innovations sheet.

When you have finished, use the Lesson Answer Key to check your work, and then place the Innovators and Innovations sheet in your History Journal.

Spark of Genius: From Hobby Horse to Automobile

Go online and follow the spark of genius from one creative idea to the next all the way from hobby horse to automobile.

Activity 2: The Wizard of Menlo Park *(Online)*

ASSESS

Lesson Assessment: Age of Innovation (*Online*)

You will complete an online assessment covering the main objectives of this lesson. Your assessment will be scored by the computer.

© 2016 K12 Inc. All rights reserved.
Copying or distributing without K12's written consent is prohibited.

Name Date 

Innovators and Innovations

Fill out the chart and answer the questions below.

Innovator	Place	Innovation	Purpose	Impact
Henry Bessemer				
Charles William Siemens				
Andrew Carnegie				
Samuel Morse				
Alexander Graham Bell				

© 2016 K12 Inc. All rights reserved.
Copying or distributing without K12's written consent is prohibited.

Innovators and Innovations

Innovator	Place	Innovation	Purpose	Impact
Thomas Edison				
Jean Lenoir				
Gottlieb Daimler and Wilhelm Maybach				
Karl Benz				
Guglielmo Marconi				

© 2016 K12 Inc. All rights reserved.
Copying or distributing without K12's written consent is prohibited.

Innovators and Innovations

1. How did steel spark a second industrial revolution?

2. People looking for new fuels to run their factories and heat their homes saw promise in ________________________, a liquid mineral found beneath the ground.

3. Why was petroleum superior to coal and wood?

4. Thomas Edison called his research and development lab the "________________________."

5. In your opinion, which innovators or innovations contributed most to the industrial development of the late nineteenth century? Make sure you support your answer with ideas, facts, and/or quotations.

© 2016 K12 Inc. All rights reserved.
Copying or distributing without K12's written consent is prohibited.

Student Guide
Lesson 4. Optional: Your Choice

PREPARE

Approximate lesson time is 60 minutes.

© 2016 K12 Inc. All rights reserved.
Copying or distributing without K12's written consent is prohibited.

Student Guide
Lesson 5: The New Imperialism

Lesson Objectives

- Explain the reasons for the New Imperialism.
- Identify key events and individuals in the expansion of the British Empire.
- Identify on a map the major areas of colonization by Britain, Belgium, Japan, France, Russia, and the United States.
- Describe the way Africa was divided among the European powers.
- Identify major countries and events in the New Imperialism in Asia.
- Describe the effects of colonization on the peoples of the colonized territories.

PREPARE

Approximate lesson time is 60 minutes.

Materials

For the Student

Reading Guide

The Human Odyssey, Volume 2 edited by Klee, Cribb, and Holdren

History Journal

Dividing Up the Riches

Keywords and Pronunciation

Benjamin Disraeli (diz-RAY-lee)

Ferdinand de Lesseps (furd-ee-NAHN duh lay-SEPS)

imperialism : the policy or action by which one country controls another country or territory; it may involve political or economic control

khedive (kuh-DEEV) : the ruler of Egypt

Sa'id Pasha (sah-EED PAH-shah)

LEARN

Activity 1: The New Imperialism *(Offline)*

Instructions

Day 1

Read

Read Chapter 4 from the beginning to "King Leopold and the 'Magnificent African Cake,' " pages 572–583, and complete the Reading Guide. When you have finished, use the Lesson Answer Key to check your work, and then place the Reading Guide in your History Journal.

© 2016 K12 Inc. All rights reserved.
Copying or distributing without K12's written consent is prohibited.

Activity 2: Building the Suez Canal *(Online)*

Activity 3: Dividing Up the Riches *(Offline)*

Instructions

Day 2

Read

Read from "King Leopold and the 'Magnificent African Cake' " to "The New Imperialism and the Map of Asia," pages 583–589.

Dividing Up the Riches

After finishing the reading assignment, complete the Africa section of the Dividing Up the Riches sheet to review how the Europeans carved up the continent of Africa and tapped its natural resources.

Day 3

Read

Read from "The New Imperialism and the Map of Asia" to the end of the chapter, pages 589–591.

Dividing Up the Riches

After finishing the reading assignment, complete the Asia section of the Dividing Up the Riches sheet to review how the Europeans and the United States staked claims in Asia and tapped its natural resources. When you have finished, use the Lesson Answer Key to check your work, and then place the Dividing Up the Riches sheet in your History Journal.

New Imperialism: Blessing or Curse?

New Imperialism transformed Africa, Asia, and Europe. Pretend you are a newspaper editor writing at the beginning of the twentieth century. Write an editorial about the way New Imperialism has affected the people of Africa and/or Asia. Take a stand on whether it has been beneficial or harmful and support your argument with specific facts and examples.

Reminder: An editorial is a brief article written to influence public opinion about an issue or event. A good editorial may include constructive criticism and offer solutions. Like other essays, an editorial should have a brief introduction, a body, and a powerful conclusion. The main argument should be well supported with facts, quotations, or evidence.

Remember to pick your topic or angle wisely and research it. Then, carefully craft your thesis statement or main idea. Write an outline that includes your supporting evidence and your conclusion. Then, write your editorial. Be sure to proofread it carefully before you send it to the press!

ASSESS

Lesson Assessment: The New Imperialism (*Online*)

You will complete an online assessment covering the main objectives of this lesson. Your assessment will be scored by the computer.

© 2016 K12 Inc. All rights reserved.
Copying or distributing without K12's written consent is prohibited.

Reading Guide

Read

Reading Guide

1. List four reasons for European interest in overseas colonies at the end of the nineteenth century.

2. The policy of action by which one country controls another country or territory is called ______________________ . What does *New Imperialism* refer to?

3. The British East India Company began to set up trading posts in India in the ___________________ century.

4. During the expansion of the empire, the ruler of England was _________________________ .

5. Explain the meaning of the expression, "The sun never sets on the British Empire."

6. What triggered the Sepoy Mutiny?

7. Describe the situation in India under British rule.

8. ______________________ was the British statesman who challenged Britain to become a great, imperial country.

© 2016 K12 Inc. All rights reserved.
Copying or distributing without K12's written consent is prohibited.

9. Some "social scientists" misused the ideas of ______________________ in order to say that some races were superior to others. How did this pseudo-scientific view of race affect the way the British treated their colonies?

10. ______________________ was the Scottish missionary, physician, and explorer who shaped the way Europeans thought about Africa.

11. As he traveled throughout Africa, Livingstone tried to convert people to ______________________ and tried to help the people find profitable businesses to replace ________________ .

12. Livingstone named the spectacular waterfall he encountered ______________________ to honor the queen of England.

13. When Livingstone returned to Britain he gave many speeches about his experiences in Africa. What were the three main topics of his speeches?

14. The Royal Geographic Society persuaded Livingstone to look for the source of the ________.

15. Why were the French so eager to build a canal across the Isthmus of Suez?

16. Who was Ferdinand de Lesseps?

17. How much time did the shortcut between East and West save?

18. When the Egyptian khedive became desperate for money, he sold his shares in the canal project to ______________________ .

19. What relationship developed between Britain and Egypt?

© 2016 K12 Inc. All rights reserved.
Copying or distributing without K12's written consent is prohibited.

Name Date 

Dividing Up the Riches

Africa

1. In 1877, King Leopold of Belgium declared "We must obtain a slice of this *magnifique gateau africain*"—this magnificent African cake. The king was inspired by the writings of _______________. What did his statement mean?

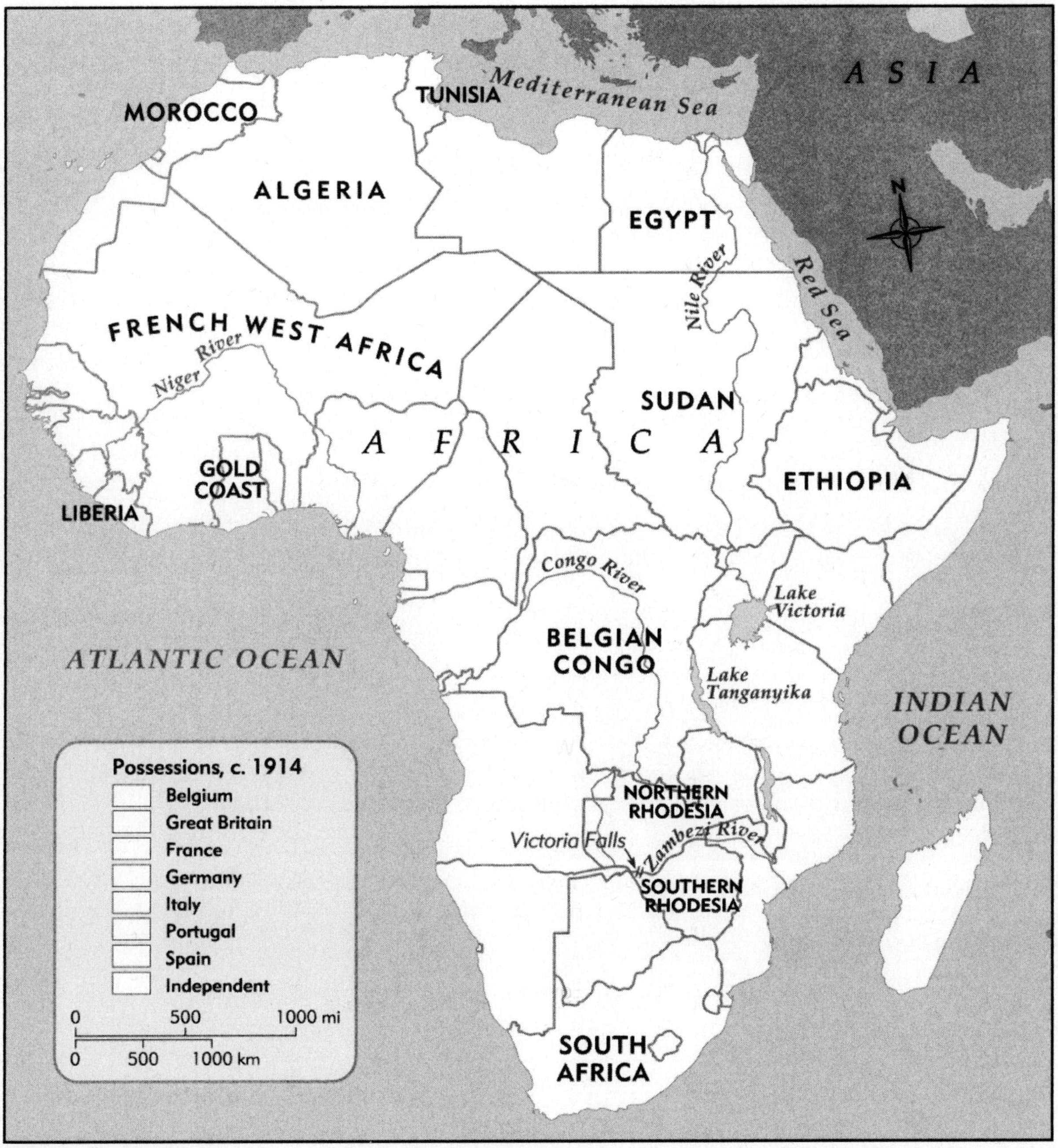

ASIA
Mediterranean Sea
MOROCCO
TUNISIA
ALGERIA
EGYPT
Nile River
Red Sea
FRENCH WEST AFRICA
Niger River
SUDAN
AFRICA
GOLD COAST
LIBERIA
ETHIOPIA
Congo River
Lake Victoria
BELGIAN CONGO
Lake Tanganyika
ATLANTIC OCEAN
INDIAN OCEAN
NORTHERN RHODESIA
Victoria Falls
Zambezi River
SOUTHERN RHODESIA
SOUTH AFRICA

Possessions, c. 1914
Belgium
Great Britain
France
Germany
Italy
Portugal
Spain
Independent
0 500 1000 mi
0 500 1000 km

© 2016 K12 Inc. All rights reserved.
Copying or distributing without K12's written consent is prohibited.

Dividing Up the Riches

2. What slice of the African cake did King Leopold claim for Belgium? Color the area on the map pink.

3. What role did the Africans play in the 1884 and 1885 conferences about the future of Africa?

4. Name at least four areas the British claimed. Color the British areas on the map red.

5. Who was Cecil Rhodes and what lured him to Africa?

6. What businesses did Rhodes establish?

7. He dreamt of expanding the British Empire, so he used his personal army to conquer a vast region in Africa. He named it ________________.

8. Which areas did the French colonize? Color the French areas on the map purple.

9. Color the areas the Spanish claimed orange.

10. The Ethiopians were able to drive out the Italians, but the Italians succeeded in colonizing other areas of northern Africa. Color those areas of the map dark green.

11. Color the German colonies yellow.

12. Color the areas the Portuguese claimed light green.

© 2016 K12 Inc. All rights reserved.
Copying or distributing without K12's written consent is prohibited.

Dividing Up the Riches

13. In all of Africa, only __________ and __________ remained independent.

Color in the boxes on the key with the appropriate colors and compare your map to the one on page 587 of your textbook.

Thinking Cap Question

14. Why were the Europeans able to gain control of nearly the entire African continent?

© 2016 K12 Inc. All rights reserved.
Copying or distributing without K12's written consent is prohibited.

Dividing Up the Riches

Asia

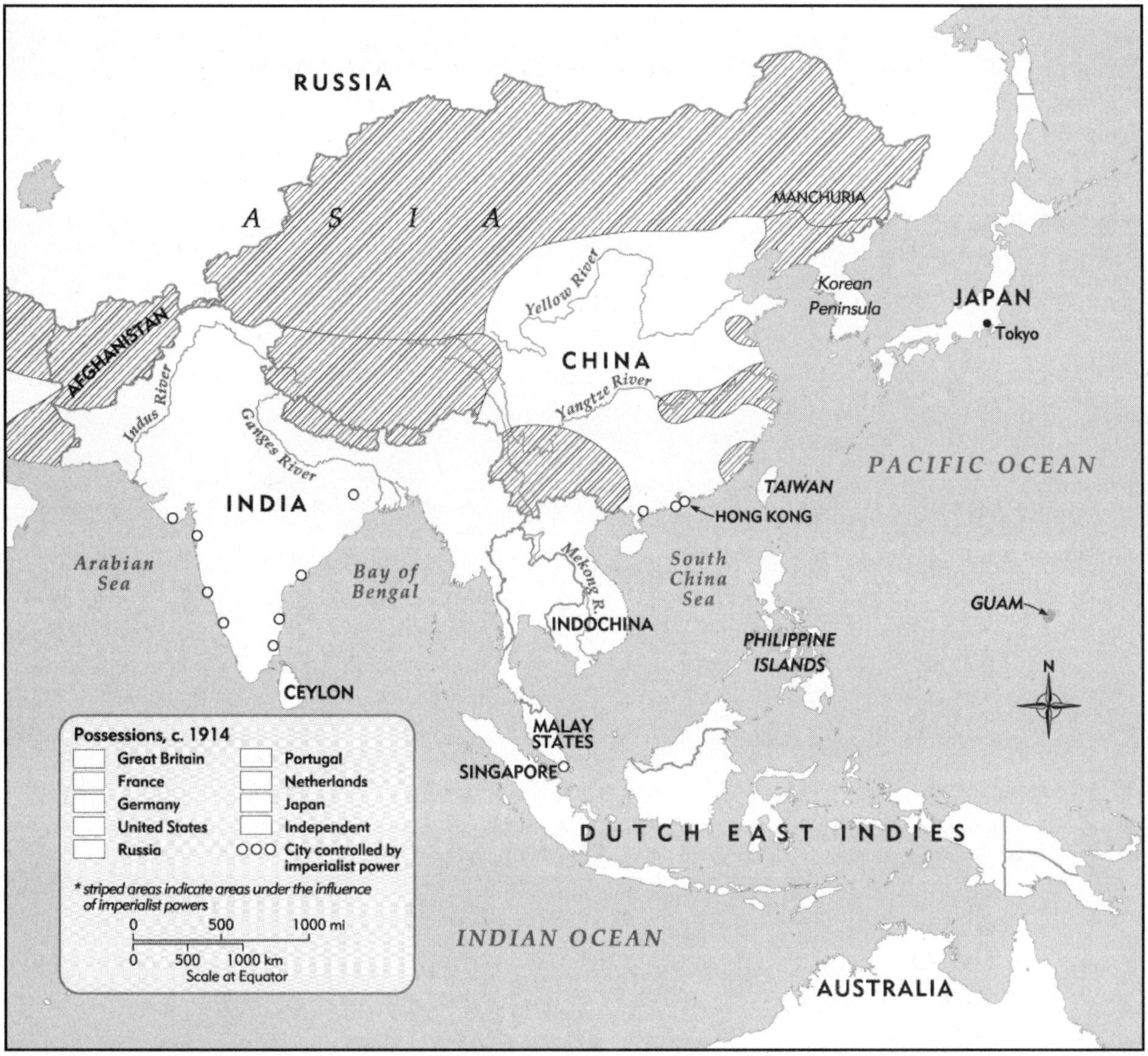

RUSSIA
A S I A
MANCHURIA
Yellow River
Korean Peninsula
JAPAN
Tokyo
CHINA
Yangtze River
AFGHANISTAN
Indus River
Ganges River
INDIA
PACIFIC OCEAN
TAIWAN
HONG KONG
Arabian Sea
Bay of Bengal
South China Sea
Mekong R.
INDOCHINA
GUAM
PHILIPPINE ISLANDS
CEYLON
N
MALAY STATES
SINGAPORE
DUTCH EAST INDIES
INDIAN OCEAN
AUSTRALIA

Possessions, c. 1914

- Great Britain
- France
- Germany
- United States
- Russia
- Portugal
- Netherlands
- Japan
- Independent
- ○○○ City controlled by imperialist power

** striped areas indicate areas under the influence of imperialist powers*

0 500 1000 mi
0 500 1000 km
Scale at Equator

15. What three areas of Asia did the British control in 1914? Color the British areas on the map red.

16. List two examples of the New Imperialism in China.

17. The colonizing countries worked out a policy that none of them would close its portion of China to trade with the others. The policy was known as an "________________" policy.

© 2016 K12 Inc. All rights reserved.
Copying or distributing without K12's written consent is prohibited.

Dividing Up the Riches

18. Rebels in China tried to end Western domination in the ________________. What happened in the end?

19. In 1853 the United States used military power to force _________ to open its door to foreign trade.

20. Color the areas Japan colonized dark green on the map.

21. To avoid conflict, Russia and Britain marked off ______________ as a land to separate their empires.

22. In the mid-nineteenth century the French sent troops into Indochina. Which three countries are in the region today? Color the area purple on the map.

23. The United States gained control of _________ and ______________________ as a result of the Spanish-American War. Color them light green.

© 2016 K12 Inc. All rights reserved.
Copying or distributing without K12's written consent is prohibited.

Student Guide
Lesson 6. Optional: Your Choice

PREPARE

Approximate lesson time is 60 minutes.

© 2016 K12 Inc. All rights reserved.
Copying or distributing without K12's written consent is prohibited.

Student Guide
Lesson 7: Unit Review

PREPARE

Approximate lesson time is 60 minutes.

LEARN
Activity 1: Nations Unite and Expand *(Online)*

© 2016 K12 Inc. All rights reserved.
Copying or distributing without K12's written consent is prohibited.

Student Guide
Lesson 8: Unit Assessment

Lesson Objectives

- Recognize major causes, events, and individuals in the unification of Germany and Italy.
- Define *nationalism* and *imperialism.*
- Identify major contributors to the second industrial revolution and describe their accomplishments.
- Explain the reasons for the New Imperialism of the late nineteenth century.
- Locate on a map major colonial claims in Africa and Asia.
- Describe the effects of colonization on the peoples of the colonized territories.
- Recognize major causes, events, individuals, and results of the American Civil War.
- Describe the second industrial revolution.

PREPARE

Approximate lesson time is 60 minutes.

Materials

For the Student

Question Review Table

ASSESS

Unit Assessment: Nations Unite and Expand, Part 1 (*Online*)

Complete the computer-scored portion of the Unit Assessment. When you have finished, complete the teacher-scored portion of the assessment and submit it to your teacher.

Unit Assessment: Nations Unite and Expand, Part 2 (*Offline*)

Complete the teacher-scored portion of the Unit Assessment and submit it to your teacher.

LEARN

Activity 1: Optional Unit Assessment Review Table *(Online)*

© 2016 K12 Inc. All rights reserved.
Copying or distributing without K12's written consent is prohibited.

Assessment Date

Unit 13: Nations Unite and Expand

Before you retake the Unit Assessment, use the table to figure out which activities you should review.

Question Review Table

Circle the numbers of the questions that you missed on the Unit Assessment. Review the activities that correspond with these questions.

Nations Unite and Expand, Part 1

Question	Lesson	Review Activity
1,2,3,4,6	1: Growing Nationalism in Italy and Germany 2: The United States Fights and Unites	Growing Nationalism in Italy and Germany Changing Nation
5,13,14,15,16,17	5: The New Imperlialism	The New Imperialism
7, 8,9,10,11,12	3: Age of Innovation	Innovators and Innovations

Nations Unite and Expand, Part 2

Question	Lesson	Review Activity
1,4,5	1: Growing Nationalism in Italy and Germany 2: The United States Fights and Unites	Growing Nationalism in Italy and Germany Changing Nation
3	5: The New Imperlialism	The New Imperialism
2	2: The United States Fights and Unites	Changing Nation

© 2016 K12 Inc. All rights reserved.
Copying or distributing without K12's written consent is prohibited.

Student Guide

Unit 14: Answers and Questions
Lesson 1: Organizing for Change

Lesson Objectives

- Describe the conditions city dwellers faced in places such as Paris, London, and New York.
- Explain the role of trade unions and describe the methods they used to improve working conditions.
- Identify significant leaders of the women's rights movement of the late nineteenth and early twentieth centuries and describe their methods and accomplishments.
- Explain the reasons for the population growth in cities of the 1800s.
- Identify Louis Pasteur and describe his accomplishments.
- Describe the conditions most industrial workers faced.
- Give examples of the ways Paris and New York addressed their problems.
- Review historical events.

PREPARE

Approximate lesson time is 60 minutes.

Materials

For the Student
- Reading Guide
- The Human Odyssey, Volume 2 edited by Klee, Cribb, and Holdren
- History Journal

LEARN

Activity 1: City Life *(Offline)*

Instructions

Day 1

Read

Read Chapter 5 from the beginning to "Louis Pasteur: Fighting Disease," pages 592–600 and complete Day 1 of the Reading Guide. When you have finished, use the Lesson Answer Key to check your work, and then place the Reading Guide in your History Journal.

New York, New York

Immigrants poured into New York City in the late nineteenth century, making it one of the most densely populated places on earth.

Population density is the term that describes the average number of people in an area of a given size. Population density is calculated by dividing the number of people in the area by the size of the area. Population density is frequently expressed as the average number of people per square mile.

What was the population density of New York City in the following years?

© 2016 K12 Inc. All rights reserved.
Copying or distributing without K12's written consent is prohibited.

Year	Population	Area in Square Miles	Population Density
1870	1,443,000	25	
1880	1,919,000	36	
1890	2,693,000	63	
1900	3,802,000	91	
1910	6,230,000	203	

Today New York City covers 321 square miles and has a population of 8.2 million. What is the population density?

Cheyenne, the capital and largest city in Wyoming, covers 21.2 square miles and has a population of 55,362 today. What is the population density of Cheyenne? The entire state of Wyoming has a population density of about five people per square mile.

The population density figures for New York are pretty impressive, but what do they really mean? How did New Yorkers live, work, and shop at the turn of the century?

To see the people working and shopping on a busy street in New York City at the end of the nineteenth century, go back online and click the New York, New York button at the bottom of the screen.

View the living and working conditions of most of the new immigrants in New York and elsewhere on the Social Reform Photography of Jacob Riis and Lewis Hine. Look at both slide shows and the analysis for each.

Write your reactions to what you learn in the activity and the website in your History Journal.

Did anything surprise you? Did you react to the pictures of both photographers in the same way? Do you think the media can have an impact on social problems?

What inventions or projects that you have read about improved the quality of life of New Yorkers in the late nineteenth century?

You may wish to visit the following websites in Resources to learn more about New York City.

Skyscrapers

Central Park

Frederick Law Olmstead

Discuss your findings with an adult.

Day 2

Read

Read Chapter 5 “Louis Pasteur: Fighting Disease,” to the end of the chapter, pages 600–609 and complete Day 2 of the Reading Guide.

Triangle Shirtwaist Fire

Why were so many people willing to take a risk and organize to demand better conditions? Many people were feeling pretty desperate. To learn more about the working conditions immigrants faced in the late nineteenth century, go back online and click The Triangle Shirtwaist Fire.

Then, answer the following questions in your History Journal:

1. How did workers and trade unions draw attention to the poor working conditions?
2. Did most people in the nineteenth century support the business owner or the workers and the unions?
3. How did the public react to the Triangle Shirtwaist Fire?

© 2016 K12 Inc. All rights reserved.
Copying or distributing without K12's written consent is prohibited.

4. Who held more power in the nineteenth century—the workers or the factory owners? Was the balance of power changing in the early twentieth century?

Women on the March

To review some of the important steps women took to obtain equal rights, click Women on the March.

If you would like to learn more about the struggle for women's suffrage all over the world, visit the Women's Suffrage website in the Resources section.

If you would like to read more about the militant tactics the suffragists eventually resorted to in Great Britain, visit the Suffragettes 1913 website in the Resources section to read an account written by Emmeline Pankhurst's daughter Estelle Sylvia.

Day 3

Pretend you have moved from a farm to a big city in the United States or Europe in the late 1800s. Some of the family members you left behind are thinking about coming to join you in the big city. To help them make up their minds, you are going to create a scrapbook about life in the city.

In your scrapbook, you want to show the folks back home:

- What the city is like in 1900
- Progress you have seen—new buildings, parks, bridges, as well as legal or economic reforms and so on.
- Problems that still exist in 1900

You may want to visit some of the following websites in Resources to print out pictures to add to your scrapbook. Be sure to write captions to explain the pictures to the folks back home.

The History Place: Child Labor in America

The Living City

Wonders of the World: Brooklyn Bridge

Brooklyn Bridge: Facts, History, and Information

Frederick Law Olmstead

When you have completed your scrapbook, show it to an adult and discuss it.

ASSESS

Lesson Assessment: Organizing for Change (*Online*)

You will complete an online assessment covering the main objectives of this lesson. Your assessment will be scored by the computer.

LEARN

Activity 2: Organizing for Change *(Online)*

© 2016 K12 Inc. All rights reserved.
Copying or distributing without K12's written consent is prohibited.

Name Date 

Reading Guide

Day 1

Read

1. In the nineteenth century urban population grew dramatically. Why did so many people move to the cities?

2. What were the working conditions like in most factories?

3. What was Paris like when Napoleon III became emperor in 1852?

4. How did Napoleon III and Eugène Haussmann transform Paris?

5. Describe New York City and its population in 1900.

6. Why did New York face a special challenge trying to handle its growing population?

7. Who created Central Park and how did it differ from most European parks?

© 2016 K12 Inc. All rights reserved.
Copying or distributing without K12's written consent is prohibited.

Name Date 

Day 2

Read

8. How did Louis Pasteur establish his reputation?

9. What happened when Pasteur injected an old culture of chicken cholera microbes into a hen? What happened when he injected a fresh culture of chicken cholera microbes into the hens that had been injected with the old culture?

10. Pasteur also created vaccines against ________________ and ________________.

11. Ironworkers, coal miners, and other workers began to organize trade unions. What did trade unions do?

12. When collective bargaining failed, employees sometimes went on ______________.

13. Why did the workers at the Bryant & May match factory in England go on strike?

14. Employers created blacklists of union organizers. People on the lists were frequently_______________ or denied ________________.

15. A British immigrant named _____________________ organized the American Federation of Labor. By 1900, it had more than a million members.

16. In 1848 women held the first conference for ________________________ in Seneca Falls, New York.

17. Who was arrested for trying to cast a vote in the U.S. presidential election in 1872? Why?

18. Why did many people object to giving women the right to vote?

© 2016 K12 Inc. All rights reserved.
Copying or distributing without K12's written consent is prohibited.

Name Date 

19. Who was Emmeline Goulden Pankhurst? Why did she become famous?

20. Which nation became the first to grant women full voting rights?

© 2016 K12 Inc. All rights reserved.
Copying or distributing without K12's written consent is prohibited.

Student Guide
Lesson 2: Reaching Millions

Lesson Objectives

- Explain the meaning of the term *mass society.*
- Explain why new leisure activities became popular in the late 1800s, and give examples of those activities.
- Identify William Randolph Hearst and Joseph Pulitzer and what they are known for.
- Summarize the methods Henry Ford used to bring automobiles to the masses.
- Identify new technologies that contributed to mass entertainment.
- Explain the role of universal education in the economic progress of Western Europe and the United States.
- Describe the changes that occured in sales and marketing and the reasons for them.

PREPARE

Approximate lesson time is 60 minutes.

Materials

For the Student

Reading Guide

The Human Odyssey, Volume 2 edited by Klee, Cribb, and Holdren

History Journal

Keywords and Pronunciation

Aristide Boucicaut (ah-ree-steed BOO-sih-koh)
Baron Pierre de Coubertin (koo-behr-tan)
Bon Marché (bohn mar-SHAY)
mass production : the production of goods in large quantities
mass society : large numbers of people
middle class : the social class of people who are neither rich nor poor, which includes most skilled workers
vaudeville (VAWD-vil)

LEARN

Activity 1: Turn of the Century *(Offline)*

© 2016 K12 Inc. All rights reserved.
Copying or distributing without K12's written consent is prohibited.

Instructions

Day 1

Turn of the Century

When you think of the late 1800s, what do you think of? What products were being produced in all those new factories? What were people doing with the free time they had finally earned?

Before you begin the reading assignment, click the Turn of the Century activity to see if you have an accurate picture of the changes that were occurring at the end of the nineteenth and the beginning of the twentieth century. What do you think the latest sensations were?

Read

Read Chapter 6 from the beginning to "Mass Publishing: Pulp Fiction and Yellow Journalism," pages 610–619 and complete Day 1 of the Reading Guide. When you have finished, use the Lesson Answer Key to check your work, and then place the Reading Guide in your History Journal.

Day 2

Read

Read Chapter 6 from "Mass Publishing: Pulp Fiction and Yellow Journalism," to the end of the chapter, pages 619–625, and complete Day 2 of the Reading Guide.

What Happened?

When inventors come up with a new product, they frequently do not know what impact the invention will have on society. There are often many unintended consequences that the inventor never even considered. Visit the How the Car Changed America website to see how the car affected society.

In your History Notebook create a diagram or chart, or write a very brief essay describing how each of the following inventions changed society.

- phonograph
- Kinetoscope
- high-speed printing press

Day 3

Ford's Revolution

Today you will write a brief document-based essay in your History Journal. The essay should answer the following questions.

How did Henry Ford revolutionize the auto industry? Why did he introduce the changes he made? How did he revolutionize the lives of millions of workers all around the world?

You will base your essay on what you know about the time period and about Henry Ford (you may want to review pages 621–625 of your textbook) and on the documents found at the websites listed below. Your essay must include quotations from Henry Ford.

You may consult the following websites in the Resource section.

Henry Ford Interview

Henry Ford's Revolution for the Worker

© 2016 K12 Inc. All rights reserved.
Copying or distributing without K12's written consent is prohibited.

ASSESS

Lesson Assessment: Reaching Millions (*Online*)

You will complete an online assessment covering the main objectives of this lesson. Your assessment will be scored by the computer.

© 2016 K12 Inc. All rights reserved.
Copying or distributing without K12's written consent is prohibited.

Name Date 

Reading Guide

Day 1

Read

Reading Guide

1. How had life in Western Europe changed between 1800 and 1900?

2. What is the middle class?

3. What is “mass society”?

4. How did stores change in the nineteenth century?

5. How did marketing to people in rural areas change during the nineteenth century?

© 2016 K12 Inc. All rights reserved.
Copying or distributing without K12’s written consent is prohibited.

Name ______________________________ Date ______________________________ 

6. As shorter work hours and labor-saving home appliances began to allow people some leisure time, people started to seek new forms of entertainment. Many headed toward "trolley parks," which offered ____________ , ____________ and ____________ .

7. Many people also began to attend sporting events. The most popular sport in the United States was__________. In Great Britain fans flocked to__________ and ____________ games.

8. In the United States of the 1890s vaudeville became very popular. What was it?

9. Technology also contributed to new forms of entertainment. After Thomas Edison invented the ________________ , people began to listen to famous singers in their own homes.

10. Thomas Edison also invented the Kinetoscope. What was it and how did it affect entertainment?

Day 2

Reading Guide

Read

11. Why did people in the second half of the nineteenth century have more and more books to read?

12. What were *pulps*?

13. The two publishers who transformed the daily newspaper into a form of entertainment were ______________ and ________________. Their newspapers included many sensational stories, sports, comics, and news about entertainment.

© 2016 K12 Inc. All rights reserved.
Copying or distributing without K12's written consent is prohibited.

Name Date 

14. When did European nations begin offering education to all children? When did the United States start public education?

15. How did education affect the economic status of most nations?

16. When Henry Ford was growing up, what did he like to do in his spare time?

17. Henry Ford became obsessed with building a quadricycle. What was it?

18. What was Ford's primary goal when he started the Ford Motor Company?

19. Ford finally figured out a way to build his Model T cheaply enough so that middle class people could afford it. How did he do that?

20. How did the car change America?

© 2016 K12 Inc. All rights reserved.
Copying or distributing without K12's written consent is prohibited.

Student Guide
Lesson 3: Culture Shocks

Lesson Objectives

- Recognize that while many people saw the nineteenth century as a time of great progress, others questioned materialism and human nature.
- Identify Freud and describe his accomplishments.
- Explain the goals and techniques of the Impressionist, Postimpressionist, Cubist, and abstract painters.
- Identify examples of Impressionist, Postimpressionist, Cubist, and abstract art and artists.
- Recognize the goals and characteristics of modernism in music.
- Identify Zola and describe his Naturalist beliefs.

PREPARE

Approximate lesson time is 60 minutes.

Materials

For the Student

Reading Guide

The Human Odyssey, Volume 2 edited by Klee, Cribb, and Holdren

History Journal

Keywords and Pronunciation

L' Assommoir (lah-sohm-wahr)
Ballets Russes (ba-lay roos)
Claude Monet (klohd moh-NAY)
Coupeau (coo-poh)
Cubism : a 20th-century style of art developed by Pablo Picasso and Georges Braque in which the artist reduces an object to its basic geometric shapes and shows it from a number of different angles at the same time
Edgar Degas (ed-gahr duh-GAH) : a French Impressionist artist
Edouard Manet (ay-DWAR ma-NAY)
Georges Braque (zhorzh brahk)
Gervaise (jehr-vehz)
Giverny (zhee-vehr-NEE)
Igor Stravinsky (EE-gor struh-VIN-skee)
Impressionism : an artistic movement in which painters gave an "impression" of a scene rather than trying to make their painting depict reality with photographic accuracy; major Impressionists include Degas, Manet, Monet, Renoir, and Cassatt
Jan Vermeer (yahn vur-MAYR)
Mary Cassatt (kuh-SAT)
Pierre Auguste Renoir (pyehr aw-GOOST ruhn-wahr)
Sigmund Freud (froyd)

© 2016 K12 Inc. All rights reserved.
Copying or distributing without K12's written consent is prohibited.

Vincent van Gogh (van GOH) : Dutch Post-Impressionist artist
Wassily Kandinsky (VAH-si-lee kan-DIN-skee)
Émile Zola (ay-meel ZOH-luh)

LEARN

Activity 1: 1889 World's Fair *(Offline)*

Day 1

- **1889 World's Fair**

To celebrate the one hundredth anniversary of the French Revolution, the French decided to host a World's Fair in 1889. They thought it would offer a wonderful opportunity to show the world how much progress had been made. If you had been in charge of planning the World's Fair (the 1889 Exposition Universelle), what would you have showcased? (Think about the time period and what you learned in the last two chapters.) Click 1889 World's Fair and jot down your list. Print your list and save it in your History Journal.

- **Read**

Read Chapter 7 from the beginning to "New Artistic Visions: Impressionism and After," pages 626–633, and complete Day 1 of the Reading Guide. When you have finished, use the Lesson Answer Key to check your work, and then place the Reading Guide in your History Journal.

Day 2

- **Read**

Read Chapter 7 from "New Artistic Visions: Impressionism and After" to the end of the chapter, pages 633–639, and complete Day 2 of the Reading Guide.

- **Artistic Styles**

When you have finished the reading assignment, go back online and complete the Artistic Styles activity. When you have completed the activity, print it out and use the Lesson Answer Key to check your work before you put it in your History Journal.

- **The Rite of Spring**

The public was shocked when Igor Stravinsky's *The Rite of Spring* premiered in Paris on a May evening in 1913. The audience hissed, booed, shouted, and even began fighting! Since that tumultuous evening Igor Stravinsky's music has had an enormous influence on modern music. Today many people easily accept some of the harsh, dissonant sounds that outraged the Paris audience in 1913. Click The *Rite of Spring* to listen to a brief excerpt of the music. Then write a paragraph in your History Journal describing the music and your reaction to it.

Day 3

- **Interview**

Choose one writer, composer, or artist from the chapter and do more research about that person's life and work. Then "conduct an interview" with that person by writing a series of questions and answers based on the research. You may want to go to Grolier's online encyclopedia or to Resources to visit some of the websites below to find more information.

Impressionism
Post-Impressionism
The Vincent Van Gogh Gallery
Cubism

© 2016 K12 Inc. All rights reserved.
Copying or distributing without K12's written consent is prohibited.

Kandinsky
Ivy's Search Engine Resources for Kids

ASSESS

Lesson Assessment: Culture Shocks (*Online*)

You will complete an online assessment covering the main objectives of this lesson. Your assessment will be scored by the computer.

© 2016 K12 Inc. All rights reserved.
Copying or distributing without K12's written consent is prohibited.

Name Date 

Reading Guide

Day 1

Reading Guide

Read

1. When the French hosted the World's Fair in 1889, what were they celebrating? What were they trying to showcase?

2. Why were the late 1800s and the early 1900s known as the *"Belle Epoque"*?

3. Despite the signs of prosperity, some people expressed doubts. Who were they and why were they concerned?

4. According to most people in the nineteenth century, what caused mental illness?

5. Who was Sigmund Freud? What did he think caused mental illness?

6. What is *psychoanalysis*?

© 2016 K12 Inc. All rights reserved.
Copying or distributing without K12's written consent is prohibited.

Name Date 

7. What did the Naturalists believe?

8. Who was Émile Zola?

9. Write a short paragraph describing Zola's purpose in writing *L'Assommoir*. Do you think he succeeded in doing what he set out to do?

Day 2

Reading Guide

Read

10. How did photography complicate the question of artistic truth?

11. What did the Impressionists think art should convey? How did they convey it?

12. Name some of the famous Impressionist painters.

13. Vincent van Gogh admired the Impressionists, but he had one criticism. What was his criticism?

© 2016 K12 Inc. All rights reserved.
Copying or distributing without K12's written consent is prohibited.

Name Date 

14. Fill out the chart below.

Style	Famous Artists	Goals	Techniques
Impressionist			
Postimpressionist		Continue to depict light, and use bright colors and short brushstrokes, but emphasize emotions. Artists' styles varied.	
Cubist			
Abstract			

15. The composer most associated with the beginning of modern music is___________________. His ballet, __________________________ , shocked the music world when it premiered in 1913.

How did modern music differ from traditional music?

© 2016 K12 Inc. All rights reserved.
Copying or distributing without K12's written consent is prohibited.

Student Guide
Lesson 4: Remarkable Individuals

Lesson Objectives

- Identify key individuals who shaped the modern era and describe their contributions to society.

PREPARE

Approximate lesson time is 60 minutes.

Materials

For the Student

Reporter's Checklist

LEARN
Activity 1: The Modern World *(Offline)*
Instructions
Day 1
The Modern World

Today and tomorrow you will create a special edition of a newspaper called *The Modern World*. The special issue will focus on some of the remarkable individuals who shaped the modern world.

Before you begin, print out the Reporter's Checklist and gather background information about the remarkable individuals listed.

Then click Newsroom and look at the images the picture editor has submitted for your special edition.

Use your Reporter's Checklist to help you choose the four individuals who most deserve a place in your magazine. Write a brief article about each of them. Be sure your articles focus on the individual and his contributions to society, not just on the pictures. Write a headline for each story.

You've got a tight deadline. Click Newsroom to pick up your assignment.

Day 2

When you have finished writing articles about four individuals who have had an enormous influence on the modern era, decide which one of the four was the most influential. Write an article explaining why you chose that person over all the others. (After you print your newspaper, illustrate your article with a drawing or a picture you have photocopied or printed out.)

After you print your newspaper, create a cartoon or caricature of "the modern man" or "the modern woman." You know what a cartoon is. A caricature is an exaggerated drawing or description. Your cartoon or caricature should show—probably from a humorous point of view—some of the activities, customs, interests, or fashions people enjoyed in 1900.

© 2016 K12 Inc. All rights reserved.
Copying or distributing without K12's written consent is prohibited.

As an example, think about today and what you would include in a caricature of today's "modern teen." Would you include a laptop computer? A cell phone? Would today's modern teen be in a car, or jogging, or shopping? What hairstyle would you use? What clothing? Is there a television show or book that is a must for today's modern person? Can you picture a cartoon drawing of a teenager with a cell phone attached to one ear, and an MP3 player to the other, as he stares at his computer monitor in a bedroom with clothes and books and everything else all over the floor? The cartoon wouldn't show teens the way they really are—it would reflect and exaggerate teenagers' preferences and habits and the time we live in.

If you don't want to draw the modern man or woman of 1900, you could make a must-have list of contemporary activities, gadgets, styles, and interests instead.

When you have finished, share your special edition with an adult.

© 2016 K12 Inc. All rights reserved.
Copying or distributing without K12's written consent is prohibited.

Name Date 

Reporter's Checklist

Who	Where	What (Contributions to Society)
Aristide Boucicaut		
Thomas Edison		
Sigmund Freud		
Frederick Law Olmsted		
Emmeline Pankhurst		
Louis Pasteur		
Pablo Picasso		
Joseph Pulitzer		
Richard Warren Sears		
Igor Stravinsky		

© 2016 K12 Inc. All rights reserved.
Copying or distributing without K12's written consent is prohibited.

Student Guide
Lesson 5. Optional: Your Choice

PREPARE

Approximate lesson time is 60 minutes.

© 2016 K12 Inc. All rights reserved.
Copying or distributing without K12's written consent is prohibited.

Student Guide
Lesson 6: Unit Review

PREPARE

Approximate lesson time is 60 minutes.

LEARN

Activity 1: Answers and Questions *(Online)*

Instructions

History Journal Review

Review the unit by going through your History Journal.

You should:

- Look at activity sheets and Reading Guides you completed in this unit.
- Review unit keywords.
- Read through any writing assignments you completed during the unit.
- Review any offline assessments you took during the unit.
- Skim through the chapters in The Human Odyssey: Our Modern World that you read in this unit.

Don't rush through. Take your time. Your History Journal is a great resource for a unit review.

Online Unit Review

Go online and review the following:

- New York, New York
- Triangle Shirtwaist Factory
- Women on the March
- Turn of the Century
- Artistic Styles
- Modernistic Trends
- Groundbreakers

© 2016 K12 Inc. All rights reserved.
Copying or distributing without K12's written consent is prohibited.

Student Guide
Lesson 7: Unit Assessment

Lesson Objectives

- Recognize changes in the way many people lived as a mass society developed.
- Identify major leaders of the labor and women's movements and their methods for achieving reform.
- Describe the goals and techniques of painters, authors, and composers.
- Describe living and working conditions in the cities of the 1800s and how they were improved.
- Identify major innovators in the new mass society and what they are known for.

PREPARE

Approximate lesson time is 60 minutes.

Materials

For the Student

Question Review Table

ASSESS

Unit Assessment: Answers and Questions, Part 1 (*Online*)

Complete the computer-scored portion of the Unit Assessment. When you have finished, complete the teacher-scored portion of the assessment and submit it to your teacher.

Lesson Assessment: Answers and Questions, Part 2 (*Offline*)

Complete the teacher-scored portion of the Lesson Assessment and submit it to your teacher.

LEARN

Activity 1: Optional Unit Assessment Review Table *(Online)*

© 2016 K12 Inc. All rights reserved.
Copying or distributing without K12's written consent is prohibited.

Assessment Date

Unit 14: Answers and Questions

Before you retake the Unit Assessment, use the table to figure out which activities you should review.

Question Review Table

Circle the numbers of the questions that you missed on the Unit Assessment. Review the activities that correspond with these questions.

Answers and Questions, Part 1

Question	Lesson	Review Activity
2,3	2: Reaching Millions	Turn of the Century
4,5,6,7,8,9,10	3: Culture Shocks	1889 World's Fair

Answers and Questions, Part 2

Question	Lesson	Review Activity
1,2	1: Organizing for Change Throughout Unit	City Life

© 2016 K12 Inc. All rights reserved.
Copying or distributing without K12's written consent is prohibited.

Student Guide

Unit 15: The Dawn of the Twentieth Century
Lesson 1: Rising Expectations in Waning Empires

Lesson Objectives

- Explain the reasons for discontent in old empires in the late nineteenth and early twentieth centuries.
- Recognize the Serbs as an example of ethnic groups whose nationalism led to independence movements within the Ottoman Empire.
- Identify Franz Josef and the methods he used in trying to maintain his empire.
- Analyze excerpts of Gandhi's philosophy of nonviolent resistance.
- Identify Sun Yat-sen and his role in Chinese independence.
- Recognize changes to the maps of empires in the late nineteenth and early twentieth centuries.
- Summarize Gandhi's development as a champion of Indian independence from Britain.
- Describe the role of nationalism in changing imperialism in the early twentieth century.
- Recognize the city of Vienna and the cultural attractions it offers.

PREPARE

Approximate lesson time is 60 minutes.

Materials

For the Student

- Cataloging the Past
- Reading Guide
- The Human Odyssey, Volume 2 edited by Klee, Cribb, and Holdren
- History Journal

Keywords and Pronunciation

Antonin Dvorák (AHN-toh-neen DVOHR-zhahk)
Antonín Dvorák (AHN-toh-neen DVOHR-zhawk)
Croats (CROH-ats)
Czechs (cheks)
Shanghai (shang-HIY)
Slovaks (SLOH-vahks)
Slovenes (SLOH-veens)
Sun Yat-sen (soun yaht-sen)

© 2016 K12 Inc. All rights reserved.
Copying or distributing without K12's written consent is prohibited.

LEARN

Activity 1: Rising Expectations in Waning Empires *(Offline)*

Instructions

Day 1

Read

Read Chapter 8, from the beginning to "India's Mohandas Gandhi," pages 640–647, and complete Day 1 of the Reading Guide. When you have finished, use the Lesson Answer Key to check your work, and then place the Reading Guide in your History Journal.

Putting the Habsburgs on the Map

Consider the great empire of the Habsburgs—as the chapter says, the largest empire in Europe after Russia. You've seen what time did to the Ottomans. Review the Habsburg Map activity to see what time did to the Habsburgs.

Cataloging the Past

Now review some of the ethnic groups, nationalists, and revolutionaries you've met in the chapter so far. Begin the Cataloging the Past activity. In this activity you'll fill out a chart that catalogs the following:

- various ethnic groups and peoples
- their political leaders
- the issues and grievances that united the people
- the tactics and techniques used by the leaders and their followers to achieve their goals
- assistance from other peoples (military help, political support, inspiration)
- what these movements won for their peoples

Complete the first two sections—the Serb and Hungarian peoples. The blanks that can't be filled in from the information in the chapter have been done for you. You'll use the completed chart for an activity later in the lesson.

Day 2

Read

Read Chapter 8, from "India's Mohandas Gandhi" to the end, pages 647–653, and complete **Day 2** of the Reading Guide.

Finding India and China on the Map

Before you go any further, make sure you know exactly where India and China are in the world. These are two important countries—the two most populous nations on Earth.

Turn to page 693 at the back of the book and locate India (purple) and China (orange). You can also see them on the Cultural Regions map on page 710—South Asia and East Asia.

For a more detailed look at these two huge countries, see the map on pages 700–701, as well as those on page 704 (South Asia) and page 694 (the Pacific Rim).

Document Analysis: Getting to Know Gandhi

Go online and analyze Gandhi through his words by completing the Gandhi's Quotations activity.

Cataloging More of the Past

It's time to do the Cataloging the Past activity. Fill in the third and fourth sections of the chart.

© 2016 K12 Inc. All rights reserved.
Copying or distributing without K12's written consent is prohibited.

Day 3

In Tribute...

Go back to your by-now-completed Cataloging the Past chart. Select one of the leaders or peoples whose accomplishments you find most noteworthy, impressive, and compelling. Write a tribute to that leader or those peoples giving emphasis to the methods used to accomplish their goals. To prepare for the tribute, carry out research online as required.

ASSESS

Lesson Assessment: Rising Expectations in Waning Empires (*Online*)

You will complete an online assessment covering the main objectives of this lesson. Your assessment will be scored by the computer.

LEARN

Activity 2. Optional: Rising Expectations in Waning Empires *(Online)*

© 2016 K12 Inc. All rights reserved.
Copying or distributing without K12's written consent is prohibited.

Name Date 

Cataloging the Past

Fill out the chart below. A couple of the blanks can't be filled in from the information in this chapter, so they've already been done for you. Try to give full answers, using complete sentences as needed.

Peoples	Leaders	Grievances	Methods	Outside Help	Accomplishments
Serbs	Karađorđe (known as Black George because of his dark complexion and short temper)				
Hungarians	Gyula Andrássy				

© 2016 K12 Inc. All rights reserved.
Copying or distributing without K12's written consent is prohibited.

Name ______________________ Date ______________________ 

Cataloging the Past

Peoples	Leaders	Grievances	Methods	Outside Help	Accomplishments
Indians					
Chinese					

© 2016 K12 Inc. All rights reserved.
Copying or distributing without K12's written consent is prohibited.

Name Date 

Reading Guide

Day 1

Read

1. In the late nineteenth and early twentieth centuries, the new force of nationalism began to motivate many subject peoples living in old empires. Nationalists did not feel allegiance to their imperial masters. Instead, they felt a sense of belonging and loyalty to their own ____________________.

2. What did nationalists seek instead of imperial rule?

3. One of these old empires was the Ottoman Empire. Name three of the four regions of the empire.

4. In 1683, the Ottomans had advanced to the very gates of Vienna before they were______________ by the Austrians. Since that time, slowly but surely the Ottoman Empire began to________________ and various subject peoples struggled for their____________________.

5. In southeastern Europe, the Ottoman Empire faced a particularly stiff challenge from nationalists. Name the ethnic group that fought for and won its independence from imperial rule in 1878.

Use the map of the Ottoman Empire on page 642 of the chapter to answer the next six questions. (As you do so, you'll also need to refer to several of the modern-day maps at the back of the book; see pages 693, 698, 699, 700, and 700–702.)

6. You've read how Ottoman troops advanced to the very gates of Vienna in 1683. After that time, the empire seemed to be in retreat. What territory did the Ottomans lose next?

7. By 1812, the Ottomans had lost two large chunks of land in the north and east. What bodies of water do they border?

8. More territories had slipped from Ottoman control by 1878. Name two European nations that had emerged as independent countries. (You learned about one of them in the chapter. You read about the other nation in an earlier chapter—and about the English poet Lord Byron's attempt to help liberate it from Ottoman rule.)

© 2016 K12 Inc. All rights reserved.
Copying or distributing without K12's written consent is prohibited.

Name Date 

9. What happened to Serbia and Greece? What is their status today?

10. The Ottoman Empire was in decline, known to the other great powers of the day as "the Sick Man of Europe." In fact, most of its remaining territory was not in Europe but in North Africa and the Middle East. Name two modern-day countries in each of those regions.

11. Ultimately, the Ottoman Empire shrunk to what was called Asia Minor, with only a small toehold in Europe. What is the name of the country occupying that part of the world today?

Now continue your reading in the text from "Franz Josef Governs the Habsburg Empire" to "India's Mohandas Gandhi, pages 643–647 and answer the following questions.

12. ____________________ ascended the imperial Habsburg throne in 1848. Immediately, he had to put down a revolt against his rule in____________________ .

13. Later, however, he maintained Habsburg power in his far-flung empire by compromising with his Hungarian subjects. How did he do this?

14. He was less successful in winning over the Czechs, Slovaks, Croats, and Slovenes of his empire. What were these people collectively known as?

15. With which ethnic group would the Habsburgs have particular trouble that would plunge the nations into a world war?

Day 2

Read

Reading Guide

16. Who was the champion of India's independence movement from Britain?

17. He was raised in India as a traditional________________________, but was educated as a lawyer in________________________, where he adopted many Western ways.

© 2016 K12 Inc. All rights reserved.
Copying or distributing without K12's written consent is prohibited.

Name Date 

18. In which country did he first practice as a lawyer and work for the rights of the Indian people?

19. Name the "weapon" that he used to "fight" against injustice and oppression.

20. Who is known as "The Father of the Chinese Revolution"?

21. Name two things that angered this revolutionary leader.

22. In 1911, he became the first ____________________.

23. All across the globe, nationalism challenged the power of imperialism in the early twentieth century. Nationalists from ________________ won their freedom from the Ottomans in 1878. The Habsburgs had to concede some self-rule to the ________________. The nonviolent resistance of Gandhi threatened Britain's hold on ________________. And Chinese nationalists drove Western imperialists out of the ________________ on the coast.

Explore and Discuss

Is imperial rule always a negative experience? Are there positive things about empires? The Roman Empire, for example, brought law and order and roads and aqueducts to Gaul. But what if the people still don't want to be ruled by a foreign power? What if some, half, or most of the people *do* want foreign rule and the benefits it brings? Is there such a thing as a good empire? Give examples to back up your answers.

© 2016 K12 Inc. All rights reserved.
Copying or distributing without K12's written consent is prohibited.

Student Guide
Lesson 2: Linking the Seas and Reaching for the Skies

Lesson Objectives

- Explain the reasons for building a canal across the Isthmus of Panama.
- Identify Lesseps as the builder of the Suez Canal who attempted to build the Panama Canal.
- Recognize the purpose and practice of selling stocks.
- Identify key individuals in the building of the Panama Canal and their accomplishments.
- Summarize the development of the airplane.
- Identify key individuals in the development of air travel.

PREPARE

Approximate lesson time is 60 minutes.

Materials

For the Student

Questions and Answers

Reading Guide

The Human Odyssey, Volume 2 edited by Klee, Cribb, and Holdren

History Journal

Keywords and Pronunciation

Chagres (CHAH-grais)
Gatún (gah-TOON)
George Goethals (GOH-thuhlz)
Louis Blériot (BLER-ee-oh)
Otto Lilienthal (LIL-yuhn-tahl)
Paul Gauguin (goh-GAN)

LEARN

Activity 1: Linking the Seas and Reaching for the Skies *(Offline)*

Instructions

Day 1

Read

Read Chapter 9, from the beginning to "Reaching for the Sky," pages 655–663, and complete **Day 1** of the Reading Guide. When you have finished, use the Lesson Answer Key to check your work on **Day 1**, and then place the Reading Guide in your History Journal.

Map Your Way Across Panama

Find out more about the great canal that connected the Atlantic and Pacific Oceans by completing the Panama Map activity. When you have finished, print the activity and then compare your answers with the ones in the Lesson Answer Key.

© 2016 K12 Inc. All rights reserved.
Copying or distributing without K12's written consent is prohibited.

Day 2

Solving the Panama Puzzle

In the chapter you read about "The Fight Against Yellow Fever" and the work of Colonel William Crawford Gorgas, a doctor with the U.S. Army. Before Gorgas arrived in Panama, another army doctor, Major Walter Reed, was given the task of curing yellow fever. Begin today's lesson by helping Major Reed figure out what caused the disease by visiting the Panama Puzzle website.

Read

Read Chapter 9, from "Reaching for the Sky" to the end, pages 663–667, and complete **Day 2** of the Reading Guide. When you have finished, use the Lesson Answer Key to check your work, and then place the Reading Guide in your History Journal.

The Wright Stuff

Today we're so used to flying that we take it for granted. But it was only a hundred or so years ago that humans mastered flight. That means that there are some elderly people alive today who were born at a time before airplanes!

Learn about a recent attempt to recreate "the Wright experience." Relive the thrill at Kitty Hawk by reading the accounts and examining the images at the Wright Experience website.

Day 3

Time for a Little Q&A

Get your chance to ask questions of one of the individuals in the chapter by beginning the Q&A activity. (Don't worry about the Plan B section at the bottom of the printout. You'll find out what this means later.)

Note: Q&A means "question and answer." It usually refers to an interview—a series of questions posed by an interviewer and the answers to those questions provided by the interviewee, the person being interviewed.

Read through the chapter again and think about the questions you posed in the Q&A activity. Now try to fill in the answer section of the activity. But only answer the questions you think you can answer from the chapter or from other parts of this lesson. Leave unanswered at least two questions—the toughest ones. You'll do them next.

Some questions will take a little more time and a little more effort to answer. They'll probably require having a Plan B.

"Having a Plan B" is an expression. It means having a plan of action in reserve in case you need it. In other words, if your first course of action (Plan A) does not work, then you have another approach (Plan B) that just might.

To answer most of the questions in the Q&A activity, you went with Plan A. Plan A involved using what you had learned in the lesson already to answer most of the questions. Plan B will involve taking other steps, carrying out other procedures, and using other resources to answer the remaining questions—the tough ones.

What might those other steps, procedures, and resources be? Write them out in the Outline of the Plan B section at the bottom of the Q&A printout. (There are spaces for six steps; you shouldn't need any more than this—and you may very well need less.) These other steps might involve more resources such as the library, the Internet, or inquiring of family members or other adults.

When you have finished, carry out the steps necessary to find answers to those remaining tough questions. Write the answers in the printout.

© 2016 K12 Inc. All rights reserved.
Copying or distributing without K12's written consent is prohibited.

ASSESS

Lesson Assessment: Linking the Seas and Reaching for the Skies

(*Online*)

You will complete an online assessment covering the main objectives of this lesson. Your assessment will be scored by the computer.

© 2016 K12 Inc. All rights reserved.
Copying or distributing without K12's written consent is prohibited.

Name Date 

Questions and Answers

Wouldn't it be great to be able to travel back in time and ask important historical figures questions about what they did and what their thoughts were?

Some of the questions might be objective (meaning they have factual answers). Others might be subjective (meaning they are less fact-based and ask for an opinion or a point of view).

Gandhi would be a good example from the previous chapter. Questions for him might include:

"When you were in South Africa, did you try to help everyone or just the Indian people? Why?"
"Did you ever feel discouraged and ready to give up?"
"Did fellow Indians fight in the First World War or the Second World War? Were they right to do so?"
"Is there anything you would do differently if you could do it all over again?"
"Name one particularly difficult challenge for you."

You've met a lot of important people in this chapter. Choose one of them, and then write questions you would like to ask that person in the spaces provided.

Question 1:

Answer 1:

Question 2:

Answer 2:

Question 3:

Answer 3:

Question 4:

Answer 4:

© 2016 K12 Inc. All rights reserved.
Copying or distributing without K12's written consent is prohibited.

Name Date

Question 5:

Answer 5:

Question 6:

Answer 6:

Outline of Plan B

Step one:

Step two:

Step three:

Step four:

Step five:

Step six:

© 2016 K12 Inc. All rights reserved.
Copying or distributing without K12's written consent is prohibited.

Name _______________ Date _______________ 

Reading Guide

Day 1

Read, Part 1

Reading Guide

1. For hundreds of years, Europeans had dreamed of a canal across the narrowest part of Central America to connect the ____________ and the ____________ Oceans. This would eliminate the need to sail all the way around Cape Horn at the southern tip of ____________ .

2. Finally, they chose a location—the Isthmus of ____________ .

3. The man tasked with building the canal was named ____________. He had a good track record, having already built the ____________ Canal.

4. What country was he from?

5. To fund the project, he tried to raise money from investors by selling ____________, which are also known as ____________. This gave the investors part ____________ of the canal company.

6. In the early nineteenth century, which country became involved in the building of the canal?

7. Ownership of the canal company shifted. ____________ arranged to have the United States purchase the French canal company and made the canal's completion a top U.S. priority. ____________ was the chief engineer who realized that the canal required a series of locks between the two oceans.

8. Name the army doctor who brought yellow fever under control in the canal zone. Who was the military engineer who completed the canal's construction?

© 2016 K12 Inc. All rights reserved.
Copying or distributing without K12's written consent is prohibited.

Name ______________________________ Date ______________________________ 

Day 2

Read

Reading Guide

9. Early aviators such as the German-born ____________________ flew heavier-than-air aircraft with no engines, known as ____________________.

10. ________________________ built a man-sized, engine-powered flying machine that they flew from the sand dunes of North Carolina's Outer Banks.

11. Frenchman Louis Blériot was the first aviator to fly across which body of water?

12. Eventually, people began to think of practical purposes for flight. Name one of those early uses.

Explore and Discuss

This lesson is called Linking the Seas and Reaching for the Skies. These were great transportation achievements in the early twentieth century. What are some of the greatest achievements in the twenty-*first* century? Can you imagine what they might be in the twenty-*second* century?

© 2016 K12 Inc. All rights reserved.
Copying or distributing without K12's written consent is prohibited.

Student Guide
Lesson 3. Optional: Your Choice

PREPARE

Approximate lesson time is 60 minutes.

© 2016 K12 Inc. All rights reserved.
Copying or distributing without K12's written consent is prohibited.

Student Guide
Lesson 4: Wrapping Up

Lesson Objectives

- Complete a project summarizing historical themes.

PREPARE

Approximate lesson time is 60 minutes.

Materials

For the Student

- Reading Guide
- The World Turned Upside Down
- The Human Odyssey, Volume 2 edited by Klee, Cribb, and Holdren
- History Journal

LEARN

Activity 1: Wrapping Up *(Online)*

Instructions

Day 1

Read

Read the Part 4 Conclusion, from page 668 to page 675, and complete the Reading Guide. When you have finished, use the Lesson Answer Key to check your work, and then place the Reading Guide in your History Journal.

A Look Back

Review some of what you've learned in this unit by completing the Show You Know online activity.

The World Turned Upside Down

Imagine you were born in 1830. Throughout your life, you witness one momentous change after another. By the first decade of the twentieth century, the world around you has been transformed thoroughly. See just how great that transformation is by completing the World Turned Upside Down activity sheet.

Day 2

Dear Granddaughter...

Now comes an important event in your life. It may not make it into the history books or the newspapers, but it's all your family members can talk about...the birth of your first granddaughter!

You've lived through a lot of changes, and you begin to wonder about how the world might be transformed during her lifetime. After all, your granddaughter might well live until the year 2000!

© 2016 K12 Inc. All rights reserved.
Copying or distributing without K12's written consent is prohibited.

You sit down to write a letter to your newborn granddaughter—something she can read in the years and decades ahead. Reflecting on the types of changes that have taken place in your lifetime, you decide to write about what you think will happen in the century ahead. Your letter will address possible changes in the four categories you looked at in the previous activity: political/military, cultural, science/technology, and social/economic.

In addition, you'll want to write about the following:

- Ways in which life might improve in the future
- Good things from the previous century that might be lost as times change
- How your granddaughter should view change, what he should resist, what he should embrace, and so on.

ASSESS

Lesson Assessment: Wrapping Up *(Offline)*

You will complete an offline assessment covering some of the main points of this lesson. Your assessment will be scored by the teacher.

© 2016 K12 Inc. All rights reserved.
Copying or distributing without K12's written consent is prohibited.

Name Date 

The World Turned Upside Down

Using the Part 4 conclusion, pages 668–675, make a list of the major innovations and events that have occurred during your life (remember, you were born in 1830). There are no particular "right" or "wrong" answers as long as the things you choose really did occur between 1830 and 1900, and they don't have to be in any order. Just make sure to give examples of changes or significant events from all different aspects of life. Assign each innovation or event to the appropriate category by putting a check mark in one or more of the category columns.

Feel free to refer to earlier chapters in the textbook, if you think it would help. But as you know, the conclusion is jam-packed with significant developments from the nineteenth and early twentieth centuries. We've added the first couple of innovations and events, just to get you started. You should have no difficulty in coming up with the others.

Innovation/Event	Categories						
	Political	Military	Cultural	Science	Technology	Social	Economic
Sun Yat-sen becomes president of the first Chinese republic.							
The opening of the Suez Canal provides a shortcut for shipping from Europe to Asia.							
Henry Ford begins assembly-line production for automobiles.							

© 2016 K12 Inc. All rights reserved.
Copying or distributing without K12's written consent is prohibited.

Name _______________ Date _______________ 

Innovation/Event	Political	Military	Cultural	Science	Technology	Social	Economic

(Political, Military, Cultural, Science, Technology, Social and Economic are grouped under the heading "Categories".)

© 2016 K12 Inc. All rights reserved.
Copying or distributing without K12's written consent is prohibited.

Name Date 

Innovation/Event	Categories						
	Political	Military	Cultural	Science	Technology	Social	Economic

© 2016 K12 Inc. All rights reserved.
Copying or distributing without K12's written consent is prohibited.

Name Date 

Innovation/Event	Categories						
	Political	Military	Cultural	Science	Technology	Social	Economic

© 2016 K12 Inc. All rights reserved.
Copying or distributing without K12's written consent is prohibited.

Name ______________________________ Date ______________________________ 

Reading Guide

Day 1

Read

Reading Guide

1. Sun Yat-sen helped set up the first republic in ______________, while Mohandas Gandhi was marching in South Africa for the rights of ______________.

2. Name the supposedly unsinkable ship that plunged beneath the waters of the Atlantic on April 14, 1912.

3. Mazzini and Garibaldi helped unite ______________, and Otto von Bismarck forged ______________ into a single nation.

4. What were the two main consequences of the American Civil War?

5. Name the canal in Egypt that provided European powers with a shortcut to Asia. Name the canal that linked the Atlantic and Pacific Oceans.

6. Which "-ism" is concerned with the building of empires?

7. It was said that "the sun never set on the ______________ Empire."

8. Which "-ism" teaches the superiority of one group of people over another?

9. Which Western ideas helped inspire revolts by subject peoples against world empires?

10. Name two great empires whose European subjects began to struggle for their freedom.

11. By the early twentieth century, ______________ powered many factories and helped light up homes and streets.

© 2016 K12 Inc. All rights reserved.
Copying or distributing without K12's written consent is prohibited.

Name Date

12. Name two ways in which communications improved links between nations.

13. What new high-rise buildings began to appear in cities? Name one new method of transportation in cities. Which New York City suspension bridge was made of twisted steel cables?

14. _______________ invented the assembly line, which produced automobiles cheaply and efficiently.

15. By 1914, which new form of travel were companies in America and Europe developing?

16. That same year, the outbreak of _______________ plunged Europe into a conflict that would involve much of the world.

Explore and Discuss

Wow! There were a *lot* of changes during this time period. Most people would say that some of those changes were very good, but that some had both good and bad consequences. Some changes had only negative results. Give an example of each kind of change and evidence to support your answers.

© 2016 K12 Inc. All rights reserved.
Copying or distributing without K12's written consent is prohibited.

Name Date

Wrapping Up

Write your letter and submit it to your teacher.

1. Now comes an important event in your life. It may not make it into the history books or the newspapers, but it's all your family members can talk about…the birth of your first granddaughter!

   You've lived through a lot of changes, and you begin to wonder about how the world might be transformed during her lifetime. After all, your granddaughter might well live until the year 2000!

   You sit down to write a letter to your newborn granddaughter—something she can read in the years and decades ahead. Reflecting on the types of changes that have taken place in your lifetime, you decide to write about what you think will happen in the century ahead. Your letter will address possible changes in the four categories you looked at in the previous activity: political/military, cultural, science/technology, and social/economic.

   In addition, you'll want to write about the following:

   - Ways in which life might improve in the future
   - Good things from the previous century that might be lost as times change
   - How your granddaughter should view change, what she should resist, what she should embrace, and so on.

© 2016 K12 Inc. All rights reserved.
Copying or distributing without K12's written consent is prohibited.

Student Guide

Unit 16: End-of-Course Review and Assessment
Lesson 1: End-of-Course Review

Lesson Objectives

- Review knowledge gained in previous lessons and units.
- Demonstrate mastery of important knowledge and skills taught in the Age of Democratic Revolutions unit.
- Demonstrate mastery of important knowledge and skills taught in the Revolutions in Arts, Industries, and Work unit.
- Demonstrate mastery of important knowledge and skills taught in the Nations Unite and Expand unit.
- Demonstrate mastery of important knowledge and skills taught in the Answers and Questions unit.
- Demonstrate mastery of important knowledge and skills taught in The Dawn of the Twentieth Century unit.

PREPARE

Approximate lesson time is 60 minutes.

Materials

For the Student

Crossword Puzzle

LEARN

Activity 1: Democratic Revolutions, Revolutions in Arts, Industries, and Work

(Online)

Activity 2: Looking Backward, Looking Forward *(Online)*

© 2016 K12 Inc. All rights reserved.
Copying or distributing without K12's written consent is prohibited.

Name Date 

Cultural World: Art, Literature, and Music

1. 2. 3. 4. 5. 6. 7. 8. 9. 10. 11. 12. 13. 14. 15. 16. 17. 18. 19.

© 2016 K12 Inc. All rights reserved.
Copying or distributing without K12's written consent is prohibited.

ACROSS

2. Created Cubism with Picasso

4. Artistic movement in which the artist breaks objects into geometric shapes and imaginatively reassembles them

7. Author of *Heart of Darkness*

9. Romantic poet inspired by England's Lake District

14. Artistic movement in which painters give an "impression" of a scene

16. A style of art that does not depict the physical world as we see it, but makes art out of line, color, shapes, light, and texture

17. French author who wrote the Naturalist novel *L'Assommoir*

18. Author of *Uncle Tom's Cabin*

19. Romantic poet who loved to break the rules

DOWN

1. Postimpressionist painter who liked to show strong emotion in his work

3. Spanish painter who broke down objects and imaginatively reassembled them

5. Russian painter who banished recognizable objects from his paintings

6. German author of *Sturm und Drang* movement who created a hero named *Werther*

8. Artistic and literary movement that emphasized an appreciation of nature, feeling, and emotion

10. German Romantic painter who painted rocky seacoasts and dark forests

11. Author who lived in India and wrote *The Jungle Book*

12. American Impressionist painter who tried to capture the movement of light and color on water

13. Leading painter of the Romantic movement in France who created *Liberty Leading the People*

15. Russian composer associated with the beginning of modern music

© 2016 K12 Inc. All rights reserved.
Copying or distributing without K12's written consent is prohibited.

Student Guide
Lesson 2: End-of-Course Assessment

Lesson Objectives

- Demonstrate mastery of the skills and concepts taught in this semester.
- Demonstrate mastery of important knowledge and skills taught in previous lessons.
- Explain why Parliament imposed taxes after 1763 and why the colonists reacted as they did.
- Identify George Washington and his contributions to the revolution.
- Identify the U.S. Constitution as the world's oldest functioning written constitution.
- Summarize Enlightenment ideas that promoted revolution in France.
- Describe the events of the Reign of Terror.
- Explain how Napoleon came to power.
- Identify major positions of the political spectrum.
- Identify significant leaders of nineteenth century Latin American independence movements and their accomplishments and failings.
- Explain why attempts to establish republics in Latin America were less successful than in the United States.
- Describe how Russia differed from western Europe in the sixteenth and seventeenth centuries and explain why.
- Identify Peter the Great.
- Identify Catherine the Great.
- Identify Alexander I.
- Identify major writers, artists, and composers of the Romantic period and the kinds of works they are known for.
- Identify the factors that allowed the Industrial Revolution to begin first in England.
- Identify Adam Smith and what he is known for.
- Describe the advances made in the textile industry in England in the eighteenth century.
- Explain the significance of the steam engine to industry.
- Describe the need for better roads in the 1700s and 1800s and the attempts to improve roads.
- Identify Fulton and his contribution to steam-powered boats.
- Identify Stephenson and his contribution to railroad travel.
- Identify Morse and his contribution to rapid communication.
- Describe conditions for factory workers in the early nineteenth century.
- Describe living conditions for poor workers in industrial cities.
- Identify Charles Dickens and the impact of his writing.
- Identify Karl Marx and what he is known for.
- Identify Charles Darwin and what he is known for.
- Describe the slave trade in Africa as it existed by 1700.
- Describe the transatlantic slave trade and its consequences.
- Identify the causes of Italian and German unification.
- Identify Jefferson Davis and Abraham Lincoln and what they are known for.

© 2016 K12 Inc. All rights reserved.
Copying or distributing without K12's written consent is prohibited.

- Summarize the results of the American Civil War.
- Identify Alexander Graham Bell and his accomplishments.
- Identify Thomas Edison and his accomplishments.
- Identify Guglielmo Marconi and his accomplishments.
- Describe advances in fuels in the late 1800s.
- Explain how steel led to a second industrial revolution.
- Explain the reasons for the New Imperialism.
- Identify on a map the major areas of colonization by Britain, Belgium, Japan, France, Russia, and the United States.
- Explain the reasons for the population growth in cities of the 1800s.
- Identify Louis Pasteur and describe his accomplishments.
- Summarize the methods Henry Ford used to bring automobiles to the masses.
- Identify examples of Impressionist, Postimpressionist, Cubist, and abstract art and artists.
- Identify Sun Yat-sen and his role in Chinese independence.
- Identify key individuals in the building of the Panama Canal and their accomplishments.
- Summarize the development of the airplane.
- Summarize Gandhi's development as a champion of Indian independence from Britain.
- Define *nationalism.*
- Recognize Napoleon's role in the nationalist movements of the nineteenth century in Europe.
- Describe the effects of colonization on the peoples of the colonized territories.
- Describe the conditions city dwellers faced in places such as Paris, London, and New York.
- Recognize the Serbs as an example of ethnic groups whose nationalism led to independence movements within the Ottoman Empire.
- Describe the role of nationalism in changing imperialism in the early twentieth century.

PREPARE

Approximate lesson time is 60 minutes.

ASSESS

Semester Assessment: End-of-Course Assessment, Part 1 (*Online*)

Complete the computer-scored portion of the Semester Assessment. When you have finished, complete the teacher-scored portion of the assessment and submit it to your teacher.

Semester Assessment: End-of-Course Assessment, Part 2 (*Offline*)

Complete the teacher-scored portion of the Semester Assessment and submit it to your teacher.

© 2016 K12 Inc. All rights reserved.
Copying or distributing without K12's written consent is prohibited.